KEEPING THEM *the* OFF STREETS

A Youth Work Story

Tim Caley

Matador
9 Priory Business Park,
Wistow Road, Kibworth Beauchamp,
Leicestershire. LE8 0RX
Tel: 0116 279 2299
Email: books@troubador.co.uk
Web: www.troubador.co.uk/matador
Twitter: @matadorbooks

ISBN 978 1789016 499

British Library Cataloguing in Publication Data.
A catalogue record for this book is available from the British Library.

Printed and bound by CPI Group (UK) Ltd, Croydon, CR0 4YY
Typeset in 11pt Adobe Garamond Pro by Troubador Publishing Ltd, Leicester, UK

Matador is an imprint of Troubador Publishing Ltd

PRAISE FOR KEEPING THEM OFF THE STREETS

Engaging and highly informative; the book covers key youth work debates that students, academics and practitioners grapple with including policy, professionalisation and perceptions of the young. Highly compelling – it draws you in from the first page!

Dr. Naomi Thompson, Lecturer,
Goldsmiths, University of London

Very good – there are few, if any, similar works that link personal practice with the wider policy arena as this does. The material on detached work and the rare section on inspection practices are especially valuable.

Tom Wylie,
Chief Executive,
National Youth Agency, 1995-2007

Concise, engaging and beautifully written – an important addition to the literature.

Tania de St. Croix, Senior Lecturer,
King's College, London

I read it avidly – thought-provoking and in an easy to read format. I think it will be a good read for student youth workers, especially with a view to keeping the youth work flame alight.

Lucy Hill, Youth Work manager, Sussex

A stimulating on-the-ground insider's insights into youth policies and developments over forty years. Enjoyable and highly informative – we have far too few contributions like this to our youth work literature.

Bernard Davies, author of the
History of the Youth Service

The book is topical and timely – hopefully its messages will speak to policy makers, civil servants and government.

Dr. Jane Melvin, Principal Lecturer,
University of Brighton

Quite an achievement… warm, insightful and presents an informed and observational reflection on a tremendous career, alongside the twists and turns of youth work over the past forty five years. The insights and anecdotes are fabulous – it's what gives the book authenticity and accessibility. A good story, told well – with important messages that deserve to be heard.

Dr. Mark Price, Principal Lecturer,
University of Brighton

A real story with a level of veracity and authenticity that others often lack. The anecdotes are warmly written, highlighting the passion and strong value base the author obviously has for youth work. Indeed, few youth workers possess the author's 'grassroots to government' profile. There is a role model here for youth workers to aspire to, learn from and shape their own professional development.

Mick Conroy, Course Leader: Youth &
Community Work, University of South Wales

It is pointless to denounce street evils, gang hooliganism or to mourn the absence of team spirit in poorer areas. Platitudinarians should live for one week where society has compelled millions to live. They will then cease to hold their hands in horror at giggling girls and boisterous youths around lamp posts, or condemn the pastimes of the young in back alleys.

James Butterworth, *Clubland*, 1932

The writer's craft must encompass a strong impulse to bring the different kinds of experience together: the abstract and the sensuous, the public and the private, the large and the small, the big issues and the small habits, the large ideas and the petty smells.

Richard Hoggart, *A Sort of Clowning*, 1990

Their accost is curt; their accent and tone of speech blunt and harsh. They have a quick perception of character and a keen sense of humour. The dwellers among them must be prepared for certain uncomplimentary, though most likely true, observations pithily expressed.

Elizabeth Gaskell, *North and South*, 1865,
on Yorkshire men

CONTENTS

PART 3: SUPPORTING GOOD YOUTH WORK

PART 4: KEEPING THE YOUTH WORK FLAME ALIVE

ACKNOWLEDGEMENTS

I am firstly indebted to Elaine Harrison – kindred spirit, committed youth worker and firm friend – without whose help and continuous encouragement this book would never have been written.

My special thanks go to a number of people (some sadly no longer here to receive them) who have supported, influenced and enlivened my youth work story. In Sheffield, to Joan Bennett, John Barnett, Mick Croydon, John Fair and Chris Strawford. In Berkshire, to John Ashdown, Geoff Hills, Detta Regan, Adrian King, Anne Atkins and Anita Mountain. In Portsmouth, to Dave Parker, Marilyn Lawrence, Brenda Tregarthen, Eric Harrington, Peter Littlefield, Paula Medd and Jacky Parker. In Hampshire, to Peter Coles, Peter Read, Val Webster and Sheila Ogden.

To Maureen Banbury, Olwyn Cupid and Clive Rowe at Ofsted, to Tom Wylie at the National Youth Agency, to David Marsland and Simon Day at Brunel University, and to Steve Bolger, Mike Counsell, Brian Parker, Angela Palmer, George Weech, Terry Ryall and Susie Grainger, fellow heads of youth services. In West Sussex, to Ken Pritchard, Penny Hardwick, Carole Aspden, Sandra Carey and Steven Tregidgo. And finally, in consultancy days, to Paddy Hall, Liz Wade, Chris Nash, Linda Deazle, Chris Garcia, Nigel Jenner, Steve Sipple, Janine Brady, Phil Cotgreave, Colin Barrett and David Wright.

My thanks also go to the staff of the youth work archives at De Montfort University Library, Leicester; to students on the youth and community work courses at Goldsmiths, University of London and the University of Brighton; to Motiv8 South for permission to use the material in the epilogue; and especially to Kirsty Robertson and her Gosport team for helping to create the cover photographs.

Finally, I'm particularly grateful to a number of colleagues who kindly offered their time and provided valuable advice and suggestions that improved early drafts of this book; in particular Elaine Harrison, Marilyn Lawrence, Detta Regan, Clare Ansell, Angela Palmer, Tom Wylie, Jane Melvin, Lucy Hill, Chris Nash, Tania de St Croix, Bernard Davies, Victoria Roddam, David Blunkett and Mark Price.

And to the many youth workers I've met and admired, too numerous to record, for whom I hope my story is of some help and encouragement.

DEFINITION OF TERMS

It may be of help to the general reader to offer the following definitions – especially the distinctions between 'youth work', 'youth service' and 'services for young people'. Please note that the book refers only to policies in England: youth services in Scotland, Wales and Northern Ireland remain different.

Youth work refers to the relationships established and programmes delivered by qualified youth and community workers with young people, normally in the thirteen to twenty-five age range. This may include youth clubs, detached youth work and project work. It can be funded through local authorities, voluntary organisations or other bodies.

Youth service refers to the youth work delivered by local authorities (councils) which employ the youth work staff (full- and part-time) and fund a range of activities under the umbrella term 'youth service'.

Services for young people refers to a range of other youth providers including schools, further and higher education, youth justice, leisure, sports, advice and guidance.

General services refers to other services which may impact on young people, e.g. police, fire service, housing, welfare, churches, hospitals, commercial, private and other providers.

See the chart below – taken from an original model by Tom Wylie,
National Youth Agency, 2006.

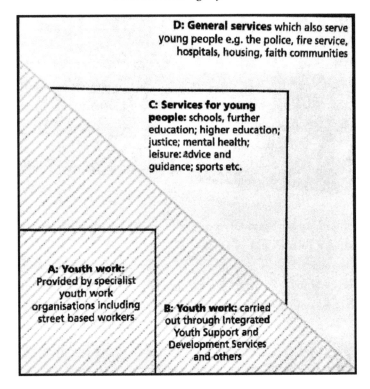

D: **General services** which also serve young people e.g. the police, fire service, hospitals, housing, faith communities

C: **Services for young people:** schools, further education; higher education; justice; mental health; leisure: advice and guidance; sports etc.

A: **Youth work:** Provided by specialist youth work organisations including street based workers

B: **Youth work:** carried out through Integrated Youth Support and Development Services and others

KEEPING THEM OFF THE STREETS: A TIMELINE

Albemarle Report, 1960: youth club building programme, national youth leader training course, establishment of National Youth Agency.

Ted Heath, 1970–1974: miners' strikes, three-day week, power cuts, who rules the UK?

Sheffield Youth Service, part-time youth worker Greenhill-Bradway Youth Centre, 1971–1972.

Kelvin Youth Centre, youth worker, 1972–1976; Kelvin detached youth worker, 1976–1979.

Youth and Community Work in the 1970s (Fairbairn-Milson Report), 1969: a hybrid, 'mixed economy' report linking youth work and the community.

Harold Wilson, 1974–1976; James Callaghan, 1976–1979: IMF loan, 'winter of discontent'.

Sheffield Youth Service, youth and community worker, Parson Cross, 1976–1979.

Berkshire Youth Service, Reading district youth officer, 1979–1982.

Margaret Thatcher, 1979–1990: Falklands War, miners' strike, privatisation, decline of unions, council house sales, poll tax, unemployment, Manpower Services Commission.

Hampshire, Portsmouth youth and community coordinator, 1983–1989.

Thompson Report (Experience and Participation), 1982: the five 'A's.

John Major, 1990–1997: back to basics, problems over Europe, 'sleaze'.

Hampshire Youth Service, County youth officer, 1990–1997.

Youth service 'core curriculum' conferences, 1991–1992.

Tony Blair, 1997–2007: New Labour, 'education, education, education', Iraq War.

West Sussex Youth Service, Principal youth officer, 1998–2003.

Libre Consulting, 2003–2005.

Connexions, 2000; *Transforming Youth Work: Resourcing Excellent Youth Services*, 2001–2002.

tim caley consulting, 2005–2014.

Gordon Brown, 2007–2010: banking crisis (2008), Libya.

Aiming High for Young People: A Ten-Year Strategy, 2007.

David Cameron, 2010–2016: coalition government, 2010–2015.

Positive for Youth, 2011; *Delivering Differently for Young People*, 2014.

Conservative government, 2015: budget cuts, austerity, Brexit.

Theresa May, 2016–present: June (Brexit) election 2017, hung Parliament, Grenfell Tower fire.

PROLOGUE

It was a cold, cheerless December afternoon in 1972 when I found myself in a small office at Sheffield's police headquarters in West Bar. I was there to present my credentials to the local police inspector as the new youth leader at Kelvin Youth Centre. He was an intelligent, middle-aged man, friendly, clearly experienced but with a rather world-weary attitude. Heaven knows what he thought about the naive young twenty-four-year-old he found in front of him. I told my story and he listened attentively. We exchanged ideas about the club members, about roles, protocols and professional boundaries.

As we talked, I warmed to his common sense and obvious support and sympathy for the scale of the task I had embarked upon at Kelvin. 'It's a tough patch,' he said. Then, pausing for a moment, added, 'Youth workers should all get medals as big as dustbin lids for the work they do.' Now that was a surprise, and a very welcome one. How often do any adults, never mind senior police officers, hold such complimentary opinions about youth workers? Remembering his words and the impact they made on me more than forty-five years ago is one of my reasons for writing this book.

I've always enjoyed being around teenagers and it's been a privilege and a pleasure to have spent my professional life working with them – not to mention a whole raft of youth workers who support them. I like young people's energy, their optimism, their fearlessness, their boisterousness, their style, their fashion, their language, their emotions, their vulnerability and their sometimes-brutal honesty. Of course, I'm a big fan of youth work and the benefits it brings to young people's lives. Naturally, I think youth workers are a unique and idiosyncratic breed who bring special skills and talents to helping, cajoling, challenging and supporting teenagers – in ways that no other professionals can. Youth work is both a rewarding and a fragile occupation: celebrating its rewards, whilst analysing its fragilities, is another reason to record my story.

This book's rationale is to combine both a cogent intellectual analysis of youth work policy and issues with a celebration of all the great down-to-earth, grassroots youth work practice that I've seen and admired over many years. It's a mixture of policy and personality. When you reflect over a longish time span, you realise that there are some common threads to government policies for young people, good and bad. You also realise how your own philosophy and beliefs have evolved and developed through hard experience and long practice. I've tried to link these two ideas together in this story. As a historian by training, I thoroughly concur with the opinion of our service's foremost critic and author Bernard Davies, who wrote that the youth service:

> *...has a very shaky hold on its own origins – even some of the most active and committed within it don't know its own history. It is our history that gives us a shared sense of what is different and special about us and of what is worth defending.*[1]

So *Keeping Them off the Streets* is about what is worth defending in youth service history. Don't let the title put you off: it is a phrase I have used deliberately, with real affection and with no sense of anger or negativity. It has pervaded most of my career, from youth club member, to part-timer, to head of service (twice). I recognise that it is a pejorative slogan on the whole, but I believe it also reflects a more positive concern about youngsters, about their needs and the tough process of growing up that is a commendable trait in a sometimes harsh adult cultural environment.

Some say there never was a 'golden age' of youth work. I've been lucky enough to have worked during two golden ages. The first was in the late 1960s after the publication of the Albemarle Report, when new youth centres were being built all over the country, not least in Sheffield (my home town), where I worked in two of them. The second was in the early 2000s with the publication of *Resourcing Excellent Youth Services* during the Blair government's era of spending priorities on 'education, education, education'. By then, I was a principal youth officer and REYS gave us all a well-deserved boost in confidence and morale. Golden or otherwise, there are some enduring characteristics that underpin good youth work and they are as important to capture and replicate now as they have always been. There are troughs as well as peaks in youth work and, in times of challenge, recounting the benefits of our particular craft for the future is even more critical.

My aim in writing *Keeping Them off the Streets*, then, is to inspire, to connect, to challenge and to remind practitioners of the professional history, critical values and continued importance of their work. Understanding your own history is a prerequisite to understanding how you got to where you are today and how you might sustain and develop strategies for youth work in the future. The narrative was never intended as a purely academic study, nor does it have scholarly pretensions other than to recall youth service policy and practice through the prism of my own personal experience and viewpoint. I have been struck during my research for this book by how there are very few similar personal memoirs that link national policies and local experiences in youth and community work. There are some histories of youth work, many dissertations on good practice and a plethora of university academic-led policy essays and theories, most of which belong to the intellectual and 'romantic' tradition of youth work advocacy. But there is not much that connects policy to personal fieldwork experience and, indeed, managerial and inspection experience in my case. I hope my work helps to fill this gap: certainly I acknowledge that writing it has been a continuing labour of love.

And also, with this book I hope to provide for the reader an entertaining and educational experience, to have some fun, to recall the anecdotes and characters that have shaped my experiences, to place my story in its proper social and political context, to try and deliver the writing with style and humour, and to remind colleagues about the enduring values of our work. But mainly I wrote it to record and reinforce my admiration and deep respect for the many youth workers, especially the part-timers, it has been my privilege to meet since those early days at Greenhill-Bradway Youth Centre in Sheffield, way back in 1971.

Tim Caley, Hampshire
February 2019

Part 1

GRASSROOTS
YOUTH WORK

CHAPTER 1

KELVIN YOUTH CENTRE: STARTING OUT

My youth work story begins many years ago. If it was not a golden age of youth work, at least it was one where the climate was much warmer and more supportive than it is now, where funding and staffing were more generous, where optimism and energy were more commonplace, and where hope and enterprise were the watchwords for youth work and youth services.

Kelvin Youth Centre was a brand-new £50,000 youth club building with a sunken disco dance floor, a floodlit football pitch outside, a three-quarter-size snooker table, a craft area, a leader's office and, of course, a girls' powder room. The only thing missing was the mirror ball globe for the pulsating disco lights, but we bought one later with club funds anyway. The fundamental problem was that it was built on the ground floor of a high-rise block of flats. Kelvin Youth Centre was built as part of Sheffield City Council's Kelvin Flats development. It was one of many similar post-war housing developments across the country. Architects, desperate to rehouse families and to replace and redevelop the streets of run-down terraced houses, looked abroad for inspiration. Specifically, to the French architect Le Corbusier and his concept of 'streets in

Kelvin Flats, late 1970s: the youth club entrance is bottom right.
Photo: Peter Jones.

the skies'. In the late 1960s, Hyde Park and Park Hill were erected on a massive hill site looking over Sheffield's city centre. Rising in the west, Kelvin Flats were built in a linear style, some ten storeys high, along the road out towards Sheffield Wednesday's ground at Hillsborough – with 945 flats and room for 2,500 residents.

At first, the tenants welcomed the flats with their inside toilets, modern kitchens and views from the heights. But soon, as the lifts broke down, as parents found nowhere safe for their children to play, and as the flats became (allegedly) a dumping ground for 'problem' families, attitudes changed and hardened. Before long, the proud civic boasts of a 'City on the Move' were replaced by a more negative picture – at one extreme the Kelvin Flats became a symbol of the ugly squalor that high-rise developments could so easily become. By the turn of the decade, the press was full of stories about the nightmarish experience of high-rise living. Replacing crowded terraced streets with brutal concrete estates had led to disappointment and disillusion on a national scale. Health concerns, children with nowhere safe to play, lack of gardens or shops, the culture of teenage bullying, drugs and gang violence were common complaints. Vandalism was a constant problem: shut up inside, many teenagers almost literally had nothing better to do and graffiti, litter and damage were everyday problems. From wherever you stood, the Kelvin Flats were an arresting and unattractive sight: the enclosed design of the blocks seemed to tower over you and hem you in. The height, the physical scale and the long, slab-like concrete lines of the layout were not very people-friendly. In fact they were rather threatening and scary: harsh blocks that rose above the landscape and darkened the residents' lives.

I'd been a schoolteacher before embarking on youth work. Just before I left my teaching job, the deputy head came into the staffroom to have a word with me. This was an unusual occurrence for a lowly probationer. 'We were surprised to hear of your decision to take up your new job on the Kelvin Flats,' he explained. 'Congratulations on your bravery,' he added, smiling.

1970S SHEFFIELD

Mind you, the industrial north of England in the early 1970s was hardly a land flowing with milk and honey. The decline and fall of working-class Britain was one of the most common themes of cultural life in the 1970s. In the television series *Whatever Happened to the Likely Lads?* Terry Collier bemoans the closure of the factory, the colliery and the pub, as well as the chapel, the co-op and his football club in the industrial north-east. Victorian buildings were being demolished to make way for a landscape of flyovers, ring roads, tower blocks, shopping centres and office buildings. Conflict between government and the trade unions led to the miners' strike, the three-day week, power cuts and (in my case) the experience of running a youth club by candlelight. In Sheffield, the steel industry was beginning its long decline into oblivion with more men laid off and families on the dole. The 1970s have not had a good press, and rightly so. They are accurately perceived as a much more drab, disenchanted and pessimistic decade than their 1960s predecessor. The heady days of the Swinging Sixties were long gone – along with Carnaby Street, hippies, flower power, the Beatles and miniskirts. It was a gloomy period of decline: industrial strikes, inflation, devaluation of the pound, the oil crisis, petrol rationing, blackouts, IRA bombs, the 'Winter of Discontent' and the government's apparent impotence in resolving any of them. 'The swinging London of the '60s has given way to a London as gloomy as the city described by Charles Dickens,' the German magazine *Der Spiegel* informed its readers. As some commentators have put it, the 1970s were just a protracted setting of the scene for the advent of Margaret Thatcher as the new Conservative Prime Minister.

There was a local symbol of this sense of national decline. In the mid - 1960s, Sheffield Council had decided to clean up its Town Hall, a Victorian stone edifice which had suffered from over sixty years of smoke, grime, coal dust and dirt. The clean-up revealed the original delicate stone mouldings and friezes of steelworkers that had hitherto been invisible, and the almost white, marble-like colour of the stone itself. By the late 1970s, however, the Town Hall had reverted to its black and grubby colour and there were no civic plans to improve it, nor any interest in doing so.

There were other Kelvins and other similar anxieties about teenagers and hooligans. Visiting an estate in Southampton, one commentator described the familiar dismal scene of tower blocks and deserted grassland 'patrolled by gangs of sub-teenage youths', with residents regularly complaining of theft and vandalism.[2] Anxiety about the increase in muggings, rival gangs of youths, football hooligans and the emergence of a new cultural group called 'skinheads' – working-class youths with shaven heads, clad in boots, braces and rolled-up jeans – filled the popular press of the time. Skinhead culture appealed to those disaffected, working-class teenagers who were seduced by its heady mixture of 'stylised hardness', violence, masculinity, resentment and tribal identity. Racism was also an element of its appeal, cementing the loyalties of those who felt adrift in a world of deep economic anxiety and social change. White working-class young men resented those 'job-stealing' immigrants who were trying to keep them down. And skinhead culture was linked with the perceived growing menace of football hooliganism. Football hooligans had history too. Noting that the word 'hooligan' first made its appearance in the English press during the hot summer of 1898, Geoffrey Pearson confirms that:

> *The modern football rowdy is simply a reincarnation of the unruly apprentice or the late Victorian 'hooligan'… we see the same rituals of territorial dominance, trials of strength, gang fights, mockery against elders and authorities and antagonism towards 'outsiders' as typical focuses for youthful energy and aggressive mischief.*[3]

Stanley Kubrick's film *A Clockwork Orange* premiered in 1972 at the height of the miners' strike. Its violent gang fights and scenes of rape and murder came to reflect the imagery of British youth culture, and amplified calls for more uncompromising methods to deal with youth gangs and 'youth' generally. It might have been subconscious, but we were influenced too by the 1970s interpretations of youth work based on class, Marxism, race and gender. There was a thread of intellectual underpinning to theories of the 'class revolution' approaches to youth at the time. This described a subclass of underprivileged and disadvantaged young people – the unemployed, downtrodden working class – for whom the overthrow of capitalism was their only salvation. Some of this reminded me of the work of Richard Hoggart and Stuart Hall at the Centre for Contemporary Cultural Studies at Birmingham University (where I'd been a student), and its theories were often the basis of many youth work training programmes in the 1960s and 1970s.

WHERE ARE YOU <u>LEADING</u> THE YOUTH TO, THEN...?

I've never had the 'proper' qualifications to do most of the jobs I ended up with. Becoming a teacher was down to having two degrees and completing my probationary year at King Edward VII School. This meant I became a qualified youth worker, too. I never undertook any training in teaching or youth and community work, and I've always felt a bit of a fraud compared to better-prepared colleagues. Not that I would ever place much confidence in paper qualifications – learning on the job (sinking or swimming, more like) has been my experience. The lack of an academic or intellectual rationale for work with young people is regrettably a theme of professional youth work, as I soon discovered. Most training courses in the early days were about safety, first aid, trips, finances and similar. Only once, on a residential programme, did a youth officer ask us the question, 'Now then, all you "youth leaders" – where exactly are you <u>leading</u> the youth to, then...?' It was the first time I'd stopped to consider the theoretical or social underpinning of our work. What exactly was our purpose and function as youth leaders? It was a question that worried me at the time and none of us students really came up with a convincing response to his question. The best we could offer were the usual hackneyed responses: social education, group work, leisure-time provision, providing new opportunities and, yes, keeping them off the streets.

The phrase 'informal social education' was becoming commonplace around this time – probably based on Bernard Davies and Alan Gibson's book *The Social Education of the Adolescent*, published in 1967. Interestingly, Gibson – who was the first head of the Youth Service Information Centre in 1964 (later the National Youth Bureau and then Agency) – had identified the need for a stronger 'conceptual standpoint' in defining the purposes of youth work even then. He was one of the first to recognise there were other professionals inhabiting the 'services to youth' field, not least teachers, recreation staff, student welfare officers and others, which made a clearer definition of what was special about youth work even more critical. Other staff and agencies have continually 'invaded' the youth work patch: teachers, social workers, probation officers, careers advisers, leisure centre staff and, of course, volunteers – Scouts, Guides and the other voluntary organisations. They too have claimed a unique or specialist purpose and clientele amongst young people. Some of them have been smarter at defining their distinctive professional culture and expertise than youth workers have. They have benefited from an intellectual, theoretical and academic base for their practice – something youth services have often shied away from.

The failure of youth work to define its distinctive professional contribution – to say precisely what it brings to the 'youth' table – is another constant in this story. There is a probably apocryphal tale from this period: a group of youth officers and workers visited Edward Heath, then the Prime Minister, to lobby him on the benefits of youth work. They spent a long time berating him about their lack of recognition, value and credibility, and sought his support for their services. He listened patiently and then asked them, 'What does youth work achieve, then?' There was an ominous silence – they found it hard to agree or to provide a coherent answer.[4]

THE ALBEMARLE REPORT:
SIGNPOST TO A GOLDEN AGE?

Though I didn't know it at the time, I was beginning my youth work career in the aftermath of the Albemarle Report, published in 1960 – the first government initiative focusing on youth services in England. Before Albemarle, most leisure-time activities for young people were run by the Scouts and Guides, or by churches and voluntary organisations, going right back into Victorian times. Local authorities had a very limited and patchy role in the proceedings. The first truly national policy guidance came in 1939 with the publication of Circular 1486, entitled *In the Service of Youth*. This commented on the neglect of the social and physical development of fourteen to twenty-year-olds, and gave the Board of Education a direct responsibility for 'youth welfare'.

Yet even as I started out in my youth work career, the Albemarle milieu seemed a bit dated. It was the age of Richard Hoggart, an Albemarle Committee member, and his defence of the publication of *Lady Chatterley's Lover*; it was the era of Teddy boys, the blackboard jungle, getting hip, 'with it' and all that jazz. Ray Gosling's pamphlet *Lady Albemarle's Boys* reflected the world of the Teddy-boy gang, the teen canteen, the Milk Bar Boys who reacted against the Scouting/campfire tradition of the voluntary youth sector and who found some theoretical support in the new tolerance of a more liberal youth policy – linked to the non-directive approach, no doubt. Gosling's message was simple: 'let's get them off the streets and out of the pubs.'[5]

Gosling's experience of running an early town-centre youth club in Leicester in the 1960s is instructive. His approach and analysis were years ahead of their time. He always saw himself as 'on the side of the underdog,' and in describing the key components of a youth club, Gosling insisted it must provide a place of their own for its members, 'the otherwise unclubbables;' somewhere apart from work, home or school, situated in a building all to itself, on the beaten track used by young people in a particular locality – and not a youth wing attached to a school. In early 1961, these were superbly prescient views on the building blocks of centre-based work. He had a natural ear, too, for the rhythm and needs of young people and a sharp perception of his own role as a youth leader. Consider this thoughtful insight, for example:

> *The relationship between a young person and a youth leader must not be one of pupil to teacher, worker to boss, or son to father – but of consumer to supplier. And the supplier must be like a novelist, an accomplice on the inside and a witness on the outside – in sympathy with the demands of his consumer, but able to stand apart and see his client, his character in perspective.*[6]

Ray Gosling was dismissive of some of the Albemarle Report's views, considering them little more than 'hot dogs and coffee – the jazzing up of the youth service to get hep *[sic]*', and that it had done little to shift power towards young people. He probably wouldn't have been impressed by the report's definition of youth work as a 'tense day-to-day walking on a razor edge between sympathy and surrender'. But mocking that analysis seems unfair: the report's authors provided some very perceptive and relevant insights. The striking contrast, for example, between what is provided for those who continue into higher education and what is available for the remainder who have only impoverished youth facilities to turn to. The disparity between the shabby premises apparently considered suitable for youth clubs and the university students' union or sixth-form common room reinforced the point. It was Albemarle that reiterated that the youth service is not negative, not a means of simply 'keeping young people off the streets' or out of trouble, but that its primary function is social or pastoral and that it offers 'places of association' which young people may, or may not, accept on their own terms. It argued strongly about 'what the youth service might do if properly supported and what it is able to achieve today.'

These comments reflected an optimistic, national view of teenagers at the time which especially noted their affluence and opportunity. In 1958, the *Manchester Guardian* reported on a conference of youth workers that concluded that 'the Teddy Boy movement is a hopeful thing.' In an era of rising wages and full employment, teenagers were encouraged to aspire not just to a steady job and economic security, but to creativity and emotional fulfilment as well. The Albemarle Committee's report sanctioned shopping, fashion, coffee bars, jiving and jazz as significant cultural activities, 'charged with emotional content,' that offered young people an outlet for creativity that might otherwise be stultified in monotonous factory and office jobs. As Selina Todd, in her powerful history of the working class in England, puts it, 'all this suggested that working class teenagers had much to offer the country and deserved to have their aspirations taken seriously.'[7] Certainly, the Albemarle Committee was the first to acknowledge that the service had some problems, not least professional uncertainty and a lack of enthusiasm about modifying its traditional practices. A particular issue was low morale amongst practitioners:

> *The Youth Service is at present in a state of acute depression… those who work in the Service feel themselves neglected and held in small regard, both in educational circles and by public opinion generally. We have been told time and time again that the Youth Service is 'dying on its feet' or 'out on a limb'.*

Greenhill-Bradway Youth Centre.
Photos: Sheffield City Council official opening brochure, September 1971.

Plus ça change, plus c'est la même chose, perhaps. But Albemarle was responding to a mixture of other issues, both positive and negative. The problem of the adolescent birth-rate 'bulge' and the lack of youth provision for growing numbers of teenagers; the ending of National Service and the need to redirect surplus youthful energies into alternative, healthy physical recreation. The growth of adult disquiet at the apparent estrangement of young people from society, especially adolescent behaviour, which seemed puzzling or shocking. 'A new climate of crime and delinquency' was how the report put it – so a common thread for youth work as early as the 1960s. Young people, they argued, were misunderstood, confused by conflicting pressures, had too much pocket money, were open to commercial exploitation, and suffered from adult and media stereotyping. 'Latchkey kids' or 'the unattached' were identified as potential target groups of socially deprived for whom the youth service might make provision. The impetus for the work had a positive and philanthropic feature also. This was the need to make the public more aware of how far it was failing to provide adequate support for those who left formal education in their early teens – compared to the pastoral care and the physical and social education available for those who went on to attend further education including universities. Our role was one of public enlightenment, as Lady Albemarle later described it, along with an intention to reverse past policies of neglect towards youth provision.

The Albemarle Report did usher in a new national capital building programme – a very early precursor of the later policy tune of 'places to go and things to do'. Dozens of new youth centres were constructed over the next ten years, based on a design pilot known as the 'Withywood model', after its location on a Bristol estate. 'Bricks and mortar, plastic and Formica' was the slogan for their design and construction. As well as the youth club programme, Albemarle established a youth leaders training course (later the

'Withywood' design youth centre.
Photo: Ministry of Education building bulletin, 1963.

National College) and a Youth Service Information Council (later the National Youth Agency), both based in Leicester. In youth service terms, these are concrete and tangible achievements – not least the development of a trained youth service workforce and the recognition that local authorities have a responsibility to deliver such services in every part of England.

Writing much later, Richard Hoggart felt that the Albemarle Report had the 'fairest of winds' from the government because it was inspired by the first wave of public concern about the increasingly dissident behaviour of urban young people. In stark contrast to later youth service reports, Albemarle's recommendations were accepted very quickly and the funding was provided. 'Not as much,' Hoggart reflected, 'as the report had recommended, but more than it had expected.'[8] Lady Albemarle herself claimed some personal credit for the government's speedy acceptance of her recommendations. In 2005, Howard Williamson recalled meeting her at the annual lecture which bore her name and congratulating her on the clarity of thought and direction in her report.

'You know why that is, dear boy?' she replied. 'The civil servants produced a draft that was absolute gobbledegook; so I tore it up and decided to write it myself.'[9] Probably this is an over-exaggeration, but whatever the reasons, the funding that followed Albemarle established a national youth-centre-building programme that was still going strong as I started my youth work in the 1970s in Sheffield. Greenhill-Bradway Youth Club and Kelvin Youth Centre were both Albemarle centres.

CHAPTER 2

KELVIN: THE LIFE AND DEATH OF A YOUTH CENTRE

So this was a youth club built in the wrong place – albeit with good intentions. I should have guessed something was amiss when I realised I was the only candidate being interviewed for the job of full-time youth club leader. And when I was taken on my first visit to the centre in the summer of 1972, they told me there had already been a number of complaints from residents about the noise and disturbance from members – and this before it had even opened. Whether they were desperate to get the building open, having spent all that council money building it, or whether they took pity on me as the only candidate, I will never know. But they offered me the job and I agreed to take it. And, because I'd obtained a 'good' degree, my starting salary was enhanced to £1,100 per annum.

My brand-new Kelvin Youth Centre opened its doors in October 1972 – over a hundred young people flooded in on the first night. It was a relief and a triumph: everyone had a good time, there was no trouble and members were amazed and delighted at the club's facilities. It was an intense period; a turning point and a milestone in my professional career which left a deep and lasting impression. At twenty-four, I learnt a lot quickly. Working for the first time face-to-face with dozens of young people from one of the more deprived areas of Sheffield, at first hand on a daily and nightly basis. Learning about the realities of their lives and homes, their parents (or lack of them), their hopes and expectations, their ambitions: jobs, money, partners, the future. I also had to learn about managing part-time staff, about political networks – councillors, tenants' groups and schools – about looking after furniture and equipment, about keys, cash boxes, safes and alarm systems.

It was an eye-opener for a bright young graduate taking on his first real new job in charge of a £50,000 youth centre: someone who had led a life relatively sheltered from this new social and cultural experience. I was pretty immature and inexperienced generally. 'He's nowhere near ready for the job,' my previous boss at Greenhill-Bradway Youth Club had told the Education Office, as I discovered much later. It was a stressful and steep learning curve – in those early days I often wondered how long I'd survive in the role. The job produced some early moral dilemmas, too. If the kids arrived at the club regularly each morning, having bunked off school – and Sue, Phil, Plug, Jack or Ian always seemed to – what was I to do? Phone the school and report them to the Education Welfare Officer? Try and keep them busy with club tasks (off to the cash and carry with me) in the hope that this would prevent them going shoplifting in town? Mostly, I felt they'd be safer with me so let them stay.

And then there was Pete. He was seventeen or eighteen, older than the majority of members: a big and muscly boy with powerful shoulders and a build like a boxer's. When he walked he moved with precision but rolled a little from side to side. Yet he had a round, open face which made him easy to read, and which belied the aura of potential aggression he seemed to carry. Reputedly, Pete was a hard man on the Kelvin. He joined the club on the first night and was a regular. Funnily enough, he rather took to me – deciding that I needed 'looking after,' protecting from problems created by other members or outside troublemakers. After all, I was only a few years older than him and he was pretty acute (and accurate) in spotting my wariness of him and how he might behave. In fact, he developed a fierce loyalty to the club and got involved in everything we did. He'd accompany me to Makro and help load my car with coffee-bar stock; he manhandled our twenty-foot-high Christmas tree into position and spent days decorating it with lights and baubles. He decided he was best placed to captain the embryonic KYC football team, and chose the shirt colours and club logo as well.

But he could still be volatile and his moods could swing from benign to violent very easily – albeit not when he was in the centre. When I reopened the club after that first Christmas, Pete was missing. The members soon told me what had happened. Over the holidays, he had brutally beaten up his parents and held them hostage in their flat for two days and nights, barricading the door. Neighbours finally broke in to release them and Pete was arrested. The *Sheffield Star* ran with the story as its front-page headline, and subsequently for some while. No one really knew what had triggered the attack and why it had involved such violence. It came as a shock to me and it was hard to know how to react. Writing a letter to the court recounting his loyalty and positive contribution to the youth centre seemed a pretty futile response, although I did my best. His parents recovered and Pete was eventually sent to Walton Prison in Liverpool. I got a few letters from him at first – mostly asking after the club and how his mates were going on – but they soon petered out. I drove his mum and dad to visit him at Walton on one occasion but they wouldn't let me in to see him: family visitors only. Sadly, he never returned to the club and I never saw or heard any more about him. One of those relationships where you think you could have made more of a difference – if only there had been more time.

Kelvin Youth Centre members, 1973–1974. Photos by Tim Caley.

We were incredibly popular and busy in those first six months of 1973, and I'd relaxed enough to begin to really enjoy the job. Football teams were formed, film shows were arranged, a Saturday-morning junior club started, and there were fashion shows, coach trips and visits galore – Derbyshire, Blackpool, Skegness. It would be tempting to claim that all these events and our regular club programme were founded on a clear rationale about the nature and purpose of youth work practice and intervention. In reality, I just copied what other youth clubs seemed to be doing, or listened to the advice of my more experienced colleagues in planning and arranging things. Certainly, the trips were offering new experiences, growing self-awareness, confidence and loyalty amongst our regular members; clearly, taking them out of their home environment broadened their horizons and awakened new interests. But that was more an accidental by-product than a premeditated outcome. They were never quite sure about me personally and what my role was. 'What do you do in the day,

Tim?' they would regularly ask me. Yet they accepted me without hesitation, unconcerned about my youth and obvious lack of experience. Like Pete, most of them were keen to help me succeed and shared my ambition to make Kelvin Youth Club a success for its new membership. In my eagerness to make the club programme a success and to increase our burgeoning membership, I occasionally responded far too eagerly – arranging events and activities that a few individuals might have suggested, but which often failed to take off. The cartoon below just about sums me up during that period at the club.

Developing a sense of loyalty took time, of course, and we never had enough of that. But it was a positive period reflecting a burgeoning youth culture: when young people could escape from their homes and join their peers to enjoy themselves out of school, in their leisure time and in a safe place they could call their own. Even our dedicated girls' 'powder room' (it felt like an old-

Youthwise by TB; cartoon from Youth in Society, 1982.

fashioned description even then) was partly a symbol of that sense of fashion, clothes and make-up that the young female members were displaying.

And there was a bonus: approaching Sheffield Polytechnic to see if any of their social work students would be interested in a placement at the youth club, I was delighted at the positive response. Ros, one of the young women who volunteered to help me, became a tremendous ally and support. She must have really enjoyed youth work because she tagged along on the coach trips to Blackpool Illuminations and the funfair at Skegness, came on the camping weekends in Derbyshire and (after the club closed) worked out on the estate with me, helped to build the carnival float and generally mucked in with great spirit and enthusiasm. I couldn't believe my good fortune in finding someone both incredibly attractive and willing to pitch in and help in my new youth work job. We were soon to spend even more time together.

There were occasional episodes that cemented our relationships as staff and members in particular ways. One evening, a group managed to get into an upstairs room, normally locked, where the hot water tank was sited. They kicked and broke the valve by sitting on top of the tank and some sixty gallons of boiling hot water cascaded down the stairs, through the ceiling and the light fittings, and onto the floor below. Chaos ensued for a while but no one was hurt and, mercifully, the lights stayed on and no real damage was caused. Interestingly, whether through guilt or otherwise, a group of members stayed with us as a staff team until after midnight, clearing up, sweeping waves of water towards the front door, trying to dry off the soaking furniture, carpets and equipment. It was one of those shared moments when your members 'come good', when a critical incident brings people together to make things right again, when they began to speak of the 'youthy' rather than the club. Many of them recalled the 'flood' at the club years later – long after the building itself had closed down.

A 'NORMAL' CLUB NIGHT

When I used to write up the programme for each week's events there were some nights called 'normal club nights'. I wondered later what I really meant by that – what was normal and what exceptional? For the staff team, a good night was one where everything passed off quietly: no arguments over music between black and white, no confrontations (or worse) in the building, and a chance to interact with members positively over the snooker, coffee bar or in the girls' powder room. A quiet chat to talk through personal issues was an oft-reported feature of a good night. On these occasions, we congratulated ourselves on the youth work skills we had displayed. (On the occasions when we had trouble, of course, we just blamed the members.) Unconsciously, here, I was tapping into an early confusion of purpose and definition around the youth work role – even in this, its simplest delivery vehicle, the youth club evening. Being immersed in the normal daily

and nightly routine of activities, organisation, programme and administration tended not to encourage much reflection about purpose. Stocking up the coffee bar at the cash and carry, getting in the bread rolls and crisps, bagging up the takings and the subscriptions each morning, booking the film shows and arranging the minibuses and football fixtures: all of these kept me busy enough.

Youth club leader, 1972; sketch by Phil Brown.

THE COFFEE BAR

The concept of healthy eating had yet to reach the youth club coffee bar. We did serve coffee, but it was only the adults who drank it. When we had the staff, we might run to hamburgers or hot dogs, but our staples were crisps – plain, salt and vinegar or cheese and onion – and packets of peanuts, along with chocolates and sweets of all varieties. Mars bars, Milky Ways, Curly Wurlys, Polos and Spangles were popular, but it was the cheaper 'spice', as the members called them, that sold best of all. Liquorice bootlaces, four-for-a-penny chews, Fruit Salads, Black Jacks, aniseed balls, cola bottles, bubblegum, pink shrimps, flying saucer sherbets – they lapped them all up. It was washed down with cola – not the real thing, but an evil, sticky-sweet concentrate that was watered down, fizzed up and piped into a dispenser that sat on the counter. Gladys, our club cleaner and caretaker, often complained about the silverfish she would discover in the kitchen cupboards. It was because of the sugar vats from the Bassett's factory that was here before they built the flats, she used to tell me. She was right: George Bassett did build a confectionery works on Portland Street in 1860, employing 'over 150 persons in the various processes of spice-making'. The factory churned out Liquorice Allsorts, Spanish juice sticks, Pontefract cakes, acid drops, mints, sweetmeats and pastilles. Once the factory closed in 1860, they probably did just leave the enormous sugar vats and steam pans where they stood.[10]

One week, in an attempt to broaden our range, I decided to buy a catering-size jar of pickled eggs, on special offer at Makro. Some three dozen yellowing, hard-boiled eggs surrounded by a faintly brown-coloured liquid vinegar. It sat on the bar for months: we sold about three in total. I often wonder what happened to that jar: perhaps it was left behind and somehow amazingly preserved when the Kelvin Flats were finally demolished in 1995.

Even now, it might be resting, miraculously unbroken, beneath someone's kitchen on Portland Court, awaiting the archaeological dig that will rediscover it, along with the remains of the Bassett's Liquorice Allsorts factory sugar vats buried three metres further down.

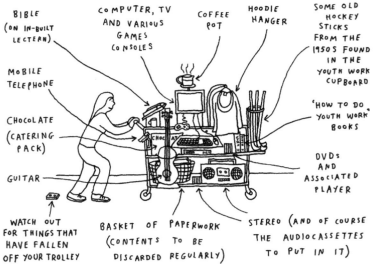

THE YOUTH WORK TROLLEY

THESE DAYS YOUTH WORK REQUIRES A VAST ARRAY OF EQUIPMENT. HAVING A SPECIAL TROLLEY IS A GOOD WAY TO CARRY IT ALL AROUND:

BIBLE (ON IN-BUILT LECTERN)

COMPUTER, TV AND VARIOUS GAMES CONSOLES

COFFEE POT

HOODIE HANGER

SOME OLD HOCKEY STICKS FROM THE 1950S FOUND IN THE YOUTH WORK CUPBOARD

MOBILE TELEPHONE

'HOW TO DO YOUTH WORK' BOOKS

CHOCOLATE (CATERING PACK)

DVDs AND ASSOCIATED PLAYER

GUITAR

WATCH OUT FOR THINGS THAT HAVE FALLEN OFF YOUR TROLLEY

BASKET OF PAPERWORK (CONTENTS TO BE DISCARDED REGULARLY)

STEREO (AND OF COURSE THE AUDIOCASSETTES TO PUT IN IT)

CartoonChurch.com

The Youth Work Trolley from CartoonChurch.com

'As long as the members are rolling up in reasonable numbers,' I was reassured by one of my more experienced part-timers, 'the youth officers won't bother you.' Implicit in this advice was that it was only when the daily routine was disturbed – by some form of crisis created by 'trouble' in the club, falling attendances, or (in my case) complaints from the neighbours – that some debate about direction, aims or objectives might follow. My youth officer boss, Joan, only ever visited once. It was in the early days, and on the night we were full to bursting: the place was a hive of activity. Showing her round with obvious pride, I noticed she had a contented half-smile on her face. She didn't stay long but it seemed like I had passed some kind of probationary test.

There was poverty in the area, certainly, and poverty of ambition apparent in many individuals. For many, boys and girls both, by around fourteen or fifteen years old, school and academic achievement was an impossible dream. Most had experienced failure at exams and looked forward to leaving as soon as the law allowed; post-sixteen education, college or university was an unrealistic target and not for the likes of them. There wasn't much crime or drugs or violence at that time – just a stifling lack of ambition, of interest in people, places or ideas. It reminded me of the social and class divisions Richard Hoggart had described in his book *The Uses of Literacy* more than a decade earlier.[11] They had little chance to be ambitious, had little sense of career possibilities or promotion, their jobs were 'spread around horizontally, not vertically' – life was not seen as a climb, nor work the main interest in it. Their lives were circumscribed by a tight geographical neighbourhood, an unchanging, humdrum routine and a constant lack of money to break out of both. But they certainly wanted (and needed) the centre and the security and relationships it seemed to provide. They turned up all the time – if we'd have opened on Christmas Day there would have been a queue. Perhaps it was that archetypal safe haven, a place for association and friendship, to talk to trusted adults who were willing to listen; maybe it was just somewhere out of the cold. That, after all, has been a key rationale and function of the youth club through the ages. One evening we took a group of loyal 'regulars' out for a special treat: a steak-and-chips meal at a Berni Inn. They were a little anxious travelling there in the minibus: it was only four miles from home, but this was new and dangerous territory. They loved it, as I knew they would, lapping up the experience, luxuriating in the novelty and pinching themselves to check that

"Who says there aren't enough after-school activities for youths on these estates?"

Cartoon by RGJ from Youth in Society, 1983.

they weren't dreaming. And at the end of the night, Ian declared gratefully that 'that was the best meal I've ever had in my life.'

Before Kelvin, I'd been a teacher for a year at King Edward VII School in Sheffield and hated every minute of it. Well, not the bits when I could just talk to pupils – at break time, after school, passing in the corridors. I liked the informal relationships with the young people, not the formal classroom work. As well as my teaching job, I was working three nights a week as a part-timer at the newly opened Greenhill-Bradway Youth Centre and enjoyed it a great deal more. The young people I met during my (admittedly limited) youth work experience to that point were friendly, enthusiastic and full of energy. It's no surprise that I preferred my three nights a week at Greenhill-Bradway to my classroom trials and tribulations in the history department at King Edward VII School. The contrast in job satisfaction and enjoyment between school and youth club could not have been greater. Who wouldn't have preferred the friendly, vibrant and positive atmosphere of the youth centre to the disciplined and sterile environment of the grammar school?

To be honest, I was never meant to be a history teacher; the realities of classroom management came as a shock to me. King Edward VII had been for generations Sheffield's top boys' grammar school – the ambition of every (male) eleven-plus exam-passer in the city. But by the late 1960s it had become a comprehensive and – much more of a shock for the traditional male staff – a co-educational school. I had just come back from the USA, having finished my Masters in American history, and they needed a history teacher. In those days, the concept of induction, probation and support for new staff was unheard of. Only once did I receive any positive feedback on my classroom skills and that was from a fellow teacher; I had organised an exhibition about Henry VIII and his wives and the pupils had produced some wonderful pictures, collages and displays. These I had conscientiously judged and awarded prizes (of chocolate bars) to the winners. My colleague told me that the class had really taken to me and were obviously enjoying my lessons with them. Rare music, indeed, to my apprentice ears. Mostly, though, I was just pitched in at the deep end and learnt to sink or swim. On the whole I managed, and I especially enjoyed teaching the younger third-year pupils. Generally, I kept a page ahead in the book for most lessons, even the sixth-form A Level groups. But I confess the prospect of double history with 4X on Thursday afternoons struck fear into my heart.

It was in one such difficult lesson that I was reduced to threatening to cane an unruly pupil who had spent the term making my life a misery. This was an era when corporal punishment was still available to teachers and, to my horror, I discovered I had the power to use a cane if I felt it was needed. To me this was an appalling prospect and I must have been seriously under pressure to have even considered the idea. Another good reason to give up on the teaching profession. Having decided my future lay outside the classroom, and having tendered my resignation in my first summer, the headmaster summoned me to his office. I'd never been there before, just as he had never ventured into the staffroom – at least not in the year I'd been in post. Sitting behind his massive desk, he exuded an air of patrician distaste for the defecting probationer in front of him. 'Your decision to leave the school is unfortunate,' he explained. 'Working three nights a week in a *youth club* [he formed the words as though they had somehow attached themselves to the sole of his shoe] is not something we look kindly upon.' Confused as to how I should respond, I just muttered, 'Yes, Headmaster.'

Working with Youth, BBC TV booklet, 1972.

And I was dismissed with a sigh, as he moved on to the more serious matters on his desk, omitting any best wishes for my future.

Youth work was something I really knew nothing about. But I watched a BBC television series called *Working with Youth* with interest. It was set in a youth club and each weekly programme provided some helpful tips and suggestions: how to approach and engage young people in conversation around the snooker table; how to support individuals who were unhappy or seemed to be in trouble; ways to handle teenage anger or aggressive behaviour. There was an accompanying booklet to the series which I also read and tried to follow. It was only when researching this book that I learnt that *Working with Youth* had been produced by Bernard Davies, whose epic three-volume *History of the Youth Service* was published twenty-five years later. I tried to follow the guidance in the series but, truth be told, I wasn't very successful. Probably I was just too young, too naive, too inexperienced. And my head was still back at the University of Kansas where I had been working on my dissertation only a few months previously. Understanding the dynamics of group work or one-to-one work seemed alien to me at the time. It was simpler and easier to give me a basic job to do in the youth centre – organising the rounders in the park or the sponsored walk for club funds. The club leader at Greenhill-Bradway agreed. He sent me off one night to represent the club at a city-wide meeting about sports tournaments despite my lack of sporting knowledge or expertise. When I got back later, I asked him why he'd sent me.

'Easy,' he replied. 'We agreed you were the one member of staff we'd least miss tonight.' So much for my fledgling youth work career. Nevertheless, I enjoyed the chance to get to know the teenage members and help or support their hopes and aspirations, involving them in the club programme, watching them line-dancing to the Osmonds – this all seemed a breath of fresh air to me. And my view was echoed by an ex-member who recalled, thirty years later, the good times at Greenhill-Bradway Youth Centre:

Great times, discos on a Friday and Sunday – people used to come from miles around. It was a top youth club – floodlit football, basketball, holiday clubs in Lowedges Park in the summer: great memories, great music, great friends. It kept a lot of people off the streets, including me...![12]

MORAL PANICS

As well as Kubrick's *A Clockwork Orange*, another early influence on me was Stanley Cohen's *Folk Devils and Moral Panics*, published in 1972. His detailed research study was based on observing the activities of groups of 'mods and rockers' in Clacton and Brighton during bank holiday weekends in the 1960s and recording the reactions of adults, the police and the press. The book received a lot of sensationalist press and television coverage. Cohen showed how the mass-media reaction to the delinquency and troublemaking created what he termed 'moral panics' about young people and 'folk devils' of youth cultures and subcultures. More broadly, Cohen argued that the most recurrent type of moral panic in Britain since the war has been associated with the emergence of various forms of youth culture – originally almost exclusively working class – whose behaviour is deviant or delinquent and often associated with violence. The roll call includes Teddy boys, mods and rockers, Hell's Angels, grebos, skinheads and hippies, but 'working-class yobs' in general are the most enduring of these enemies. These particular adolescent groups occupy the position of folk devils, symbolising in the eyes of the establishment and the popular press a threat to order and society.[13]

I saw plenty of that during my time on the Kelvin estate. But none of the youngsters on the flats were criminals or delinquents, and collectively they offered no threat to society. Most of them simply craved someone to talk to, someone who would listen to them, someone to support and encourage them, someone to treat them fairly or to provide them with new ideas and activities. At heart, these young people just needed the care and attention they failed to get at home and the chance to learn something new, meet their mates, have a laugh, expand their horizons and achieve something positive to make them feel good about themselves.

Very occasionally, it was easy to gain a glimpse of how they felt. During the hot summer of 1976, sitting one afternoon on the kerbside with a group outside the club, idly chatting, I suddenly said, 'Why don't we go and vandalise something, do a bit of damage?' I don't know where the words had come from: prompted by a flash of boredom, or maybe empathy with the depressing tedium of what we were doing and the need to inject some excitement, however antisocial or illegal, into the moment. Not that we did it, of course.

COMPLAINTS ABOUT NOISE

But I had a more pressing local problem at Kelvin Youth Centre – and that was the growing chorus of complaints from residents about noise. The club's official opening ceremony was postponed. We had opened in October 1972, but by the following autumn residents' meetings were being held, complaints had reached the local press, and tenants were compiling petitions to close down the centre. Sound recorders were brought in to measure decibel levels, extra soundproofing was installed in the roof and disco sessions were banned. In October, the tenants even served a Nuisance Abatement Order on me. Being caught in the middle of this particular political storm was not much fun. I started to get a bit worried as there was no sign of my Youth Office managers riding to my aid and rescuing me from the problems. As a trade union member, I contacted the Community and Youth Service Association for advice. To my amazement, the general secretary herself personally travelled to Sheffield to meet me and support my predicament. Her arrival triggered a more proactive reaction from the Youth Office, but I was ever after impressed and grateful for her intervention.

One afternoon, around this time, a bright and buzzy young woman came to see me in the centre office. She introduced herself as the prospective Liberal candidate for the local ward, adding that she'd heard the club was going to close down. 'It's terrible,' she said; 'is there anything I can do to help?' Unexpectedly seduced

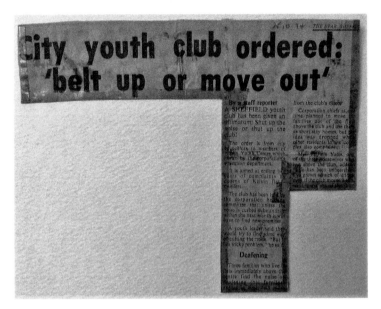

Sheffield Star, October 1974.

by her sympathy, I suddenly felt encouraged and hopeful. 'Where have you been all my life?' I heard myself replying. I recounted the story of the centre's problems and she listened closely, promising to go away and get the decision on closure reversed. Of course, I never saw her again. I should have realised that the chances of a Liberal councillor being elected in the Socialist Republic of South Yorkshire were, to put it mildly, unlikely.

We also had a visit from a group of London youth workers soon afterwards – a kind of exchange visit arranged by the National Association of Youth Clubs. They obviously supported my cause too, and on returning to the capital they wrote a very strong letter to the *Sheffield Star* deploring the decision to close Kelvin Youth Centre and deprive local teenagers of somewhere to go. I was grateful, but truth to tell, it was all too late and all in vain.

Trying to sustain my loyalties to the members and the thriving programmes that were developing, and to include discos as part of the club's repertoire, was ultimately doomed. In reality, the residents had a strong case: the fabric of the concrete pillars which ran the length and breadth of the flats inevitably transmitted noise and vibration – of every kind. Even had the music been abandoned, the complaints would not have stopped. By the end of 1973, the council conceded that building a youth centre within the flats had been a 'very big mistake'. The members – all three

Press coverage, Sheffield Star, 1974.

hundred of them – wanted to fight it out and began their own campaign to resist closure of the club. This put me in an even more exposed position as a council employee but local youth worker. Together we arranged a march on the Town Hall with a petition protesting about the plans to close down the centre.

In the midst of this campaign, I arrived at the club one afternoon and was accosted by three of the regulars. 'We've been speaking to that Hattersley woman,' Plug informed me. 'She rang you, but you weren't here, so we gave her a reight mouthful about closing the club,' he added forcefully. This was Councillor Enid Hattersley, mother of Roy Hattersley, later Deputy Leader of the Labour Party in the 1980s, and a powerful woman in the city council of the time. 'Fine, thanks, Plug,' I mumbled feebly, horrified at what he might have said to her and how far it could have cemented the club's fate. But secretly I was quite proud of his new-found political activity on behalf of the centre and his fellow members.

Over the years, some of the regular and loyal Kelvin members had become something of a surrogate family for me. Plug, Phil, Ian, Sue, Jack and a few others were always around, daytime and evenings; what's more, they were on my side. We'd been through a lot together in quite a short time. They travelled in my car to the cash and carry and on trips to town or out into the Derbyshire countryside. When I couldn't make the home games at Bramall Lane, I might give one of the lads my Sheffield United season ticket, so they could go to the match. Once, Phil and Leslie decided they wanted to bake me a cake, so we drove up to my house, bought the flour at the local shop and used my kitchen to make and eat the Victoria sponge they created. Yet this fragile little family soon melted away once the club closed. I bumped into Jack a couple of years later at an outdoor centre in the Peak District when I brought a group from Lindsay Road Club, but most of them I never saw again. Like me, they'd moved on – they too had the rest of their lives to lead.

I knew there were dangers and pitfalls in becoming 'friends' with club members in this way, of course. Dangers in getting too close to individual youngsters: in establishing favourites who could be identified as one of the leader's 'chosen few'. These risks had been around when I was teaching, but the youth centre was a much more private and informal arena than the school classroom. That hadn't prevented some awkward situations at King Edward's. Teaching a third-year group a lesson on the Tudors and Stuarts one afternoon, I was pleasantly impressed with their rapt attention and diligence in answering my questions. Until, at the close of the lesson, a group of girls surrounded my desk to invite me to the school's end-of-term disco. I made my excuses, deciding the risks outweighed any potential loss in popularity. That response was based solely on some kind of internal, instinctive awareness of the boundaries and hazards in the job; certainly not on any training or guidance I'd received. Relying on instinct or common sense was (and is) a dangerous practice – this was the era of Jimmy Savile, remember; a man who was much in demand to visit youth clubs in the 1970s. In fact, we had invited him to do the official opening of Kelvin Youth Centre, but he'd sent me a postcard regretting that he couldn't come because his volunteering activities were concentrated at the Leeds Hospital where he was a porter.

As far as the political protests about the club closure were concerned, my bosses were probably unaware and didn't seem too concerned about any potential collusion with the club members. On the march to the Town Hall, it helped that the local press described me as the 'social worker' at the centre of the youth club protest movement. It was the club's last hurrah as far as I was concerned, with the centre finally shutting its doors in March 1975. We closed before we had even officially opened. And maybe it was just as well Jimmy Savile had never come.

The story of Kelvin's closure is not that uncommon or unusual; the pressures and dilemmas for politicians and officers in trying to resolve two compelling and competing sets of interests – young people and local adults – are hard to underestimate. Well, the adults almost always win, but that's a political reality too. For me, there were some harsh lessons learnt over the closure of Kelvin – lessons that stayed with me into my later time as a head of service. Firstly, that it was critical to get your elected members 'on side'; and secondly, that it is equally important to balance the sometimes-conflicting demands of two competing constituencies: local teenagers and local adults. Finally, that it is difficult to tread that fine line between advocacy and visible support for the aspirations of young people whilst remembering the professional duties of an employee.

THE THEORY (OR LACK OF IT) BEHIND YOUTH WORK

As a new entrant to the youth work profession (albeit only a part-timer in 1971), there wasn't a lot to read to help me understand my new craft. The literature of youth work is pitifully small and often weak. The ethos of non-judgemental, non-interventionist, uncritical thinking has been too influential on youth work college training courses and their students. Person-centred approaches, transactional analysis methods, facilitative leadership styles – all have characterised youth work training from the 1960s onwards. Even the National Youth Bureau (later Agency), which might have taken a lead, has a poor record in sponsoring improvements in the academic rigour of youth work theory or research into theory and practice developments nationally. While the contribution of those academics and writers from *Youth and Policy* has been important – not least Bernard Davies, Mark Smith, Tony Jeffs, Tom Wylie and others – unfortunately their work has had a limited readership and has barely scratched the surface in shifting the thinking of the average practitioner. Sometimes youth services have been complicit in their own weaknesses and low priority perceptions. The service has often accepted an anti-intellectual tradition, with little sustained and critical attention devoted to the development of the professional craft of youth work. For youth workers, 'being there' is more important than 'understanding.' The only good theory is that which derives from experience – anything else can be dismissed as jargon. Youth work seems stuck in the realm of feelings, participation and empathy, all of which limit theoretical understanding and application to the development of thinking and challenge on the youth work role: 'Never mind the quality, feel the relationship,' as we tended to describe it.

Sometimes this tradition becomes a badge of honour, to be upheld on all occasions. Academics and theorists are viewed with some suspicion by youth work practitioners. The gold standard of youth work currency is fieldwork, grassroots, coalface experience – not degrees, diplomas or certificates. This set of attitudes has a long history – my own youth work experience in Sheffield was influenced by these same person-centred approaches and the 'non-judgemental,' 'non-directive' philosophies in vogue at the time amongst training agencies and local authorities. At Greenhill-Bradway Youth Club, struggling early on as a part-timer to come to terms with some of the behaviour and attitudes of the teenage members, I asked for help and advice from the full-time leader. He did his best to reassure me, but mainly by reiterating that all these difficulties were valuable 'learning experiences' for me. Later, I was to discover that many inspection reports noted that youth club provision was often indistinguishable from leisure or recreational activity. The policy vacuum that all this created has left the youth service highly vulnerable to demands that it needs to respond to whatever the current moral panic concerning young people may be.

It soon became clear to me that this professional 'brittleness' – it is tempting to write 'inferiority complex' – sometimes led to a defensiveness of attitude and sensitivity, especially with other agencies and professionals. Our perceived lack of status and confidence every so often led us into unnecessary overcompensation, into adopting an antagonistic view of allied colleagues including teachers, social workers and (later) Connexions personal advisers. This brand of belligerent behaviour sometimes proved politically counterproductive, alienating potential allies and undermining the good work that was being achieved. It was on display during the curriculum conferences of the early 1990s, and largely responsible for the generic over-exaggeration of youth work's potential and, in particular, for the hopelessly unrealistic Statement of Purpose produced for the service at that time.

It was accepted that youth workers worked with young people in a style different from that of the formal school curriculum – usually characterised by the phrase 'non-directive youth work', probably from T.R. and M. Batten's *Non-Directive Approach to Community Development*, published in 1967. This approach appeared to rely on the young person taking the lead, suggesting the agendas, revealing their feelings, hopes or fears – with a 'passive' adult youth worker friend listening and empathising with them, helping them to form their own conclusions and make their own decisions. Nothing much wrong with that, and the non-directive approach was very popular in the 1970s among youth workers like me. This is not to confuse 'non-directive' with 'laissez-faire' – deciding not to intervene is often a considered option in youth work practice. But I sense that it chimed firstly with our wish not to be like teachers or other social-work-type professionals who clearly had a more structured or directive role with young people, including one that more directly represented the state. And secondly, with the fact that we did not have any well-defined role or responsibility with our own youth club members or contacts anyway. By definition, we preferred approaches that avoided the implicit direction of policy or authority agendas and desired social outcomes. Again, that might have been just because we were pretty young and immature, professionally, ourselves – too much like our clients, critics might argue.

There were times when I blamed myself for the closure of Kelvin Youth Club. Had I been too naive and inexperienced in my approach? What if I'd tried harder to work with the residents? Could we have changed the programme – reducing the noise of discos and music, perhaps developing work with an older age range? But in the end, I concluded that I was simply the unfortunate club leader: a pawn caught up in the middle of a political conflict not of my own making and with little influence on its outcome.

Fortunately, there was a silver lining, professionally speaking, for me. I was to become a detached youth worker for the Kelvin Flats area, working both with young people and community groups. I received a letter from the authority commiserating with my plight.

> *It is regrettable that a youth centre has to close through no fault of the leader and his staff. You worked through a great deal of difficulty during the last few months before closure and your application was much appreciated by the youth officers.*

More honestly, the city's senior officer said to me informally, 'You've done your apprenticeship; now you can go detached!' Even more honestly, one of the detached worker team complained to me, 'How come you manage to get promoted for *failure*? You close down a perfectly good youth club and they give you another, better job…'

YOUTH AND COMMUNITY WORK IN THE 1970S: A CONFUSED HYBRID?

While I was wrestling with the pressures of the closing campaign at Kelvin, I'd found time to read a report called *Youth and Community Work in the 1970s*, often referred to as the Fairbairn-

Milson Report after its two authors. My fledgling detached youth work career was partly a result of this report. It was responding to a time of student unrest and political revolutions and protest during 1968. Albemarle's anxiety over Teddy boys had been replaced by rising concern about the disengagement of the young and 'hippy' protestors. What was the youth service doing about it, was the question? And more critically, had the youth service got a future? The report's answer was yes, but as a service that could not be isolated from general community activities. The report attempted to create a new, all-purpose youth *and* community service – one which added to the traditional youth worker's role a vague and unspecific responsibility for 'community development', 'neighbourhood work' and other concepts; concepts which embraced all sectors of the education service as well as the police, social services, trade unions, commercial provision and others. There was little in the way of details addressing how this new community dimension would be funded or measured, however.

The report was also, critically, split in outlook between its two authors. One of them, Andrew Fairbairn, a Director of Education, wanted an expansion of school-based youth work, with more youth wings and youth tutor posts in every school. He was more than happy to see a separate youth service 'atrophy and disappear' as the growth of school-based provision made it irrelevant. The other, Fred Milson, from a voluntary youth organisation background, was dead against such a move, arguing from a youth work perspective that for many young people, school was part of the problem and they were unlikely to return there in the evenings. There was also plenty of opposition at the time to the dangers of diluting and distracting youth work by incorporating it into the rather nebulous edifice described as 'community work' or 'community education'. One critic was David Marsland, who complained that someone or other is always wanting to reorganise the youth service. Marsland was sceptical of the procession of demands for the service to become something other than a youth service. 'In my view, the Youth Service has an important job to do and is quite capable of doing it well,' he declared, 'adding that the concept of community education was vague, weak and impractical.'[14]

Fred Milson held firm to a similar focus for youth work, reiterating his belief that its primary purpose was to provide support and opportunities for the individual young person. The youth service, he wrote, needed above all to rediscover those simple realities which are its essence: it had no need of new structures or reorganisation. The service was never intended as a social work rescue agency, nor to function as a political lobbyist. It provided an educational and pastoral service for those many youngsters who have had a rough deal, the relatively deprived, often victims of a meritocratic society. It was – and is – a voluntary association: bringing old and young together in a relationship of mutual respect, joint learning and common endeavour. Warning of the dangers of unrealistic expectations, he feared the service could become 'the rag bag for the frustrations and fears of society as a whole'. Youth workers must hold firm in limiting their ambitions to what they can deliver – not trying to pretend they held long-term panaceas or short-term instant solutions to 'the problem of youth'. 'We should say no with courage and confidence,' he stated, 'so lessening the pressures which come upon us.'[15]

These were wise and welcoming words for a youth worker still learning his trade and sometimes feeling buffeted by the pressures of the seemingly endless competing demands from local groups and organisations, from managers and other agencies. Having the confidence to 'say no' or 'draw a line in the sand' over the ever-increasing expectations of others was advice I regularly repeated to many youth services in my consultancy roles twenty years later.

For a number of reasons, the *Youth and Community Work in the 1970s* report met with little sympathy from the government and many of its recommendations were shelved. It met with hostility from senior civil servants who viewed the youth service as a 'fringe activity,' and their views probably influenced ministers in the Labour government. Fears about the potential costs of undefined community services added to the delays in response. Margaret Thatcher, the new Conservative Secretary of State for Education, confirmed that the government was not minded to set up 'a youth and community service with not very clear responsibilities'. And she also subsequently abolished the Youth Service Development Council, whose members had worked hard to develop the report and the youth service nationally. Nevertheless, some of the report's recommendations were craftily linked by youth officers to the expanded geographical areas established at the same time by local government reorganisation. Many suddenly called themselves 'youth *and community* officers', awarded themselves a pay rise and, to the fieldwork staff, appeared to alter their role or responsibilities not at all. The only change I noticed was that my salary slip was now headed 'South Yorkshire Metropolitan District Council' instead of 'Sheffield City Council'.

On the ground, therefore, youth workers were left to deal with the policy inconsistencies and contradictions of the report. Some developed the youth and community line, others the youth in the community model – a confusing position. Critically, as later became apparent, where authorities adopted a 'community education' model, there was a continuing danger that the primacy of youth work could be lost or sidelined to wider priorities. But the *Youth and Community Work* report does still resonate with me for a number of other reasons both political and personal – especially bearing in mind what I'd just been through at Kelvin Youth Centre. It validated the view that we need to get away from the 'club is the youth service' approach; it argued that the service should be setting target and priority groups of young people who have left school or are from 'inadequate social environments'.

And it made no bones about the youth service's poor image and publicity. For the man in the street, it argued, youth clubs were 'rowdy,' youngsters were 'undisciplined and irresponsible' and the youth work job was about 'keeping the young off the streets'. It highlighted the service's 30% take-up rate, the decline in membership and the comparative success of the voluntary sector. The report fundamentally reinforced social education, partnership and new approaches that saw the youth club as a 'base of operations' in a neighbourhood, and which legitimised – maybe for the first time nationally – detached and community youth work styles of operation and delivery. For me, this was just what I needed to hear as I moved from the club into the wider estate.

CHAPTER 3

DETACHED YOUTH WORK

It was a liberating feeling to be released from the tyranny of the youth club's bunch of keys. It was my good fortune to have the advantage of knowing most of the young people on the Kelvin estate already, whilst now seeing them in a wider context – their schools, families and the other adult or friendship groups in which they operated. I had to start thinking more carefully about what a detached or a community youth worker was supposed to be doing – now I had the freedom to do it. My new job description was magnificently vague:

> *The worker will be expected to develop relationships with young people living in or relating to the Kelvin Flats area. These will be used to further the development of young people, either through direct work with adolescents or as a result of changes made by working with the adult community and agencies affecting the lives of local people.*

To be truthful, I was looking forward to doing detached work, having heard it described as probably the most exciting and effective way of meeting the needs of young people, but also one of the most demanding to accomplish well. I wasn't too sure *how* to do it, but it seemed like a 'promotion' of some sort to be allowed out of the youth club building into this pioneering new world with its dangerous, unprotected and exciting work on the margins! Back in the 1960s, the Albemarle Committee had acknowledged that many young people were too wary or estranged to accept the commitment of youth club membership, or simply rejected involvement and belonging – at least in the conventional sense. The report felt that youth workers should develop *more experiments to cater for their social needs in the unconstrained way they seek. We have in mind the coffee bar sited strategically at the places they congregate, the 'drop-in' club… the experimental youth centre or workshop.* It went further, suggesting there was also a need for an

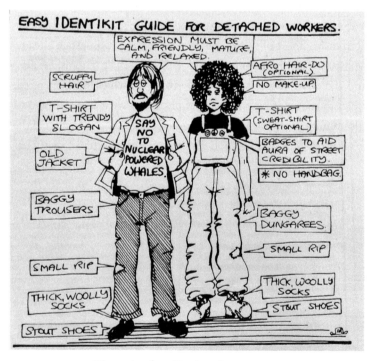

Illustration from Youth in Society, 1980.

experiment with peripatetic youth workers, not attached directly to any organisation or premises, who would work with existing groups or gangs of young people. By definition those groups who rejected youth centres might be seen as a tougher breed – more difficult to reach and form relationships with. Detached work had something of an aura about it: it was 'harder' – as the northern terminology of the time had it – well, harder than running a youth club, certainly.

So detached work was not new and there was a clear recognition of the needs of young people who did not join centres. Sometimes they were called the 'unclubbables' or the 'unattached'. The latter label was taken from Mary Morse's seminal book of that title, published in 1965. Her work was influential: between 1967 and 1970 the Youth Service Information Centre in Leicester published over forty-five youth work project summaries described

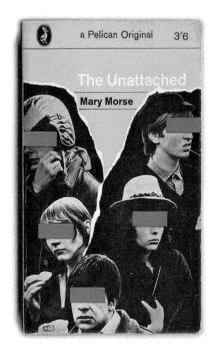

as 'experimental projects in the informal education of young people'. Even this early, there seemed to exist a plethora of youth work on the margins: experimenting with different styles of delivery.

The idea of contacting young people on their own territories – the street corner, the shopping precinct, the parks and playgrounds – was seen as an alternative. Sometimes workers were called detached workers,

'The Unattached' Mary Morse, Book Cover, Penguin 1965

sometimes outreach workers. The former was seen as the more 'purist' approach. It required a period of 'reconnaissance' in the patch, contacting young people out on the streets, getting to know them slowly through establishing friendly relationships and then offering whatever support or help they needed. Outreach work, on the other hand, literally 'reached out', usually from a youth centre, to develop similar relationships with local youngsters, but also used the centre as a meeting point or small group work venue. Outreach was viewed as less perfectionist than the 'cold-calling' street work style of delivery. But it had one inestimable advantage (which I was to be grateful for on the Kelvin Flats): access to and use of a building for the client group – very important on a cold winter's evening.

Ray Gosling as a young man. Photo: The Independent.

Understanding the 'tribal' nature of youngsters and their loyalty to the gangs that inhabited particular streets or areas was important here. Ray Gosling (again) had some helpful messages for those starting out in detached work – although the term wasn't in use in 1960 when he was trying to get to know young people in Leicester city centre. He described the process in what must be one of the earliest and most honest accounts of detached youth work methodology in existence:

Alone, I sat or stood at different bars, hot dog stalls, coffee houses and dance halls throughout the city for weeks, speaking to no one until I felt I was beginning to come to terms with the climate, the atmosphere of the people...Slowly, from snippets of conversation overheard, from moving from one dance hall to another...after months of haphazard and intermittent getting around, I had a reasonably accurate picture of the city and was using a pub in the suburbs as a regular. The young people in general kept themselves to one corner and I found myself shifting towards the corner. In time, I was invited to come upstairs on Monday nights and hear the band practice. It was an open invitation and I took it.[16]

Gosling is the kind of man you would have loved to talk to about the 'art' of youth work and the skills he saw as essential to the job description. But these niceties of thinking were not particularly clear to me at the time, nor did they seem especially important in my work. I was fortunate to have access to the youth centre building and other nearby youth clubs if I needed them, but could also operate independently – using the Sheffield detached team's minibus, our package of sports equipment and other resources available to borrow for work with small groups. I had the best of both worlds, in fact. But there was little in the way of theory, training or expertise in detached youth work, even nationally, to call upon as a fledgling practitioner in 1975. The Sheffield service employed a small group of workers with similar job briefs to mine, and we met for mutual support and sharing of practice. But like me, they came from a diverse range of professional backgrounds. And like me, I suspect they had rather 'ended up' doing detached work rather than being employed through a coherent policy or strategy on the part of the local authority.

My early detached work experiences raised themes and issues that still have a currency today. For example, even at the youth club, taking youngsters on trips to the seaside usually involved the dilemma of how to respond to shoplifting, antisocial or criminal activities. Establishing boundaries on acceptable behaviour in order to sustain relationships with clients is nothing new. There was a body of learning and recorded practice to which we might refer, albeit a limited one. What seems disappointing in retrospect, remiss even, was that none of our managers or youth officers seemed aware of this potentially valuable resource to guide and develop our own thinking and practice as fledgling detached workers. Perhaps it is simply a reflection of the paucity of academic and intellectual rigour that characterised much youth work in that period. Most of the time, as workers we were all left alone to make up our plans and strategies as we went along. Whilst our managers were not unsupportive, they were far from proactive or critical in their oversight and management supervision.

Sometimes that self-sufficiency as a team paid dividends, professionally speaking. Agreeing that we needed to explore what was going on in the world of detached youth work, a bunch of us climbed into our minibus and headed off for a visit to the National Youth Bureau in Leicester. In those days, the bureau offered guided tours and even provided a dedicated member of staff to show you round. But the first adventure was parking the minibus in a multi-storey car park and, misjudging the height restrictions, almost tearing the roof rack off. Once we'd got inside number 17–23 Albion Street, things got better. Much better, in fact. The bureau was a revelation: I suddenly discovered this treasure trove of books, magazines, pamphlets, information packs, resources, facts and figures, contacts for youth work and youth projects across the country that I'd never known existed before. Not to mention the friendly and accessible bureau staff, who seemed as pleased to meet us as we were to see them. It was an eye-opener, and we spent a wonderful time amidst this profusion of new ideas and information, trying to take it all in. On the return journey, we were like a bunch of excitable teenagers returning from the seaside, sharing the experiences of the trip and reminding each other of what we had found out or what we planned to do next. Subsequently, in my officer roles I made a point of taking youth workers (especially the part-timers) to visit Leicester whenever I could. The benefits and rewards seemed self-evident – 'we never normally get the chance to see a place like this,' one of them gratefully informed me later.

LESSONS IN STREET CRED

My Sheffield managers paid for me to go to Keele University where I attended some valuable seminars called *Starting Out in Detached Work*, which were very helpful. They were led by Harold Marchant of the Manchester Youth Development Trust. His particular expertise was in analysing the skills of making contact: that 'cold-calling' element of detached work that we new practitioners were probably most anxious about. He was supremely helpful in providing us with the kinds of insight – and practical tips – in adapting our dress, behaviour and approach to young people on the streets. He warned us that we might '…spend the first year making contacts, and the second year regretting them'. Making contact, he reminded us, was very much about how workers use themselves: the skills of body language, non-aggressive stances, tone of voice, use of eye contact and humour. He warned us about how not to do it:

> *I approached a group of three young people and asked politely if I might join them. There was a pause, and the man turned and offered to throw me down the stairs. I assured him this would not be necessary…*

The sessions looked at recognising the cultural norms and values of the clientele – their use of nicknames, hairstyles, clothing, jewellery, tattoos, 'hardness', bad language, 'in' words or phrases – and how we should tune into them. How, too, we might use tools or 'hardware' on the streets, carrying magazines or football programmes, using cigarettes or matches, having change for telephones, packs of aspirin – all these might be used to help enquiry and initial contact. These simple techniques and suggestions felt immensely helpful and comforting. They also, unconsciously, reinforced some of those key youth work skills and mechanisms that I had been using in the youth club and was now developing and honing out on the streets. Naturally, being sensitive to the personal interactions going on around you and picking up on the signals given out by young people was a skill that bridged both centre-based and detached work. Finally, Marchant reminded us that young people are not always used to dealing with adults who are not in positions of authority over them – schoolteachers, work bosses, or parents – and might well initially be suspicious and wary of our approaches. We needed to remind ourselves that encountering an interested adult and a sympathetic listener willing to take teenagers as they found them was not a common experience for many young people.[17]

I did my best, but there were some afternoons when I came home from a fruitless morning session and wondered what on earth I was doing and what benefit or value it might be offering to young people. Measuring youth work outcomes was an activity yet to be invented in the mid 1970s, but we were still alive to the troubling question of benefit and impact. How effective could our detached work interventions really be? How could we measure the changes in the young people we worked with? Even Mary Morse, a decade previously, had the honesty to admit she struggled to answer this question convincingly. How effective her work with the 'unattached' really was must remain undetermined, she conceded, especially in the absence of any follow-up work, any control groups and any qualitative techniques for measuring attitude change. Nothing unusual there, then, for us defenders of the youth work flame, even fifty years later. She did feel detached work provided a 'holding operation' to tide over many delinquent youths *[sic]* from more serious problems. Echoing Marchant, she added that some derived support and encouragement simply by being able to talk with the workers:

> *The presence of an understanding adult who had become a significant person in their lives and with whom they could feel free to talk about anything at any time was undoubtedly one of the best services that could have been offered to them.*

There are some encouraging echoes from the past, in this definition at least, for practitioners today. It confirmed some of the key components of my own emerging thinking and values regarding the work. Indisputably, the worker's personality is a vital factor contributing to success or failure – especially so in detached work. There is consistent evidence that the personal characteristics of warmth, ease with people, humour, imagination and tolerance are all vital. To get on good terms with the unattached, Morse specified – in a memorable phrase – that workers needed *a willingness to like and a readiness to understand*. In terms of methodology, she reinforced the value of an approach that made no attempt to provide ready-made solutions or to pass moral judgements. Instead, both individuals and groups were encouraged to think for themselves about what was involved and the consequences of any actions they were contemplating. Morse summarised it in a passage that remains eloquently relevant, incorporating both youth work's underlying philosophy and a set of practice skills:

> *The workers' relationship with their contacts was essentially a 'Socratic' relationship, in which asking the right questions*

was more important than knowing the right answers and more useful than any lecturing and moralising. In fact, some of the most effective communication was not with words at all but, for example, with a questioning silence, an approving glance or a simple gesture.[18]

Approving glances might have found favour with Socrates, but what would our bosses in the Sheffield Youth Office have to say? Or, more pertinently, our youth work colleagues? At a residential, we detached workers formed a small subgroup when our task was to present examples of our current work practice and the issues we were dealing with. The youth centre staff, in their response to our presentation, described us politely as 'looking down the wrong end of a telescope'. It was a perceptive analysis.

'THE FIGHT'

Whether my detached work practice matched up to the methodology, standards or quality of Morse's standards or those of other practitioners, I never knew. Early on in my first summer out on the Kelvin patch, there was an incident on the grassy slopes in full view of many of the flats' adult residents which seemed important enough for me to write up later as one of my recordings.

Arrived with minibus to find groups of young kids running up towards the Springvale area, obviously intent on something. Got out of the minibus and was told by some youngsters there was going to be a 'right fight'. There was going to be 'police cars, ambulances' and God knows what. On walking out to the flats there were, it seemed, hundreds of kids: in fact I counted them, there were 82 sitting or standing around on the grassy bank close to the Youth Centre. They were looking very threatening and the atmosphere was tense and rather frightening. The porters were standing around, not quite sure what was happening. Some of the kids had sticks. There were kids I'd never seen before.

Not without hesitation, I went to sit down amongst the ones I recognised. I talked to Ian, Sparky and a group of teenagers. Apparently what had happened: two girls had started off by egging on some lads from Springvale; then something had happened; there had been an argument, and it had been decided that the Springvale 'mob' was going to 'do' the Kelvin mob. The Springvale mob apparently wasn't big enough, it is a very new estate, so they had gone off to Parson Cross to sort out some reinforcements and the Kelvin mob was getting out brothers and sisters, elder, bigger lads to reinforce them. There were indeed a number of older lads who I'd never seen before on the flats, who were sitting there, just waiting for trouble.

There were tenants looking out from windows, balconies and landings at what was going on and clearly some of them saw me sitting amongst the kids. My immediate thought — well, I had confused thoughts — one was that this was bound to happen because of the club closing. There was nowhere for the kids to go, nothing for them to do; it was a warm evening and many of them were simply looking for an excuse to get into a bit of bother. And this incident was the perfect alibi: it offered the group adventure, excitement with the hint of violence, plus the pride of the Kelvin territory — offended by strangers — could be vindicated. So, in a sense, I understood them and perhaps I sympathised with them. On the other hand, conscious of the adult onlookers and my own personal responsibilities as a worker, I did have a minibus which I thought I could use to take some of the kids away, somewhere or other, to take the heat out of the situation. Also, after sitting for a time and talking, I began to judge the atmosphere more objectively: I felt, in fact, that a fight would not happen. Obviously this is a matter of opinion, but as the only adult prepared to actually go into the group and ask them what was going on, plus my own experience of crisis situations like this in the past, I felt instinctively that they would not come to blows.

Anyway, for over an hour things just went by; nothing much happened, we were all waiting to see if the Springvale mob would return. Smaller groups formed, sub-groups from the main 'Kelvin' mob, sporadic play fights broke out among younger kids: maybe as preparation for the battle to come. At one stage, two strange teenagers walked up and the whole mob, tensed, seemed to move towards them; but they were not the Springvale kids.

Eventually, some of the older ones were beginning to get fed up. At this point, I said to Phil, Leslie, Ian, Plug et al, 'Let's get out to Dam Flask or somewhere', which we did, not after much persuading on my part. I think, though, the teenagers themselves realised that there was not going to be any fight. I took about ten of them, including some younger ones, with the swing ball set, out to Bradfield and we played out there for an hour, returning to Kelvin about 9pm. Meanwhile, someone had called the police, apparently; we found out when we got back. But I learnt from the porters that there had not been any fighting and it seemed this action had been unnecessary on the part of the tenants. By this time, the kids had almost all disappeared from the flats.

The aftermath of this incident was interesting. I discovered that I was the subject of a complaint by a number of tenants who had seen me sitting out with the kids. Their argument was that I had not adopted the characteristic 'adult' role of dispersing the group, breaking it up and moving everyone off back home. As one tenant put it, with typical northern force, 'bloody youth leader were sat in middle on 'em, doing nowt about it.' My failure to intervene was clearly the result of a mindless alliance with teenage behaviour, in his view. How to explain my judgement that the mock-preparations for battle, the gathering of weapons and reinforcements, the displacement activity of energetic subgroups – how all of this was a cathartic enough activity for the group? There was no need for actual physical violence. Justice had been done and honour satisfied by an impressive show of 'Kelvin' strength. The Springvale mob did not turn up: victory went to Kelvin by default. There was no need for me to intervene as a worker or try to disperse the group in the style of a police officer. Mind you, as one perceptive teenager said to me later, 'If they *had* turned up, half of this lot would have run a mile.' But the lesson for me was that my engagement and intervention were pitched accurately and timed right; taking them away reduced the temperature and defused, for some of them, the potential danger. It seemed like a good piece of detached youth work.

Years later, by way of comparison, visiting a detached youth work project in London, I was impressed by the skills of the workers I observed. All of them seemed to display far more experience than my own amateurish efforts that evening on the Kelvin Flats (although I was a lone worker with no team members for support):

On the Lydgate estate in North London, over seventeen young people were spoken to in an hour; an impressive contact rate. The worker knew most of them by name and they had positive relationships. They were a friendly group and he balanced challenge and support well in the encounters, not allowing young people 'off the hook', knowing when to intervene and when to allow conversations to flow. Their detached policy was to balance proactive and reactive styles; they responded to individual 'hotspot' demands from police or councillors and would always undertake one visit – then report back on

*whether they could develop work further or not. They stuck to
their policy rationale and decisions on the estates they worked
in.*

*On my second night's visit, they contacted nine young
people on the Klinger estate, engaging in discussion and
conversation for almost forty-five minutes. They knew this
group well and the youngsters looked forward to the sessions.
The discussions ranged over personal, family and educational
issues. One young man spent some time debating the potential
implications of a court appearance for a driving offence,
including a custodial sentence. Three young women discussed
college options. The team were able to move into a focused
'work mode' as soon as young people were contacted, sustaining
group conversations skilfully and deploying themselves with
separate groups when necessary.*

In contrast to my rather fumbling and uncertain efforts out on
the Kelvin Flats that night, this example seems to my eyes much
more focused and purposeful – more 'professional', if you will.
Perhaps the passage of time and the improvement in training and
techniques available to youth work staff is one explanation. Or
maybe I'm just being too hard on myself.

*Press report, Sheffield Star, May 1976,
reproduced with kind permission of the South Yorkshire Press.*

CHILDREN AND PLAY ON KELVIN

During my second summer out on the flats, I tried to get more involved with the local middle school and members of the tenants' association. My plan was to give the voices of young people a chance to be heard on the estate: to find out how *they* felt, not least to offer a counterweight to the powerful chorus of adult criticism that was the norm. The idea was to undertake a survey with young people on how they felt about living in the Kelvin Flats – particularly how and where they played and how they perceived adults and adult reactions to them as young people. My final report – called *Children and Play on Kelvin* – received significant local press publicity, balanced and favourable.

The dearth of play provision on the estate, antipathy between young and old, how young people stick to well-defined territories in their play, an active dislike of teenagers from many adults – these were all inevitable themes to emerge from the survey. There were positive signs of tenants providing junior clubs and holiday play schemes, but the overall picture was a bleak one. Most of the young people had an accurate perception of the environment they needed and would like, and they were more closely aware than any outside observer of how inadequate the Kelvin Flats were in providing it. At the time, moving families from the substandard and overcrowded 'slum' properties of the post-war city into new modern blocks of flats seemed a sensible policy for the council to pursue. If only they had listened earlier to the voices of the young people I interviewed in 1976. They could tell me with easy articulacy that the flats were not the kinds of places to live and grow up in. One respondent wanted 'better grass for playing on,' a second requested 'a big field to play in with a big forest,' whilst a third said he 'would like a wood provided in our area.' In a terse commentary on the architecture of high-rise living, one eleven-year-old replied simply that he would like some 'bungolows' *[sic]*.

Because most of the children who had filled in my survey forms were from the local middle school, I presented my final report to the school's governors one afternoon. Congratulating me on my account, one of them commented that writing it had clearly been a 'labour of love' for me. I hadn't really thought about it like that, but he was right. It is true that my own feelings about how adults viewed young people coloured some of the judgements in the report. I had been struck by watching mums bring their children to the sandpit and then stand around waiting until they had finished playing so they could take them home again. It was the parallel imagery of 'walking the dog' that came to my mind. I wanted to reiterate the

Front cover artwork by Phil Brown, club member, 1975.

evidence that many adults were tolerant of junior youth clubs and younger children, but once adolescents appear, their sympathy disappears. The word 'teenager' then becomes a synonym for 'vandal' or 'hooligan' in a totally unthinking way. I ended the report by saying …*perhaps if we listened to them more often, our vision of places where families should live and grow up might not include so many Kelvins.*

THE DEMONISATION OF YOUNG PEOPLE: A LONG HISTORY

Fear or envy of young people, apprehension about their behaviour, the link between them and the risks of crime and social disorder, and the need to produce leisure-time facilities to 'keep them off the streets' – these are perennial themes in any debate about teenagers. Richard Hoggart recorded similar views in the letters to the newspapers he surveyed in the late 1950s bemoaning the behaviour of 'young thugs' in drainpipe trousers and winkle-picker shoes. The sympathies of the average reader with this kind of delinquent teenage behaviour were severely limited. Nor were they interested in adolescent psychology or trying to understand their upbringing or behaviour. 'All this psychology is nonsense,' one aggrieved correspondent wrote, '… they should all be whipped.' That writer would probably have agreed with Aristotle, writing some two thousand years earlier:

> *The children love luxury. They have bad manners, contempt for authority, they show disrespect to their elders… they contradict their parents, chatter before company and are tyrants over their teachers… The young people of today think of nothing but themselves. They have no reverence for parents or old age. They are impatient of all restraint. They talk as if they alone knew everything and what passes for wisdom with us is foolishness with them. As for girls, they are forward, immodest and unwomanly in speech, behaviour and dress.*[19]

Whatever young people do, they get blamed for. Even when they are just 'hanging about' and doing very little, the rest of society seems to come down on them like a ton of bricks. It always struck me, as a youth worker in Sheffield, how young people standing around doing nothing much seemed an affront to social order, and yet adults propping up the bars of every pub in the city were no problem at all. There are enduring public concerns about young people's presence on the streets. One recent researcher described a common set of assumptions that detached workers regularly experienced in their patches:

> *This entrenched 'moral panic' is echoed in everyday language, where the street is a metaphor for trouble. If someone is 'on the streets', they may be taken for homeless; if 'working the streets', they are assumed to be sex workers… Young people who spend time on the streets with their friends are spoken of as 'youths', 'vandals', 'sluts', 'hoodies', 'drug dealers', or 'binge drinkers'; whatever they are actually doing, they are said to be 'hanging around' and 'up to no good'.*[20]

As a society we seem to allow very little 'public' space for young people; it seems we would really rather they did not exist. It seems, too, that we live in a culture of blame. When news is slack, editors and newspaper headlines, television and magazine features can always fall back on the 'problem of youth'. In the 1970s, as in other decades, teenagers were the focus of considerable social anxiety, blamed for everything from street crime and promiscuous sexuality to the decline of patriotism and the plight of the economy. They were even blamed for being too young to fight in the war. Young people, wrote J. B. Priestley in his 1973 survey *The English*, were 'inept, shiftless, slovenly, messy, because unlike their fathers and grandfathers they have not been disciplined by grim circumstances.' Recounting the responses of young people, the social historian Jeremy Seabrook took his tape recorder to Blackburn two years earlier to talk to adults and young people about their views. Interviewing Alan, a twenty-year-old apprentice in a local pub, he asked whether he felt he was very different from his parents. 'I think we've got more freedom now than anybody ever had', was the reply, and he continued, more emphatically:

Cartoons by Wilf Roberts and Sebastian Buccheri in Youth in Society, *1980 and 1996.*

*Older people don't like it. They're right jealous, some of them.
If we have a good time, they get your back up at times, get
in a right narky mood, they say, 'If it wasn't for us, where
would you be now? You'd have been overrun by the Germans
and then you wouldn't be able to do what you wanted.'*[21]

Young people have always suffered from the envious criticism
of their elders. Much of the academic writing on youth cultures
and subcultures focuses on social life and allegedly wild moral
values. This has reinforced the definition of 'youth' as a social
problem, particularly since the end of the Second World War and
particularly focusing on adolescent working-class males. The period
of adolescence in teenage years is one of stress and insecurity as
young people make the transition from childhood into adulthood.
Rites of passage are important steps in this transition – from legal
consents (voting, having sex, drinking, drugs, driving, marrying)
to social and emotional development, work and employment,
friendships and partners. Some sociologists have also linked youth
subcultures with distinctive music and style (groups like the Teddy
boys, mods, skinheads, bikers and punks), interpreting young
people's behaviour as a rebellion or resistance to the traditional
working-class life of their parents and the new temptations of
capitalism and commerce – which recognised the new spending
power of young people.[22]

Further, the notion of a youth 'underclass' has a long history in
England, beginning with the Victorian concept of the 'undeserving
poor.' For most governments, of whichever political affiliation,
the underclass was primarily depicted in terms of youth, using
the stereotypes of the antisocial, violent or drunken lout or the
teenage single mother – a figure of moral mockery. This is an
age-old theme – swathes of ordinary, working-class young people
being branded, corralled, herded, moved on, labelled as 'trouble'
simply for passing their evening leisure time in unremarkable, un-

troublesome friendship groups. If the same teenagers wear hoodies and loiter menacingly on street corners, it reinforces the anxiety. Boredom is another factor; places where young people could meet or congregate were disappearing – not just youth centres, but swimming pools, leisure centres, sports clubs, libraries and pubs amongst others. Overall, young people were loosely and carelessly lumped together in the public consciousness as 'yobs', 'thugs', 'feral youths' and other such phrases. This impression of a society slipping out of control and needing the firm hand of an authoritarian government to restore order recurs throughout our social history.

It was this corrosive impetus that characterised the Thatcherite 'law and order' debates during the 1980s. Later, the New Labour government of the 1990s began to codify some of these more jaundiced and stereotyped views of young people into punitive legislation, through the use of Antisocial Behaviour Orders or ASBOs. The epithet 'chav' was also adopted to represent the same social grouping: generally a working-class, antisocial youth subculture. It was often associated with the character Vicky Pollard from the *Little Britain* television programme, whose personality epitomised many of the negative traits associated with the 'white working class' – violence, laziness, teenage pregnancy, racism, drunkenness and the rest. It was not dissimilar to the way public schoolboys called townies 'oiks'.[23]

These perceptions and stereotypes reflected a more sinister and negative version of 'keeping them off the streets'. Previously the phrase had retained a more liberal interpretation, including a recognition of the need to provide leisure-time facilities – youth clubs, sports centres, 'drop-in' cafés – for young people who might otherwise be hanging around the street corners or outside the One Stop shops. Now, simply being on the streets presumed an antisocial agenda or criminal intent that required police intervention. The target was those who might 'cause offence' rather than those who committed offences. There were some reports that having an ASBO was regarded as a matter of pride by teenagers on some inner-city estates. As author Anthony Horowitz put it, ASBOs add up to create a 'cumulative vision of a Britain full of yobs, with crack houses on every inner-city estate; drunken youths running amok in provincial towns, and so on'.[24] As I was beginning to discover on the Kelvin Flats in the late '70s – and subsequently to rediscover in the late '90s – there is a long history to the demonisation of young people.

YOUTH WORK IN THE COMMUNITY

My time on the Kelvin Flats came to an end in 1977 when the authority asked me to take on a new role in Parson Cross, a large pre-war council estate in the north of the city. The full-time worker at a small local youth club had left and, instead of replacing him, the service decided to transfer me to the estate to support the part-time team and continue my community youth work role on the wider estate. It was to be an 'experiment' – to trial the idea of an area youth work role which included supporting the local youth centre. The staff team at Lindsay Road Youth Club took a pretty dim view of this experiment. They felt seriously short-changed in losing their leader and being given instead some kind of detached/community worker. My initial reception was lukewarm, at best. But slowly even the youth club staff warmed to me a little, as I put in some shifts each night at the club, organised a summer play scheme and generally mucked in with centre-based work.

I was also encouraged by the positive reception I got from the Family and Community Services area team, who welcomed me with open arms as a potential ally and new resource in their work with children and families on the estate. We soon joined forces to develop an information and advice centre in an old shop front

Buchanan Road Advice and Information Centre, Parson Cross, 1976.
Photo: Tim Caley.

premises close to the local secondary school. This also served as a contact place and meeting room for my links with young people in the area. I also found myself getting involved in welfare rights, citizens' advice and consumer protection issues in the sessions when the shop was open.

It was here that the local ward councillor, David Blunkett, later to become Home Secretary in Tony Blair's Labour government of 1997, started to use the centre for his councillor surgeries, and he, too, became an ally and friend. David once took some of us detached youth workers into the Town Hall to attend a council committee meeting to explain our work. It wasn't a success – the debate got bogged down in civic bureaucracies, but I was thoroughly impressed that the chair of the Family and Community Services Committee (as he was then) was prepared to invite a group like us into the council chamber and actually consult us on our views and our work with young people in the city.

ROSLA AND THE MSC

My role also engaged me in city-wide ROSLA (Raising of the School Leaving Age) youth programmes, run jointly between secondary schools and youth work teams.[25] The purpose and rationale of these schemes was never particularly clear. Amongst the young people that I worked with, raising the school leaving age to sixteen simply created an unwilling, resentful cohort of teenagers for whom staying on at school was a pointless exercise. Many heads agreed, and schools were more than happy for such groups to be taken out of class one day a week to visit youth clubs and participate in sports or other activities. Schools were already colluding with the absence or truancy of these pupils anyway – 'wagging it' had been the norm for a hard core of Kelvin Youth Club members since 1972.

The content or curriculum of these joint ROSLA programmes was mostly limited to an 'average youth club session' plus a few trips and visits (ice rinks, parks) thrown in. There was almost no discussion about the overall policy of the project, the potential contribution that the youth service might make to educational qualifications, to school achievement, or of careers or job advice for individual pupils. We rarely met as a joint staff team to discuss our links with our feeder schools or individual needs or progress. Not that getting a job for these young people was ever going to be easy. After a while, my disillusionment and unhappiness with the ROSLA project had increased. So when the head of the local secondary school decided, without consultation, to end our role as youth workers in the project, I was happy to leave the scheme altogether.

Unemployment rose to more than two million in the first two years of the Thatcher government from 1979 onwards – and youth unemployment was a serious issue. *The baby boom of the 1960s has turned into the youth gloom of the 1980s*, noted the *Daily Mirror*. The expansion of the Manpower Services Commission, developing job creation and youth opportunity programmes, dates from this period. In Sheffield, we ran gardening schemes using young people to get involved in local community projects on the estate: wheelbarrows and spades cluttered up the office for many months. But these schemes were like the ROSLA projects, hastily established and poorly managed, and they used teenagers as cheap labour – helping to reduce the unemployment figures for the government, but failing to address the underlying structural causes of unemployment. Nor did they give young people the 'proper jobs' they wanted. It was simply a temporary fix – just papering over the cracks.

The young people themselves were thoroughly alive to this reality. 'What's the point of digging old biddies' front gardens and clearing up the muck all over the estate for seventeen quid a week, Tim?' as one asked me. For local youth workers like me, this was a difficult question to answer. The local authority and its youth service had bought into these schemes and we were charged with trying to make them work at a grassroots level. The startling growth of the Manpower Services Commission and the scale of its funding and intervention in the lives of young people was a significant factor in this period. Job creation programmes and youth opportunities programmes spread across the country. Not just for young people: 'trainee' youth workers and university lecturers were employed under the schemes, too; indeed, the youth service in Sheffield appointed a number of these young staff – mostly women – and they undoubtedly brought a breath of fresh air and new ideas to the work. The commission's espousal of 'social and life skills training' for unemployed teenagers raised early questions about social education and the voluntary relationships that were fundamental to youth work thinking and practice.

Most youth workers recognised that unemployment was not the fault of young people and that no amount of training in 'life skills' (presentation, interview techniques, punctuality and so forth) could alter the fact that there were simply not enough jobs for them. I was helped in thinking these dilemmas through by reading Bernard Davies' influential report *In Whose Interests?*, published in 1979. This was a rather uncomfortable exercise: Davies presented a powerful polemic challenging those of us involved in sponsoring the Manpower Services Commission's job creation and youth employment schemes, as to who actually benefited from such activities and how they were affecting youth work's traditional principles of social education. His was a prescient analysis and an early wake-up call to later threats of a similar and sharper nature.

THE YOUTH EXCHANGE

My time in Parson Cross was important for another reason. I had been keen to develop the emerging concept of 'youth work in the community' in this new patch – being influenced by a number of articles written by Terry Powley in *Youth in Society* around this time.[26] Powley was a strong advocate of detached youth work in particular and the role of the local youth worker as an advocate for the needs of teenagers in general. His work followed and built on the Fairbairn-Milson report, but the model of practice he described seemed to be more coherent and realistic to me. Especially the need for the local youth worker to engage and influence the adults and agencies which impacted on youngsters' lives, notably schools, social services and the benefits system.

My aspiration to follow Powley's model led to one particularly difficult experience. I had agreed to link up with a city youth club colleague and organise a joint exchange visit with a group from a German town in the Harz Mountains. I'd blithely promised to find suitable young people on the estate, arrange the host families and get involved in all the planning. It was soon apparent that I'd bitten off far more than I could chew. Trying to engage youngsters (and their families) from a working-class housing estate in Sheffield with an aspiring, middle-class group of German teenagers was hugely overambitious. The wheels came off early on in the proceedings. On the second morning in Sheffield, a distraught German teenager came to see me. The house she had stayed in was not good, she told me; the host family had shared their breakfast with their dogs at the table. Graciously, she had presented them with the bottle of wine she had brought as a gift to her host family, but now wanted to move out, please. Luckily, we were able to offer her an alternative home through the help of one of our job creation programme workers on the estate. A steep learning curve in my first youth exchange experience.

But this was a one-off problem, caused by my own lack of foresight. Overall, the mixture of youth and community work I undertook in Parson Cross seemed to be successful in implementing the Powley model. I was supporting the part-time team at Lindsay Road Youth Club, I had opened up the advice and information shop to help local residents, set up a community newsletter for the estate and supported the growth of a tenants' association. I had worked with the secondary school on ROSLA schemes and I was managing the employment of young people as youth opportunities programme workers on the estate. I also used the shop as my base to make contact and work with local young people as a detached worker and to involve some of their parents and local residents in the issues they raised with me. And I still managed to find time to run a summer play scheme in the park, and to build a float for the Lord Mayor's parade in my last memorable summer on the estate in 1979.

PART 2

MANAGING
YOUTH WORK

CHAPTER 4

BECOMING A YOUTH OFFICER

After eight years in Sheffield, I felt the need for a change – certainly a break from face-to-face work. I was ready for a fresh challenge. David Blunkett wasn't pleased to learn of my departure from the city and his ward. 'Why you want to go and work for these Tory authorities down south, I'll never know,' he berated me.

Being interviewed for my first youth officer job in Reading, I was tested on my prospective management skills: how might I deal with potentially recalcitrant youth workers, the County Officer asked me? Thinking quickly, I replied that I would probably take a hard line in such circumstances, adding, with a weak attempt at humour, that I must be getting more right-wing in my old age. His eyes lit up with pleasure and I realised this was the right answer. My starting salary was £7,700 – a sevenfold increase since I began at Kelvin Youth Centre seven years previously.

My new job was a promotion: a vertical career move up the greasy pole of youth service management. I'd probably burnt my bridges now when it came to street credibility with the face-to-face workforce. I'd joined the 'other side', the 'management side', from which there was no return. I became a district youth and community officer; there were two of us in the Reading district, and together we managed the staff team of centre-based, detached and youth counselling provision, as well as supporting our partners in the voluntary sector and getting along with the borough council and its leisure department. At a time of growing youth unemployment, we also had a large role in working with the Manpower Services Commission on youth action and other youth opportunity programmes, and with Urban Aid projects in the town. This latter development signalled an early shift in the balance of power and funding for work with young people, nationally and locally. As budget constraints began to impact on local authorities, these new government initiatives provided us with valuable sources of alternative funding for youth work. This was to become an important theme for local youth officers like me to be aware of – and to exploit – wherever we could in the interests of young people in our local patches.

The change from youth worker to youth officer was an uncomfortable conversion for me. I wrote in June 1980 that: 'it seems difficult to believe that twelve months ago, I was standing in a Sheffield park organising a play scheme for a bunch of noisy 12-year-olds. And now here I am: a real Youth and Community Officer.' Suddenly I'd swapped the challenges of working with real 'youth' for the new challenges of working with budgets and policies. And with adults: head teachers, councillors, officers, chairs of voluntary organisations, assorted parents and members of the public. Not so much of the discos, the days out, the nitty-gritty of fights, homelessness and work on the streets any more. No trips out in the minibus with groups from the estate, no afternoons (or mornings) off to recharge the batteries. Now I had to be at my office desk by 8.30am every morning, whatever time I'd been out till the night before. And my new 'field' was to be politics, management, funding and officialdom. How well would I manage this new transition? Would it prove just as stressful a role as club leader or detached worker? Were my new adult clients likely to prove just as difficult and idiosyncratic as the teenagers I'd been used to?

THE POLITICS OF INSTITUTIONAL PRESSURE

The discomfort was partly around the hard edge of my new officer management function and wanting to stay close to my youth work roots and fieldwork practice, resisting the insidious socialisation process I sensed was implicit in becoming part of 'management'. In my head, I had started to write an article whose tentative title was to be *The Youth Office and the Politics of Institutional Pressure*, which would have fleshed out some of my anxieties about moving from the grass roots into management. The article never got written, but the themes were stark at the time and have remained with me since. I did articulate some of them in an early report to my bosses in Berkshire:

> *I do not want to be part of a service that puts its collective head down and lies low until the danger passes; I really do consider that detached youth work and social education and neighbourhood work and caring for young people and sensitivity in counselling and group work and community development and providing a quality service for young people is what we are about as a Youth Service and what we do best.*

This reads now like a political manifesto – or just plain 'swank', as Alan Bennett would put it. Maybe I was just preening my revolutionary northern feathers amongst my softer southern youth officer colleagues – or trying to raise my 'street cred' with the workforce. At my first county youth officer meeting in the new Shire Hall, the regular hurly-burly of the boisterous discussion and debate I had been used to amongst my Sheffield workmates seemed notable by its absence. This meeting was strangely devoid of any energy: flat and monotonous. Turning to the person next to me, I murmured, sotto voce, 'Are all the meetings as boring as this?' Only I clearly hadn't spoken softly enough, as my comment was picked up and passed on to the chairman with some glee. He forgave me later, agreeing that my analysis of the proceedings had been perfectly accurate. That prompted him to offer me some advice, reassuring me that 'intelligence and ability, allied to hard work' was an unbeatable combination. He might also have mentioned tenacity, attention to detail and a generous helping of low animal cunning. It was a message I took to heart.

But I had a point about the political naivety of some of the youth work staff in my new team. I was unapologetic about my view that it was the responsibility of every worker to educate, challenge and influence those politicians, councillors and committee members who help to make policy or control resources of the value of the youth service and the needs of young people in our areas. It was worrying to discover that many colleagues did not know who their local councillor was or the ward in which their club was situated, and had the scantiest knowledge of the committee structure that controlled the service they worked in.

In one of my early reflections on my new officer role, I noted the strange norms created by being based in the Civic Offices. 'The Civic Centre with its colour-coded lifts, its contract-watered rubber plants and its open-plan functional furniture,' I wrote, 'provides a difficult working environment. It is noisy, distracting, de-personalising and cheerless.' More importantly, I felt that the longer you spent working in the Civic Offices, the greater the danger of your isolation from real people in the real world. It was easy to forget – as you parked your car in the private car park, used the Dictaphones and typists, arranged your committee meetings, travelled up the lifts to eat your subsidised lunch and generally merged into a form of institutionalised behaviour and habit – that most people didn't live like this. If you've read Erving Goffman's book *Asylums*, you'll recognise the sinister process I'm trying to capture here.

ON THE STREETS

Some of my most valuable times as a new officer were spent simply walking round neighbourhoods, getting a feel for houses, shops, schools, bus routes, parks, pubs and the people who created the informal and organic networks of communities in the town. Acting rather like a detached youth officer, on reflection. I might have become part of the bureaucracy now, but I still hoped to find time to see places for myself and listen to the people who lived and worked there. This was easier said than done: district officers were not supposed to be found wandering the streets 'inducting' themselves into their new jobs. They should be visibly hard at work at their desks in the Civic Offices, nose to the grindstone, or at night attending one of the interminable centre management committee meetings, or at the very least visiting their youth centres to raise morale amongst the workforce. Luckily for me, on one of my walking tours I passed South Reading Youth Centre – only to spot the county youth officer and the chair of the Youth Service Committee waving at me from the car park. Probably a good omen for my career, I thought.

As an ex-detached worker, I had a natural affinity with Reading's detached project, based in No. 5, the youth counselling agency in the town. It was good to spend time with Adrian around his patch in the town centre, talking through issues he was facing in his work. His location in the counselling centre extended his repertoire for the young people he met on the streets. Adrian, Anne, Anita and I spent some time trying to record the 'nuts and bolts' of this work, more for our own benefit than anything else, but we were pleased when the National Association of Youth Clubs asked us to contribute our deliberations as part of its publication *Starting Out in Detached Work.*[27] My 'youth in the community' experience in Sheffield also came in handy on two Reading housing estates. Here I got involved in the creation of two 'community house' projects which served as playgroups, children's centres and contact points for meeting local teenagers. The scheme partly mirrored the model of my previous advice centre shop front at Parson Cross. Later, flushed with its success, I wrote an article about the houses which was published in *Youth and Society* in 1982.

As I acclimatised to all this new officer culture and my new role, I was much taken by an article published in the Community and Youth Workers Union journal *Rapport* entitled *Spearhead of the Youth Service*. It provided a cogent analysis of the changing role of the local youth officer, from initially being a fieldworker, leader and manager in the post-Albemarle era, to a much-weakened, desk-bound, bureaucratic defender of the status quo in the 1970s. Many youth officers, the piece argued, were completely out of touch with

Youth in Society, November 1982.

the work as field staff experienced it. Those staff identified them more with the 'education power game played by the local authority employers' than with the youth service. The article confirmed some of my new fears as a junior officer with still-recent fieldwork expertise. But it also gave me hope when it argued that full-time workers 'lucky enough to be in an area with such officers' needed to support them. Certainly being closer to my own fieldwork experience gave me greater credibility with the staff team.

Joining Berkshire taught me one important lesson: the need for a strong management structure that ensured everyone was accountable. Compared to my previous work styles, this service had a well-established and compulsory system of support and supervision for all staff. Weekly forecast sheets had to be completed in advance, with follow-up reports of work completed with comments on progress and issues raised. My officer job included the responsibility to monitor all my staff and ensure they all followed the system religiously. We all moaned and groaned about it at the time, but it enabled me and my bosses to know what everyone was doing and how they were feeling about their work. And this formed the agenda for all our regular supervision sessions. I liked the discipline and regularity of these arrangements. Another lesson that stayed with me was the value of recognising that consultation did not imply consent – an important distinction when every youth worker always wants a say in every decision to be made. With hindsight, these were the hallmarks of sound leadership in the service and evidence of effective, quality assurance for staff at all levels. And many years ahead of its time, compared to other places.

The other convention I valued was the opportunity to have an 'induction lunch' with the County youth officer, offered to all new appointees to the service. This was a rare and much-appreciated opportunity to meet and talk informally with the head of the service and to pick up some of the current issues and key personalities. Indeed, in my own subsequent county officer roles,

I have offered all my new youth work staff the same chance of an induction lunch with me. Except that in my case in Berkshire, it was more of an 'induction pub crawl'. Meeting me on the steps of his office, the boss confessed that, with all the other important things he should be doing, taking time out for lunch with me felt a bit like Nero fiddling whilst Rome burned. Anyhow, we jumped into his little, bouncy camper van and set off north beyond Henley into deepest rural Oxfordshire. The first pint was from the one-room bar at Fingest, followed by another at Skirmett and a third at Turville. Two hours later, we had a meal in Watlington (I think) and then decided to head back to the office. Only we set off on the wrong side of the road. For a split second, I wondered if this was a special privilege accorded to senior county officers out on country lanes. Then I saw the lorry approaching and decided to speak.

'John, I think you're on the wrong side of the road,' I muttered.

We lurched leftwards as he jerked the steering wheel quickly. He gave me a lopsided grin.

'Thanks.' He smiled. 'We've just come back from holiday in Italy in this.'

THE 'EMMER GREENIES'

One of the ways to help bridge those gaps and improve my role as an officer was to extend communication and staff meetings, to encourage staff to publish examples of good practice, to walk the patch myself to see the issues at first hand, and generally to support and inspire good practitioners where I found them. And at Emmer Green Youth Centre, I found an excellent example. Here, Detta, Anne, Paul and the staff team had created a vibrant, buzzing atmosphere that engaged and motivated the membership. It's not always easy to explain how this can happen in youth work. Why should one centre and one set of staff manage to achieve such a culture of positive engagement and 'ownership' whilst others can't? It's a bit like football clubs – when you get the right manager (full-time worker), the right mix of experienced and youthful staff (players), the right policies and ground rules, along with high standards and expectations, mixed with high energy levels and enthusiasm – then anything can happen. Sometimes, the youth centre buildings themselves take on a life of their own. Continuing the footballing metaphor, like the committed home crowd at a football club, they become the twelfth man – their support providing a separate and important impact on the success of the team. There is something about a youth club building not just being 'fit for purpose', but having a distinct sense of being 'owned' by the members. This could take many forms – colour, decoration, images, messages, topicality, personality, energy, vibrancy: all reflected, and seemed to me to be indicators of (and contributors to), high-quality youth work practice.

At Emmer Green, this was usually the case. We published some of the centre's youth work experiences, taken from diaries written by both Detta and Anne, in *Youth Service Scene* in 1980 and 1981. They were 'slice of life' recordings of club sessions – often pretty raw and unedited. But they served a real purpose in validating and celebrating the role of part-time staff, showing the realities of centre-based work and reinforcing how young people valued the relationships they had with these workers. I was especially pleased that *Youth Service Scene* published three of Anne's articles because they provided solid evidence of reflective practice – by a part-time worker. Anne was even more delighted: suddenly her professional contribution, previously taken for granted, had not only been taken very seriously, it had received national recognition in the youth work press.

Detta had 'graduated' from the local youth and community work training course and Emmer Green Youth Centre was her first full-time post. Her youth work philosophy was simple, pragmatic and effective: young people needed somewhere to be with their

Youth Service Scene, 1981.

friends, and to have their own space where they had access to new opportunities and learning. She gave short shrift to some of the prevailing '–isms', as she called them, of race, class and gender, which had been drummed into her at college. Detta felt she never quite fitted in as a youth worker because of her own culture and background: her instinctive recognition of the need for *respect* – for young people and adults – derived from her parents, not from any academic training. But she also recognised the importance of creating an attractive building – repainting the club, buying new furniture, replacing all the curtains, putting checked tablecloths on all the tables, building a cosy sitting area and a proper meeting room. Making Emmer Green an attractive and modern centre, in other words.

The centre soon attracted a large and regular clientele, not least because of its Friday-night discos. There was a noticeably strong group of girls – young women – who soon developed into a powerful presence and lobby, supporting Detta and the staff and beginning to influence the programme and activities. This group – they later became known as the 'Emmer Greenies' – was partly one result of Detta's experience at college and the strength of feminist activity on the course. As someone who had come into youth work from being 'just a housewife' (again, her phrase), the importance of being a woman and of providing a role model for her youth work members – giving them more space, more responsibility and a greater voice – became a powerful feature of the youth club.

Some of these ideas were crystallised and reinforced when, with my help as the junior district youth officer, the club organised an exchange visit to Rotterdam in 1981. The group from Reading was essentially the Emmer Green girls and the staff team, plus me and a borough councillor. It was an amazing experience for all of us – not least the young people. With hindsight, the youth exchange model provided Detta with an influential template for the delivery of youth work, both then and for the future. Youth exchanges inevitably involve intense experiences: the luxury of being with young people twenty-four hours a day for a week or more. This offers potent chances to really get to know them, often in a different relationship to the normal youth work setting in the club. The shared excitements of planning the trip, of seeing new sights and having new experiences, meeting new friends, travelling, eating, sleeping together – all in a foreign country. Interestingly, power in the group ebbed and flowed during the Rotterdam exchange. Those who were normally quiet and withdrawn sometimes took on a leadership role as they were able to master a few words of Dutch to assist with arrangements. Others, normally more voluble, now took a back-seat role. Confronted with new things – religion, food, transport – some blossomed in their willingness to accept and try things out; others were more reticent and hung back. All of this is the meat and drink of good youth work, of course. Experiences outside their normal sphere naturally spark conversations and reactions within the group. These are not

Emmer Green youth exchange, 1981. Photo: Reading Chronicle.

about 'issues' or 'curriculum'; they arise naturally from shared experiences and are the bedrock of the youth work process.

After a tearful, musical farewell evening with our hosts – my skills on the keyboard on display as I extemporised *Rotterdam* to the tune of *Yesterday* – we all arrived back in Reading on a high. The borough councillor wrote a letter of thanks to the County youth officer praising our excellent skills in organising the exchange. The girls and the centre buzzed for weeks afterwards with the souvenirs, memories and photographs of our exploits in Holland. Plans for a return visit of the Dutch group to Reading were put in hand immediately. That exchange set in place an important theme – a golden thread – for youth work at the centre. It led to many subsequent international visits and youth exchanges; it led to the strengthening of the bonds of friendship and collaboration amongst the group of Emmer Green girls; it cemented a style of practice associated with the club and its team for many years into the future. That thread extended to other youth centres as Detta and the girls' group moved on together, became friends, moved to new locations and were recruited into new youth work jobs.

GOOD YOUTH CLUB WORK

By now, I had begun to realise that recognising good youth work is not difficult once you can find it, but finding it is not as easy as you might think. Youth workers' own descriptions of their practice are not always the most helpful or accurate indicators of quality. It is more useful first to look for the vital surrounding characteristics – leadership, expertise, sensitivity, enthusiasm, empathy, good humour, resilience, strength of character, patience, experience. Spending time with Detta and Anne at Emmer Green reminded me of that wonderful feeling you get when you witness really good youth work. The hairs on the back of your neck stand on end and the adrenalin surges as you watch powerful relationships between adults and young people unfolding, moving, fizzing and changing in front of your eyes. Afterwards, usually in the cool of the club car park, you begin to come down from the buzz and the high; if you are charged with recording the work (and later grading it as an Ofsted inspector), you need to check out the strength of the evidence before committing it to paper; you try to reflect on what made this special; you have to try to make a fair judgement and appraisal. Inevitably, it seemed high quality was primarily down to the personal skills of individual youth workers. The National Foundation for Educational Research, after a thorough survey of the realities of youth work in eighty-four local authorities, later came to the same conclusion:

> *The personal qualities of the youth worker were generally agreed to be the most important single component of successful youth work. Quite simply, no amount of additional funding,*

curriculum planning or new facilities could compensate for
youth workers who did not engage with young people in a way
that they found acceptable.[28]

Likewise, identifying the key components of good youth club practice is not difficult. Young people display a strong sense of ownership and pride in their centre; they have high standards of self-discipline, respect and good humour; they are self-confident, friendly, welcoming and regular attendees; they display positive relationships with each other and with staff; they speak clearly about the benefits of attending, about their learning; and they are well motivated. Many of them 'graduate' to become senior leaders and trainee youth workers. They can often, easily and unprompted, describe what continues to draw them to membership and attendance:

> *There's different varieties of stuff…educational things…*
> *everyone's friends, you can have a laugh…the staff are really*
> *good to talk to – not like teachers.*

> *It's a nice atmosphere, youth workers are friendly, they set the*
> *boundaries, run trips and a rota of things to do – it's never*
> *boring.*

The best youth workers are thus both relaxed and purposeful; they nurture the culture of ownership and participation; they have a warm, friendly and proactive style. And they have that unusual ability to establish a sense of calm, respect and mutual control in the relationships between staff and young people. They treat young people as adults. They take young people's views and comments seriously. They are always concentrating when they're at work: always looking for a sign, a 'way in' to extend the discussion or support decision-making. This is not an easy trick to pull off on your average club night, I can tell you.

Sometimes young people's judgements on quality are proclaimed with a more startling simplicity. One evening in Liverpool, I was accosted by a number of teenagers hanging around outside the youth club. They were clearly expecting me: 'You the inspector, then?' they enquired. I confirmed that I was. 'It's great, this youthy: you'll see,' they assured me. They were right.

Later, during my inspection years, those components of good centre-based youth work became easier to identify and analyse. At a small, rural club in Somerset, the first thing you noticed was the strong sense of possession and pride that young people showed, and the achievements they had documented in the club's feedback book. It was here that a club member who couldn't be present on the night of my visit left me a two-page letter: *To the Inspector*. It was a powerful paean of praise to the club leader and her staff team, to the excellent programme, to his fellow members and to the youth service in general. He hoped I would be able to appreciate the quality of the club during my short stay. I wrote a reply in the same manner (creating much anxiety later about protocols for my lead HM inspector), thanking him for his kind words and concurring in his judgement on the club's excellence. I've no idea if he ever read it. On another visit I recorded my view that the members had high standards of self-discipline, respect and good humour, and that they were able to resolve differences of opinion amicably and sensibly. These kinds of judgements cropped up regularly in many of my evidence form reports. It was certainly the case during my visit one night in Cheshire, where the link between the quality of practice was mirrored in the environment of the building. Unsurprisingly, the youth club was well used and highly valued by its members:

A warm, welcoming environment – the centre was decorated with curriculum materials, evidence of achievements, summer programme outcomes, graffiti boards, healthy living displays,

> *promotion of different cultures, photographs and testimonies. The youth work team displayed energy and empathy in their relationships with young people; they have created a positive and powerful culture in the centre which is reflected in the behaviour and attitude of members. Staff were observant, intervened when needed, encouraged and challenged young people and set high standards and expectations for them.*

It remains true that in the fifty years since the Albemarle Report, open-access youth work has been, to a large extent, the modus operandi of youth work. It is the spiritual and pragmatic home and the key delivery point of most youth work practice – good and bad. This book cannot pretend to be a history of youth centres or of open-access youth work, nor is there space to detail the changing fashions and the variety of buildings and projects that have been used as youth centres. From Albemarle and the Withywood design of the 1960s, to the 'youth and community centres' of the 1970s, to the rediscovery of 'places to go, things to do' in the late 1990s, and in *Transforming Youth Work* in the early 2000s; to the policy for every local authority to provide 'a safe, warm, well-equipped meeting place within reasonable distance of home, accessible to young people at times which suit them', to the state-of-the-art Myplace centres built before the budget cuts began to bite in the late 2000s. There remain some key components of centre-based work. Both Howard Williamson and Sue Robertson identified them as association (somewhere to go), activities (something to do), advice (someone to talk to) and autonomy (space of their own).[29] An important aspect of association was acceptance – young people frequently commented how they felt accepted in the youth club and how this differed from other areas of their lives. The youth work process was important, too – 'the youth workers are really easy to talk to and we can just come in and do whatever we want, like hang out with our mates.'[30]

STUTTERING STEPS

As a youth officer in Reading, I was forced to think harder about some of those basic beliefs that had underpinned my career thus far in youth work. Moving from Sheffield – a northern, solid Labour city council – to a Tory shire county (albeit at an urban end of it in Reading) brought me up short, philosophically speaking. Ever since the days when that youth officer in Sheffield had asked us that critical question – where we were 'leading' all these youths – I had not had to set out my core beliefs or motivation as a youth worker. These were simply based on a view about the inequality of opportunity within the educational system, which was one manifestation of social inequality, and that that system obstructs or perverts the potential of many young people, providing an experience of fear and failure rather than one of enjoyment and learning. I also felt that our service could not isolate young people from the neighbourhoods in which they lived and the adults and institutions to which they related. Nor could it ignore the realities and pressures of adolescence: pressures related to growing up, adult and sexual roles, material acquisition, commercial blandishment, the economic reality of enforced leisure – to quote but a few. Thus, if we believed in the youth service and what it had to offer, we needed (as officers) to vigorously oppose threats to its effectiveness by political antagonism or financial restriction. I wrote in a similar vein about the growth of the Manpower Services Commission's youth opportunities programmes: our response should reinforce our traditional, professional role and youth work skills in social education. In practice, youth workers have always got alongside 'difficult' young people, the socially deviant, those who don't accept 'acceptable' social norms and behaviour. We have tried to welcome those and other young people to youth clubs, or to work with them on the streets via detached youth work.

I recount this thinking not because it was (or is) particularly perceptive or new – but it was received with some scepticism by some of my Berkshire officer colleagues. I was seen as some kind of political activist, and one with dangerously radical or militant views, at that. As far as I was concerned I was simply expressing the things I believed in – and assumed others did too. My awareness of the value of a high profile for youth services and a political strategy to achieve it dates from my Berkshire days. Even in the early 1980s, the continual monitoring of effective delivery of a quality youth service was a priority for local youth officers.

We know that our armoury of professional skills is perhaps small – often we use ourselves alone: our personality, our sensitivity and listening skills, our non-judgemental attitude, our acceptance of youngsters. And this is possibly our greatest strength, especially in inner-city areas where we have singular and substantial experience in permeating the informal social networks of frustrated groups of young people and forging positive relationships with them. Of course (as I had discovered previously on the Kelvin Flats), this is often mistaken as collusion or identification with young people, especially where antisocial or criminal behaviour is involved. But our youth work expertise was already seen as a valuable input to youth employment programmes. I was beginning to develop and formalise some of my previous youth work thinking into a more coherent set of principles and philosophy – with some implications for good practice, evidence and the evaluation of quality, too. Stuttering steps, maybe, towards a set of youth work values and a shared curriculum (not that we used that word yet) – but it felt like I was going in the right direction.

THATCHER'S SECOND TERM

In 1983, Margaret Thatcher's Conservative government was voted back for a second, successive term. Published around the same time was the third national youth service review: *Experience and Participation*, popularly known as the Thompson Report after its author, Alan Thompson.

Margaret Thatcher was a politician who evoked strong reactions – she was adored and reviled in equal measure throughout much of her three terms as Prime Minister. To her supporters, she was the woman who had single-handedly won the Falklands War, destroyed the power of the trade unions, won the battle with the miners, allowed tenants to buy their own homes and hold shares, and brought a renewed sense of prosperity and economic strength to the nation. To her detractors, she was defined by her well-publicised view that there was 'no such thing as society', and by her relentless pursuit of policies that increased unemployment (especially youth unemployment), destroyed local communities and increased the gap between the rich and the poor. Not to mention her later nemesis, the community charge or 'poll tax'. Mrs Thatcher was no fan of local government and public services. The welfare state was, in her vision, simply a basic safety net providing essential services to those unable to afford to look after themselves. 'Rolling back the frontiers of the state' was an oft-quoted principle of her premiership: this meant slashing public spending and reducing the size of the public sector. Early on in her government, she had set out her views on what she described as 'municipal socialism'. Her fixed view, that local government was socialist and spendthrift, permeated policy development – she opposed and mistrusted localism in all its forms, preferring centralist control. Councils were forced to put local services out to competitive tendering, were set spending targets and were banned from increasing expenditure. 'There is no alternative,' she constantly intoned.

For the Thatcher government, reducing the inflation rate was a higher priority than reducing unemployment. Ministers seemed indifferent to the continuing unemployment of young people – allegedly reaching up to 90% of young people in Liverpool in the early 1980s. Norman Tebbit, the Employment Minister, famously advised those out of work to 'get on their bikes' to look for jobs.

Homeless young people were also much more visible on the streets in this period. This level of social dislocation was partly responsible for the riots that occurred in Bristol, Brixton and Toxteth in the early 1980s, though this was exacerbated by poor relations between the police and young black people. These events caused injuries and millions of pounds of damage and drew parallels with the American urban riots of the 1960s. At the time, John Cole, the BBC's respected political editor, noted that:

> *The casus belli of a youth war therefore lies in unemployment, bad housing, the breakdown of morality and of family/school discipline, a more rebellious attitude to authority in this generation, over-reaction by the police, the violence of youth culture... the list trails on to infinity.*

Coinciding with Thatcher's re-election, rising unemployment and the urban riots was my move to take up the new post of youth and community coordinator in Portsmouth. It was a time of unrest: Lord Scarman, who wrote the government's report of enquiry into the riots, came to Portsmouth Guildhall a little later and I went to hear his presentation on the causes of the disturbances and his recommendations for improvement. He was an elderly and rather other-worldly law lord, prone to using Latin phrases without translation in his speech. He was critical of the police and recorded many examples of the extremely hostile attitudes towards them, caused by 'the racial prejudice of some officers on the streets'. But he stopped short of describing the Metropolitan Police as racist, and recommended greater efforts be made to recruit black officers and for racist behaviour to be made a disciplinary offence.

Attending his talk as a young youth officer, previously in the royal county of Berkshire and now on the south coast, it suddenly dawned on me that the riots, the unemployment and the social upheavals that he was describing in London, Liverpool and Bristol were completely outside my professional experience. They were events I had never witnessed or had to reflect on in any of my jobs so far. It made me realise how my experience was very different from those of some of my colleagues in the north or in many London boroughs. Certainly, my home town was Sheffield and I'd worked in Reading and now Portsmouth, both urban areas with their fair share of disadvantage and social issues, but at times it felt uncomfortable describing youth work with some of my peers from Brixton or Moss Side or Knowsley at principal youth officer conferences. Theirs was a comparatively tougher job than mine, it seemed.

The concept of the north/south divide was fairly well established long before Mrs Thatcher's government, of course. It could be presented in a humorous way – as the caricature of a television announcer on one of Victoria Wood's television sketches put it, 'We'd like to apologise to viewers in the north. It must be awful for them.' But Thatcher's leadership and her policies were clearly exaggerating and reinforcing the differences. As the south-east grew in wealth and affluence, so the mines, the steel industry, shipbuilding and the heavy manufacturing base of the north declined in proportion. And with it the political balance – London and south-east Conservative supporters welcomed their new-found wealth, while Labour's long tradition of being the party of the industrial working class meant it was representing a declining northern base, linked in the public perception with the past, not the future.

PORTSMOUTH: BACK IN TIME

It was against this political background that I decided to leave Berkshire. Coming to Portsmouth was like moving back fifteen years in time – as far as youth work went, anyway. Unlike Berkshire, Hampshire had no history or culture of youth services or much understanding of youth work. It did have thirteen 'institutes of adult, youth and community education' – most of which were based in colleges and run by college principals – and what youth provision existed was delivered as a low-priority appendage of the adult education service. There was no county officer and the thirteen institute principals were accountable locally to area education officers, with further education advisers having some responsibility for youth at a local level. This was not promising ground.

But I began my job in Portsmouth with a clear idea of what lay ahead. It felt like a fresh chance, an opportunity to build up a youth service almost from scratch. Somewhere, in other words, I might make my mark. The main issues that needed to be tackled were the lack of any clear policy for the service – which meant that political leverage, knowing the right people and pulling the requisite strings were how decisions were made – and the yawning chasm between youth workers at field level and the hierarchy of officers and committees at County Hall that made decisions affecting them. Luckily, my new boss in Portsmouth had been a school youth tutor in Crawley in a previous life, so was not just an experienced youth worker but also someone who was sympathetic and supportive to me in my new task. Indeed, he often rescued me from the politically difficult situations I created, caused by my impatience or naivety. This was a reassuring and fortunate position for me.

As in Berkshire, Dave was keen on induction, too. In his case my introduction to the job included an evening tour of the city's highlights including Southsea Castle, the Round Tower and Spice Island, with drinks stops at the Still & West, the Spice Island Inn and (finally) at the 5th Hants Volunteer Arms, his local watering hole. It seemed to me like a good start in the job. From the outset, Dave was a great boss: probably the most supportive I'd ever worked for.

On a personal as well as a professional level, this was a happy time for me too. Ros – that young social work volunteer who'd walked into Kelvin Youth Centre to help out back in 1976 – had agreed to marry me soon after we moved to Hampshire. And it was on Bonfire Night in 1987 that our first son was born, becoming a Portsmuthian and Pompey FC fan in the process. Dave's response was typical – he sent me a telegram reading:

> *Result of the census Clan Caley*
> *Add Nicholas Simon (baby)*
> *Guy Fawkes natation to great jubilation*
> *Weighing in at 3kg 20!*

Trying to inform and empower the staff team in Portsmouth was my initial focus. 'Information is power' was a common catchphrase at the time. There were so many basics missing: job descriptions, staff meetings, training courses, policies to allocate resources or identify priority groups of young people, links with the voluntary sector. The task was to dig out the foundations and put the footings in place on which to build a youth service. So we cracked on in getting it all in place. Booking a minibus and my favourite residential centre on the Ridgeway in Berkshire, I collected up all the staff and took them away on their very first team residential. As we pulled out of the Civic Offices car park, Dave rushed out with labels he'd prepared for the minibus windscreen: *Portsmouth Youth Service On Tour*, they read. One of our exercises on the residential was to write up on paper pinned to everyone's backs a list of their individual skills and talents. There were two of mine I especially appreciated. The first was from one of the school youth tutors: he described me as 'a very Good Shepherd of his Flock'. The other, with commendable bluntness, contended that I had a 'well-developed bullshit-ometer'. These were both helpful skills to possess, of course.

Another valuable political lesson that had stayed with me from my previous officer roles was the need to spot promptly what's important in your in-tray and needs to be dealt with urgently and what can wait a while. The ability to recognise potential 'time bombs' liable to explode if you don't defuse them promptly – complaints from the public, requests from councillors, anything from young people – was a lesson I took to heart and filed away for future reference.

Sometimes, however, the bombs go off anyway. Like the time the staff at Hillside Youth Centre decided to kidnap the Mayor of Portsmouth in a fundraising stunt. A team of members, wearing balaclavas, had 'snatched' him from his mayoral car and taken him off to the centre where he was being held ransom, pending the payment of a large grant from the city council to club funds. The first I knew of it was when the phone rang and the *Portsmouth Evening News* wanted an explanation. Seconds later, Hampshire Police were asking the same question of my bosses. Hyperventilating quietly to hide my rising panic, I heard myself saying that I was unaware of the incident but would investigate immediately and get right back to them. I called Peter at the club and demanded to know what was going on. Syd (the mayor) and he were just having tea and toasted teacakes with his kidnappers in the club coffee bar, he said. Then, with a growing sense of guilt in his voice as he began to realise the enormity of what he had let loose, he explained everything to me.

The mayor was the local Labour ward councillor and a member of the club's management committee. They had all agreed the idea and planned the staging of the 'snatch' beforehand; it was all done with the best intentions and seemed a great idea for publicity and club funds. At the Civic Offices, we moved into full disaster management and damage limitation mode. The press office helped me draft our explanation and grovelling apologies. Teenage prank gone wrong; the mayor knew all along and was unhurt; overstepped the mark in their enthusiasm to raise money for the voluntary centre; profoundly sorry to the police and public; won't ever happen again. Of course, it all blew over soon enough and Peter was afterwards eternally grateful to me for my support in his hour of need. But the incident reminded me of the remark attributed to Harold Macmillan when asked what he feared most in politics. 'Events, dear boy,' he replied, 'events.'

MARILYN IN PORTSEA

It was sometimes hard work shepherding my Pompey flock to the sunlit uplands of good youth work practice. Half my staff team were community centre 'wardens' and did no youth work anyway. Three were school youth tutors accountable to their head and governors. Two club leaders were veterans, each with thirty years' experience and both coming up to retirement. Another worked for the YMCA and one was attached to a local church. But there was a brilliant part-time detached worker linked to a city centre youth club who saved my professional sanity. Marilyn knew where I was coming from and was keen to shift the youth service in the same direction. Early on in the job, I met her one rainy night on Queen Street in Portsea and was 'inducted' into the youths of the area. She was mortified when one lively teenager snatched off my flat cap, ruffled my hair and ran off chortling into the night. I got the cap back and we ended up at Portsea Rotary Youth Centre: a tough but thriving club run (with Marilyn's support) by the redoubtable Brenda and Shane. My hopes for success in Portsmouth leant heavily on these three people, although they didn't know it.

Marilyn described the young people she worked with as seeing her as a friend, an adult they could talk to and someone who would make no judgements on them. 'I do not have all the answers to their problems,' she said, 'and, more importantly, I do not pretend

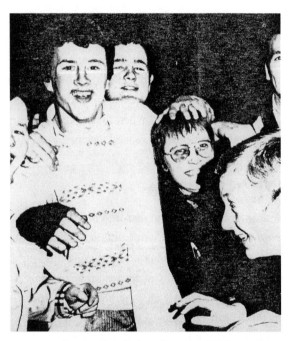

Portsea detached work report, 1984.

to.' The main topics of conversation with the young people on the streets of Portsmouth were unemployment, trouble with the police, school, sex, politics – 'just about anything and everything, really,' as she put it. Her analysis of her own role as a detached worker is worth recording:

> *My stance on all this has been to listen (remembering I have two ears and only one mouth) and allow them some valuable space to express themselves, without criticism. This is not always easy, as my own personal views do not always agree with theirs. I have always been completely honest about my political and social opinions, something I feel is very important when working with young people.*

And her views on the job? 'I now know what detached work is and it is not about not getting involved,' she noted; 'it is about involvement at a different level to club-based work. It is work where the people are bigger than the 'institution'. It is work that can be very isolated at times, especially as a lone worker, and it is hard to measure in terms of 'success' apart from a 'gut feeling' of satisfaction that I sometimes find hard to explain.'

Despite some of the obvious drawbacks, Marilyn reported that, 'I have very much enjoyed my involvement with the people of Portsea whose warmth, friendliness and community spirit towards me has been amazing.' Marilyn was an unqualified part-timer when I arrived in Portsmouth. An early target was to encourage unqualified staff to undertake youth work training – either as part-timers or in full-time trainee posts in the city. This route had been severely underused (despite there being training budgets still) in Hampshire, and we were fortunate to support three or four staff to become qualified. This method of 'growing your own' was often the most productive and effective way to capture the skills and experience of local workers and give them a well-paid job with potential career options.

WHAT DO YOUTH WORKERS ACTUALLY DO WITH YOUNG PEOPLE?

In 1984, I undertook some research at Brunel University's Centre for Youth Work Studies on youth work interventions with young people. I've always been interested in what youth workers actually do on that archetypal 'wet Wednesday night' in the youth club; those evenings I'd described at Kelvin a decade previously as 'normal club nights'. What are the theories or concepts that they operate on, and how are they translated into fieldwork practice? Simplistically, it was an investigation into the gaps between theory and practice – but especially I wanted to explore the skills and techniques that youth workers used in their work. Taking my Portsmouth staff as guinea pig interviewees, I started exploring these ideas at some length.

Questioned on the rationale underpinning their work, most referred to a version of 'social education' provision – mostly without any explicit outcome in mind, but with some implicit moral standpoints. One referred to 'helpful nudges' to setting standards, another more straightforwardly referred to 'teaching them what's right and wrong'. Some were clear that they used themselves, their own personalities, as a key tool with members – 'they can take me or leave me', 'I'm the same person inside and outside the club'. Defining what influence they might be having proved more difficult – 'it's a shot in the dark, an unknown factor' – although they could evidence individual cases and most agreed that '…they come back years later and tell you.'

The research revealed some fascinating practical skills, techniques and gambits used in interactions with young people. Examples included 'boxing clever' (establishing ways of creating learning), 'being subversive, an agent provocateur' (in eliciting group discussions), and other methods characterised by the phrases 'you have to be five minutes in front of them', 'you have to lean and push without them realising,' and 'you've got to choose your time.' Or, as one put it, 'I would justify provoking a reaction that made them think for themselves, make their own mind up.' There was considerable emphasis on availability, offering yourself, on observation and sensitivity skills, enabling in a passive, non-directive manner. And, fruitfully, there was a strong strand of the enjoyment of being with youngsters, of listening to them and learning what makes them tick. On being asked (rather bluntly) why they thought the local authority paid them, responses varied from 'society doesn't provide non-judgemental, caring adults any more' to 'fifty years ago there weren't people like us, except the local vicar' and 'the need to have an adult independent of parents or teachers.'

Providing a safe haven and someone to talk to (who wasn't a teacher or a social worker) cropped up often. Many felt that authentic relationships with teenagers could only develop where there were no statutory obligations present. Where, in other words, the young person's agenda was paramount – not those of other agencies. This sets us at a different level of engagement; as one experienced worker explained it to me, 'whatever young people bring, we work with; or if we can't we refer them – but only on their terms and with their permission.' There was an element of 'youth work as gut reaction' in some of these answers: as one worker said '…you forget the theory after college; you just go and do it.'

My Brunel research crystallised some of the ideas I'd long held as a centre-based worker myself. There are some 'unwritten rules' of youth club engagement and activity. It was the routine of the 'normal' youth club night that I was observing. Some evenings would provoke an analysis no more profound than 'letting off steam,' of basic recreational activity, fairly well organised, offering some choices, but with no apparent evidence of intentional aim or objective beyond providing young people with satisfying, simple pleasures. Some interventions might occur 'on the wing', as it were (conversations at the snooker table or coffee bar), but these would be transitory and limited in impact. Others, though, were clearly planned, well thought-out, based on evidence of need, targeted to specific individuals and implemented with determination and skill. Again, non-intervention could be a planned strategy too. But critically, throughout all my interviews, the most important component was that relationships with young people were always voluntary and on young people's terms. This was a unanimous and non-negotiable element of good youth work for these Portsmouth staff. As a youth officer, this type of research helped me to reflect on the issues of programme content, targeted groups and curriculum – long before those words were being routinely used in the political context of youth service delivery.

It was also in Portsmouth that I first did some work on 'matching resources to need' – trying to target our scarce youth budget in the areas where it was most needed. County officers at the time belittled this work, describing it as simply a futile exercise in 'equalising misery' and 'robbing Peter to pay Paul.' That made me even more determined to proceed. It was also in Portsmouth that I began to take an interest in strategic issues affecting young people and youth work. I produced a strategy outline document for the city; I encouraged staff to write up their own work with difficult young people on some of the less salubrious Portsmouth housing estates. The latter got me into trouble again when the council took exception to a part-timer's report describing her area as 'Trolleyland' – because of all the trolleys from Tesco which she saw abandoned on her patch. Again, using already published statistics in support of an Urban Aid bid for the city, the press attacked me for painting an unduly pessimistic view of things. This time the leader of the council got involved, too.

These episodes reminded me of the pickle I had got myself into at Kelvin Youth Club with the march on the Town Hall alongside the club members. Maybe there was a streak of political protester inside me that occasionally exhibited itself. Perhaps I was happy to create the odd political scenario that encouraged criticism of those bosses who patently failed, in my view, to see the benefits of youth work or were unaware of the needs of local youngsters. Certainly, I judged that too many of the county officer hierarchy at the time – based at the remote County Hall in Winchester – simply wanted a quiet life and were uninterested in youngsters on council estates in Portsmouth. This kind of 'politicking' nearly led to my downfall. I was receiving some support and encouragement at the time from a local Labour councillor who served a housing estate in the north of the city and was one of the few non-Conservative county

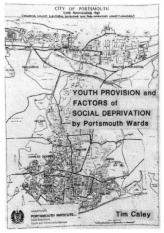

Portsmouth Evening News,
September 1983.

councillors. He was a rather short, dumpy man who carried his official council papers around in two plastic bags and whose shirts always seemed two sizes too large for his neck. Dangerously, he rather began to 'adopt' me as his favourite officer because I shared his advocacy for greater provision for young people in his ward and some of his antagonism to his less supportive Conservative county council colleagues. Maybe, between us, we sometimes overstepped the mark in our enthusiasm for change and action. Some weeks later in the Civic Offices, I opened a personal letter from the Director of Education warning me about my activities with this councillor and threatening me with disciplinary action unless I ceased discussing county policy with him. Luckily, this threat was speedily defused by my local bosses (particularly Dave), who denied that I had been acting improperly but promised to keep an eye on me in future. The lesson for me was twofold: firstly, be careful who you choose as allies and of the boundaries you establish with them; and secondly, a certain combativeness and energy on behalf of young people is no bad thing if you're committed to moving a service forward.

THE THOMPSON REPORT: A DEAD DUCK?

Early on in my Portsmouth days, a new national report on youth work had appeared. The Thatcher government was probably stony ground on which to launch a review of youth services in 1982. Mrs Thatcher's Secretary of State for Education, Sir Keith Joseph, was even less enamoured of local councils than she was and took a remote, patrician view of services to young people, seeing it as a very low priority for state involvement at all. He was certainly influential in Mrs Thatcher's political philosophy, notably through his involvement with the Centre for Policy Studies, a right-wing 'think tank'. And he had spoken controversially in the past of the 'cycle of deprivation' that led to the chaotic lifestyles of the poorest people, or the 'underclass', as they were soon described in the press.

By the early 1980s, national youth policy had remained drifting and unaltered for decades – it had been ten years since the Fairbairn-Milson report and twenty years since the Albemarle Report. Left without direction or guidance, local authorities reverted to their default policy position: doing their own thing. There had been the hints of potential civic disturbances caused by rising youth unemployment, and a number of MPs now felt the time was ripe to provide a policy response. The origins of the review that led to the Thompson Report lay in the continuing efforts of these MPs to use the device of a private member's bill to try and achieve a statutory basis for the youth service.

They never achieved that aim, but a review of the service was promised as an alternative. There were suspicions that the members of the review group had been vetted carefully by both Joseph and Thatcher – hand-picked for their Conservative sympathies, some have argued. This is probably unfair as the members included some able and experienced national names: Eric Hopwood and Francis Cattermole, for example. In some ways, the Thompson Committee was a classic, old-fashioned gathering of the great and the good. At least the review group was formed, set to work quickly and its report was promptly delivered to Sir Keith in August 1982.

Like the Albemarle and Fairbairn-Milson reports before it, the structure of the Thompson Report was familiar. A bit about the brief (advise on value for money), a bit on young people today (changing world, anxiety of youth), a bit on assessing what exists (wide variety, dedicated volunteers), a bit on the service of tomorrow (challenges, potential, age range, training), and finally a bit on money and the government's role (need for action/ legislation). Thompson is renowned for his definition of the five 'A's of youth work, but like the report as a whole, almost no one can remember them all. (They were association, activities, advice including information and counselling, action in the community and access to life and vocational skills.)

Thompson was good on specific youth service methods: the experiential curriculum, participation in decision-making, voluntaryism and non-directive relationships with young people. He was also tough on the failures to deliver: no coherent social education policy, patchy response to emerging needs (unemployment, racism, homelessness), no proper evaluation or monitoring, nothing much for the over-sixteens. While Thompson conceded that 'money hasn't been thrown at the Youth Service,' he couldn't decide if it needed more, although noting the inequality between local authority provision. With hindsight, the Thompson Report's structure and its analysis of policy assumed a somewhat liberal view of the enabling state. To put it simply, its authors felt that the government would share its assumptions about the social needs of young people, about the value base and benefits characterised by the report's strapline *Experience and Participation*, and about the likely support it might receive from the minister. Unfortunately, however, Mrs Thatcher was quite uninterested in these sets of liberal assumptions.

With this backdrop it is surprising that the Thompson Report ever saw the light of day at all. Sir Keith Joseph took almost two years to formally respond to the report and, in reality, sidelined any attempt to implement its recommendations. In his introductory welcome in the ministerial foreword, his comments were lukewarm in the extreme. Deciding about *ping-pong on the rates* was never going to be a priority for him. In my own copy of the report, I added a schoolboy, graffiti-like addition making Joseph appear to say, 'I haven't read the report, of course, but I'm sure it's jolly good...' Writing an analysis of the report for colleagues in Portsmouth, I headlined my article with the question: *Thompson – a Dead Duck?* It was a bit harsh, maybe, but simply a recognition of the government's low policy priority attached to youth services of any kind, and to reform, or the allocation of additional funding. There was one positive element for me (in my second youth officer job), and that was Thompson's definition of good youth work management. There is no mystery about good management, the report declared – it has four basic aspects: *defining objectives, assigning roles, allocating resources and monitoring performance.* At least that was something simple to take away with me. But on the whole for the practitioner, Thompson offered nothing new or helpful – indeed, it tried to have its cake and eat it, too, promulgating a generic and expansive role for youth workers while also demanding specific attention to targeted groups.

At the time, my overall verdict on the Thompson Report was one of disappointment. It failed to point a direction, to give an energetic lead with the political force to back it up. Thinking harder about the issues, I was also conscious that such a direction was probably impossible, given the pluralistic and idiosyncratic nature of what we term the youth service. Thompson had done his best to paint an honest picture, but it was not exactly an inspiring one and it lacked a pay-off. But then maybe (I wrote at the time) that is an accurate perception of our service. My definition of a dead duck seemed quite prophetic and accurate. By now, I fear, I was becoming a bit jaded as a local youth officer. I wasn't alone.

By 1987, Mark Smith felt that the rationale for a distinctive and educationally based youth service looked bleak:

> *While there may be occasional peaks of optimism, perhaps as a minister throws the Service a few pennies to demonstrate the government's commitment to 'solving' some political problem, the underlying trends suggest its demise… a withering away of a distinctive statutory service.*[31]

CHAPTER 5

NUMERO UNO: HEAD OF HAMPSHIRE

The chance for Hampshire to develop a proper county-wide youth service came in the late 1980s. A new Director of Education had been headhunted from Kent, which had always had excellent youth provision, and he was keen to see youth work emerge from beneath the umbrella of the adult education institutes. One of his first acts was to set up a review of youth work which proposed the appointment of a new county youth officer post to lead a new service across Hampshire. My old boss in Berkshire had always said I was 'the prince who wanted to be king' and there was some truth to that. But ambition has not been a major driver in my professional life. On the contrary, sometimes I feel as if I've slipped by accident into jobs – or happened to be in the right place at the right time. Although, technically, becoming head of a service is about as high as you can go if you're in youth work, it's not exactly a well-known or well-understood position. Long after I became a head of service, I frequently told audiences the story of how my mother still hoped that, one day, I might get a *proper* job.

Hence it was with some trepidation – knowing what I already knew – that I applied for and was appointed to the new job. I was asked at the interview how I would handle the transition from 'lobbyist to lobbied'. It was a good question – I was moving from the relative calm of a local post where criticism without responsibility was easy, to the top job where my role was to provide both the questions and the solutions. Just as I was about to answer, a clock on the table behind me chimed four o'clock, much to my surprise; it was disconcerting but it gave me a few helpful seconds to compose my answer. My response reflected my previous view – there needed to be policies (approved by elected members) for budgets, people and programmes; without them any organisation was at the whim of individuals or vested interests. It seemed to satisfy the interview panel: I was Hampshire's first county youth officer and I began work in late 1989. Having reached this professional peak (in youth service terms, anyway), my annual salary had now reached the dizzy heights of £23,500 – three times as high as my first officer post in Berkshire exactly ten years before.

Setting up a new youth service from scratch, from a background of further education colleges, adult education advisers and powerful school head teachers, was always going to be hard work. Indeed, at first it felt like a nightmare scenario: 'getting the Northern Ireland portfolio' was how I described my role to my

Prizewinning youth service logo design, 1991.

new colleagues at The Castle (yes, that was what County Hall was called). And worse, I wasn't really in charge: the post was located in the Inspection and Advisory Service, which meant I didn't control the youth service budget or manage the staff; that was done by the four area education officers. So I was 'a bull with no balls,' as one colleague rather painfully put it. But I was undeterred: this was my big chance and I wasn't planning to lose it; I might not have been ambitious but I was keen to hit the ground running.

There were difficulties in being a successful internal candidate: people often suspect you may not really be up to the job, but were appointed as an easy option. And then when all your senior managers have to be appointed through internal competition, you end up with a hierarchy that is essentially a compromise – well, less than ideal. Thus there were moments of pessimism and depression as I wondered whether I'd made the right decision. It certainly felt worse when the full extent of the budget problems became apparent. The director invited me to meet him early on in the job to ask how I was faring.

'Well, there are days of great elation,' I said, 'and days of black despair.'

He smiled and said, 'Yes, it's the same for me.'

In my dealings with him (which were infrequent), I recalled the words that Margaret Thatcher had used in describing one of her favourite ministers, David Young. 'Other people bring me problems, David,' she told him one day, 'but you bring me solutions.' As a strategy for managing my managers, I took that advice to heart – by always offering them some solutions to develop my new youth service in Hampshire. Most of my bosses have been easy to please: all they want is advance notice of problems and conflicts, preferably long before they happen and especially if they involve the press or elected members. Even more simply, they want me to deal with them first and quietly solve them, so their hands remain unsullied by youth service nuisances.

This was probably the second most intense period of my professional life, after Kelvin Youth Centre. My second major milestone, my most substantial learning curve, my biggest professional challenge to date. The job, essentially, was to drag Hampshire out of the 1950s and into the 1990s as far as youth work was concerned. We bravely spent time calling staff conferences and residentials to agree on what should be youth service policy, curriculum and practice. Only those who have ever been responsible for managing youth workers will understand the levels of masochism involved in running these kinds of events. By which I mean that the task of managing youth workers has often been compared to herding large groups of strong-willed cats – with the additional burden that the youth workers answer back. There is a school of thought that acknowledges the similarities in working with young people and managing youth workers. The latter retain that youthful independence and autonomy of spirit, and (from time to time) that degree of bloody-minded obstinacy that is not dissimilar to the testosterone-fuelled behaviour of some fifteen- and sixteen-year-olds. Dealing with both groups requires a quiet firmness, a reminder of the boundaries, an encouragement to express their opinions and a willingness to listen and respond – though probably at a more opportune time.

Our conferences were not without incidents of such idiosyncratic behaviour amongst staff teams. One afternoon at the residential centre, a group from Southampton refused to return after lunch in protest at some aspect or other of the proceedings. They continued their separate deliberations out on the lawn for the rest of the day. This seemed to me to be the easiest way to handle their complaint. Interestingly and gratifyingly, some years later I received a letter from one of those Southampton staff who recalled those early county policymaking days.

I do remember when you took over the County Youth Service and held that bold residential at Gurney Dixon when you invited us to help to formulate the county policy – and invited the County Education Officer! As a new member of staff, and without a track record in statutory youth work, that event made a big and very positive impression on me.

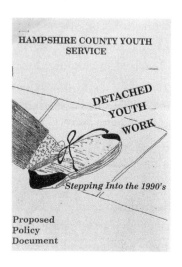
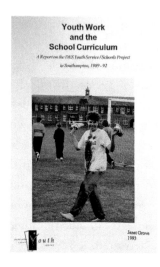

Hampshire Youth Service policy documents and reports, 1990–1995.

In a profession where measuring impact and providing evidence of outcomes is difficult, and where the processes of consultation can be fraught with difficulties, her letter was especially welcome.

Producing our service policy documents was a successful first move as it cemented a sense of ownership amongst what previously had been a diverse group of staff that rarely met together about anything. Now, at least, they had been consulted and had agreed on a set of critical policies and guidelines that were to be the bedrock of practice for the fledgling service. We published and circulated them all as widely as possible, not only internally but to partners in the district and town councils and to the voluntary sector. In the early 1990s, local authority youth services churned out countless policy and publicity documents. They varied immensely in quality and quantity – often there was a direct and inverse relationship between the glossiness of the cover and the quality of the contents. But our Hampshire ones were first-rate. I was given a remarkable level of autonomy and freedom to develop policy, practice and approaches for the youth service. It reflected the power that individual local authorities and their elected members possessed in this arena – for good or bad – in the absence of agreed national standards in the early 1990s.

BUDGETS, POLICY, STAFF, COUNCILLORS, PARTNERSHIPS

These five simple words soon began to represent every waking moment of my professional life; each one reflecting a critical constituent part of the job. Regarding the budget, I needed to find out how much money there was, where it was being spent and whether it provided good value. Protecting it and trying to get more of it was a key element of the job description. Sorting this out was seriously difficult: I discovered the youth budget had been plundered for years by various outposts of the Education

Department. We were even paying for the 'Hampshire Theatre Wardrobe'. More important, overspending had been rife and uncontrolled, especially in school and college caretaking costs. I was assigned my own personal treasury officer to help me unravel this financial shambles and together we spent a year sorting it out.

Even when things had become a little clearer, they remained fairly depressing. Hampshire was always near the bottom of the league table of spending on thirteen to nineteen-year-olds nationally: my budget at the time was about £2 million. When I had the chance, I'd explain to councillors and colleagues that the whole county youth service cost about the same as one secondary school. If I was feeling confident, I might add, 'and we're not closed for thirteen weeks of the year.' But I never complained about the comparative poverty of our resources and instructed my staff not to do so either. It was a pointless and self-indulgent exercise. Showing how good you could be with a little was the best way to encourage people to give more. At every meeting, I would hammer home the same point: if you want to increase the budget, make sure the work is good, that you can prove it makes a difference and you write it up and report it widely. Without doubt, there were times when this was hard, especially if I had to report difficult decisions or apply unpopular policies. Sustaining the morale of staff groups while being the bearer of unwanted messages and being personally uncertain about the future is no fun. But the memory of one of my part-timers from the early days at Kelvin was ever present: 'You can't be popular all the time, you know,' he used to remind me.

Policy seems a simple thing to resolve, but it accounted for major continuing headaches and debates. What should the youth service be doing? With which young people? And to what end? What were our priorities? And how much should we spend on them? Agreeing a consensus on those questions was impossible to achieve even amongst my officers, never mind the rest of the staff.

You would get a different answer every time you asked. Hence the need for our policy and curriculum conferences. Managing staff – starting with my four divisional youth officers – took up inordinate amounts of physical and mental energy. Because of the divisional structure, these key officers often resembled the feudal barons of medieval England, operating with lordly independence and autonomy as they saw fit within the boundaries of their own empires. They only occasionally acknowledged the existence of the King's writ (that is, me) in their territory. I didn't really blame them because the county structure encouraged such autonomy: I would have probably acted just the same. But trying to establish some degree of consistency in policy and practice was well-nigh impossible in these circumstances. Annual budget allocations were my worst nightmare: arguing for hours about the relative needs of Southampton, Aldershot, Andover and Portsmouth and trying to divide the budget 'cake' fairly amidst ferocious lobbying from all four of them was often a bad-tempered experience. These sessions I termed my 'two Nurofen' meetings, and afterwards, I needed to lie down in a darkened room for a couple of hours to recover. Fortunately, the divisional structure was changed after I made it clear to the director that I had to be in charge of both the staff and the youth budget. In reality, because no one else wanted the job anyway, there was little opposition in agreeing a change to my officer role. The de facto position was formalised: I became the head of the youth service in reality, taking the power away from the area education officers and ending the pretence of being an adviser or an inspector.

Learning to operate effectively in the world of council budgets was a critical skill. My introduction to financial years, annual budget-setting and budget-making timetables, the threats of budget reductions and generally fire-fighting on resources for youth work was not completely new. I had after all been a youth officer in Reading and Portsmouth. But the job of protecting your budget was a constant and all-encompassing one. At one end of the spectrum this was just ensuring the service was properly resourced and equipped to deliver the results councillors wanted. But at a more altruistic level, as head of service, you held significant responsibility for the well-being, the jobs and the salaries of many people, hundreds of whom in Hampshire were part-timers. One ill-conceived strategic blunder, one political error, one poor public performance in committee or interview with the press might have significant budget consequences for your service and thus for the livelihoods of your employees. Hence, always being ready to fight your service's corner, being alert to dangers, recognising and heading off the threats, ensuring your pre-emptive strikes were oiled and ready for action – all these things became second nature and a constant, relentless pressure. The occasional budget growth, however small and infrequent, was a cause for joyous celebration and much publicity.

Partnerships were interesting: it was a word that could hide a multitude of sins and mean different things to different people. For example, I soon discovered that all district or borough councils (not to mention the whole host of town and parish authorities) were experts on the needs of their young people and on the failure of the county council to understand and provide for them. And they all took a particular pleasure in inviting county officers to their local meetings and conferences to explain themselves. The local elected members loved these events, of course: they were the closest thing to bear-baiting they were ever likely to experience. Watching county officials squirming under local attack gave them inordinate pleasure. It was futile to resist these trials: your function was inevitably predetermined – you were the appointed sacrificial victim, the dartboard onto which their political arrows thudded incessantly. You just had to grin and bear it as part of the job. Strangely, some of the local council officers who invited me began to feel a grudging admiration, respect even, for my bravery and fortitude under such regular fire. 'Sorry if we were a bit hard on you today,' they would tell me as they saw me off, 'and thanks for coming along.'

Another early and urgent task was to resolve the pressing issue of who controlled the twenty-one youth centres on school sites in Hampshire. Was it the head and governors or the youth service? No one had ever asked this question before, so it required some historical research. Part of the task in proving my argument involved rummaging in the dusty archives in The Castle's hidden attics, stairwells and storage cupboards for evidence of past practice in years gone by. Had the youth wing building always been used for teenagers, or could it be turned into a sixth-form library or children's crèche if the governors so determined? Clambering onto ladders to dig out ancient school files of typewritten memos from the 1960s and 1970s, I got filthy as decades of undisturbed dust ended up all over my suit, my shirt and my hands. Most schools had changed their names as well – from ordinary local comprehensive secondary schools to more important-sounding titles: technical schools, colleges or academies. But the dust and dirt were worth it, because custom and practice seemed to support my case. Finding the right paperwork to buttress my argument was a powerful help when I had to appear before the members of the committee. My mission was aided, too, by a report from Her Majesty's Inspectors on a survey of school-based youth and community work which had concluded that:

> *The best work is usually found where there is a qualified youth worker with clear professional accountability to a discrete youth service. Initiatives are successful where youth work is accepted as a valid educational approach and the youth service is seen as an equal partner.*[32]

These words were sweetness and light to my ears, of course. Armed with a copy of the HMI report and my dusty evidence from the archives, we thrashed out a draft policy for the management of youth work on school sites which put in place annual agreements and contracts to deal with the real and sometimes competing needs of both school and youth work.

The job of getting it past the elected members was my first taste of appearing before the Education Committee. I was pretty nervous. My boss' secretary wished me good luck as I walked over to the committee chamber, which increased my anxiety even further. The county council chamber was an impressive wood-panelled and gilt-decorated Victorian municipal masterpiece. It had high, mullioned, leaded windows, an ornate pendulum wall clock and wooden rafters on the ceiling. You might enjoy visiting it as a tourist, but it was not a comfortable or natural workplace for discussion and debate. It reminded me of a courtroom, with the council leader sitting on a raised dais like the judge, a public gallery in the gods high above, and space for the press along the side. We officers sat on uncomfortable, tip-up wooden benches behind the leader's chair until it was our turn to be called. My turn took forever to arrive; with some hesitation, I explained my report and its plan for local annual agreements with schools. I was delighted to obtain the critical support of members for this new policy: this was an important turning point for the service, especially for all the youth workers on school sites. These annual agreements stood the test of time, although negotiating them was never easy.

Nor were we immune to staff problems in those early days. Before the first twelve months as a new county youth service had elapsed, I had to appear at an industrial tribunal, along with other senior officers, to defend a case brought by a part-time worker in Southampton. She claimed that the authority had acted in a racist and sexist way in failing to support her application for funds to attend a youth work training course. The youth workers' union, CYWU, backed her claim and hired an expensive lawyer from London to support her at the tribunal hearing. From my perspective, the decision on her claim was simply that the training budget was limited and the panel decided there were other applicants that attracted a higher priority. The chair of the industrial tribunal agreed, and we won the case without a problem. But not without wasting many weeks preparing papers, attending meetings and generally being annoyingly distracted from the business of running a youth service. It was an early baptism of management fire – although it provided an experience that had political advantages in the future. I was pleased that our developing management and policy systems had been vindicated.

As a thank-you gift, I bought a bottle of champagne for the education personnel officer who had guided us through the tribunal preparation and hearing. *To the Perry Mason of the Department*, I wrote on the card. He turned down the gift, quite sensibly, telling me to enjoy it at home with my wife. It seemed an appropriate gesture. For it was while working on the tribunal case that my pager bleeped one afternoon in the corridor of the Education Department. In the days before mobile phones, my wife had equipped me with this latest technology: she was expecting another baby and wanted to ensure she could contact me in an emergency. Sure enough, this was the emergency: our second son, Matt, had decided to arrive three weeks early. Another Pompey FC fan to join his brother, Nick.

COMPETING PERSPECTIVES

Once a head of service, it is impossible not to sort out your relationships with councillors and politicians. Their support is crucial, not just to funding but also to agreeing policy focus and direction. Fighting the youth service corner becomes a way of life – a raison d'être. At the start of my Hampshire post, I was much influenced by a conference speech by Dr Liz Hoggarth on what she termed 'the competing perspectives and rationales on youth work within a local authority setting.'[33] Our professional rationale for the work shared some common ground: a social education perspective, relationships with and participation by young people. For elected members, expectations are more pragmatic – peace, an absence of problems, keeping young people off the streets, minimising their nuisance value. Members can identify with activities and equipment, with resources being well spent and producing results, with young people being well trained and joining the workforce, with services that create a good image of their town or city. There were further facets to consider: funding bodies may also have clear expectations, and the views of young people as to what they themselves require of the service need to be uncovered. What Hoggarth highlighted persuasively was that if these two or more sets of perspectives were out of kilter – were pulling apart, even – then it increased the 'irrationality' of our jobs as managers of youth services. This was often compounded by our professional 'isolationism': our endemic failure to explain our role to others and our occasional arrogance or remoteness – we professionals know best. Local councillors, she warned, often knew their local patch much better than we did. Therefore, retaining a practical, common-sense approach for elected members, nurturing their support, eschewing all youth work jargon: these were powerful lessons.

Hampshire was a relatively old-fashioned and philanthropic authority as far as providing for young people was concerned. It had a strong voluntary tradition and a genuine care for the county's youth, including those who were disadvantaged or in need. As county officer, I realised how fortunate I was to have the support of my chief education officer and to have forged really positive links with the voluntary sector. This was an archetypal rural, Tory shire county – among other things there was an important 'ceremonial' role to the head of service appointment. The job included regular contact with royalty, Lord Lieutenants, assorted 'great and goods', chief executives,

Chief Scouts and Guides, amongst others – these things were still important in Hampshire. The Lord Lieutenant at the time explained that helping and supporting young people to grow up required what he described as a 'three-legged stool'. He always repeated this image at public events when I was with him. One leg represented parents or guardians, another stood for teachers, and the third, just as valuable, was a friendly adult figure like a youth worker, he used to declare. I rather warmed to Sir James and his implicit support for youth work.

I spent a lot of time, often at weekends, at countless ceremonies, wearing my best suit, in front of an assortment of audiences, trying to look and sound intelligent on behalf of the county council. This 'performance' role was one I always treated seriously because I viewed it as a significant element of my leadership duties and responsibilities as head of service. It was important to appear confident, in charge and optimistic – whatever the situation. It didn't even matter much what you said as long as it sounded convincing. As an aside, although I had no training in public speaking or presentations, my previous (and brief) acting career stood me in good stead. There were some simple rules: stand still, ensure they can see your face, don't start until everyone goes quiet and make certain they can hear you at the back.

Often these events took place in the council chamber, appearing before the Education Committee answering questions about the youth service or youth issues that were exercising the minds of councillors. Usually, my agenda item was buried towards the end of a very long meeting; the press and public had long since departed as the interesting or controversial topics had been dealt with and, sometimes, half the committee members seemed to have gone too. But I learnt how to take advantage of this pattern of events. First, you had to write a simplified adaptation of your report with an easy-to-understand summary and recommendation – this was called the 'Janet and John' version for members. Second, if you could get some coloured charts or diagrams into the report, you were off to a good start – councillors loved coloured pictures. Third, if you were patient and polite in waiting your turn to speak, they often took pity on you. And finally, if they were exhausted after a lengthy session and you looked and sounded confident, they almost invariably agreed all your proposals without any debate or difficulties.

THE *DAILY MAIL* 'SO WHAT?' QUESTION

Protecting the youth service corner meant establishing the quality and credibility of the work, especially for local councillors. It meant developing a higher profile for youth work. It meant putting your money where your mouth is. It meant making partnerships with others real. It meant demanding high quality and taking rigorous action where provision was below standard. It meant telling staff that they had to listen to councillors' views on the needs of young people in their wards. It meant learning some humility as professionals. It meant remembering that there was a client-led electorate that could not be ignored: the constituency of ordinary people.

On many occasions I would remind colleagues, as they waxed lyrical about some pet project or particular piece of work they were undertaking, that they needed to ask the *Daily Mail* question. Which was – *So what?* What was the impact or effect of their project? What difference was it making, and where was the evidence? Who cared about it, anyway? In taking this line, I was not seeking to devalue good youth work or demoralise hard-pressed staff: I was demonstrating that our responsibilities, and not just as managers, involved reconciling the competing rationales, interpreting fieldwork successes to elected members in a language they understood, lobbying positively on behalf of the service and providing the evidence that youth work worked. Completing a training course on writing a press release was mightily helpful to me, both then and later in my consultancy roles. I learnt how to produce a template that included a headline that encapsulated our story, text that always answered the questions: *What? Why? Where? When? How?* and *What happens next?* along with a quote and a photograph. I advocated this model endlessly to youth work colleagues and (subsequently) clients forever afterwards.

In pursuit of these aims, a concerted effort went into establishing all our policies and procedures for the new county youth service. From the competition to design the new logo, to the publication of policy and curriculum documents and writing a protocol for the inspection of youth work – before Ofsted got round to it. And beginning the tradition of annual reports called *Snapshots of Practice,* which set out examples of effective youth work and were modelled on the recently published national HMI booklet *Effective Youth Work.* They were all part of an effort to raise the profile and unashamedly to use whatever public relations skills and good-news stories we could find to tell people about how the youth service helped youngsters in Hampshire.

In 1991, we decided to hold our first birthday party as a youth service. Tim Burke from *Young People Now* came along to report on the event. It was something of a high-risk affair – bringing together different youth groups to perform music, dance, poetry, drama and exhibitions in front of a raft of assorted dignitaries from the county hierarchy, all planned by the young people themselves. We launched our new logo and the Lord Lieutenant cut our birthday cake. More importantly, the *YPN* report was very positive, repeating my view that we needed to show off examples of good practice because 'youth services are very good at under-selling themselves.' It also told the story of why Hampshire had established a youth service and given a much higher priority to youth work across the county. I was quoted as feeling that policy priorities were developing soundly, and that *we are saying this is what the service is and being tough about what it isn't… Only time will tell,* I added, *if those who count can be persuaded to increase support for our work.*

youth *service*

Tim Burke profiles two counties, Hampshire and Devon, that have been celebrating their young people and their youth services.

year for youth

i t is the first birthday of Hampshire County Council youth service, and 200 people from all over the county are in Winchester's Guildhall to attend an evening's entertainment entitled 'A Celebration of Youth'.

It is a high risk kind of event but county youth officer Tim Caley sees it as very important: 'The only way I see the service being able to develop is by showing examples of good practice to the people who count. That's why we've commissioned a new logo and arranged birthday celebrations – youth services are very good at under-selling themselves.'

After one year the benefits of having a discrete youth service within education are starting to emerge. 'There is now a degree of clarity,' says Tim Caley. 'People share a common understanding of what youth work is, and it should now be possible to support priorities.'

Before 1990, youth work was administered through the Further Education division, answerable to the council's FE committee. Under the old system there were 13 institutes with an adult, youth and community education brief. Work with young people varied greatly in quality and quantity – and often had a low priority. 'By and large it would be number 14 on the agenda for the institutes' management committee meetings,'

● Joining in the 'Celebration of Youth' evening is Lord Lieutenant for Hampshire, Commander Henry Bruce, Tamara Baggot, a member of Beyond Graffiti, and Tim Caley, county youth officer.

cont. on page 36. ▶

Hampshire County Youth Service, first birthday party,
Young People Now, August 1991.

PARTNERSHIP WITH THE VOLUNTARY SECTOR

One of my concerns from the outset was to avoid the patronising, 'statutory' view of voluntary youth organisations which was common amongst some of my regional colleagues at the time. While mouthing the philosophy of 'partnership' and support for the Scouts, Guides, Boys' Clubs, voluntary, church and community groups that abounded in their patches, in reality they felt that the local authority youth service represented the 'professionals', and that really they knew best. The statutory service would provide the occasional small revenue grant to voluntary clubs as pump-priming or support, though they had to jump through lots of hoops to apply, but the council kept most of the money and power to itself.

Now, this seemed to me an absurd policy stance. Firstly, because most of the voluntary groups had been around a lot longer than the youth service and would probably continue long after it had disappeared, but also because it seemed much cleverer to have the voluntary sector on your side, rather than as your enemy. And secondly, in a shire county like Hampshire, volunteering and voluntary groups held strong political power and public support in equal measure, not least from elected councillors of all political persuasions. Thus, a policy of genuine support for voluntary organisations was a priority.

It took a number of forms: we retained capital grants to build Scout huts, parish council youth clubs and repair church hall roofs, and we disbursed revenue grants to help all kinds of youth provision at local, community level. We managed to establish a youth service grants panel which gave me unfettered access to elected members and allowed them the particular pleasure of disbursing money to deserving youth projects and young people – sometimes in their own wards. The money went on attending training programmes, participating in international exchanges, joining the Tall Ships experience, introducing young people to gliding courses, developing apprenticeships and career ambitions – or just doing things that no one else seemed to fund. It is instructive that this latter programme to help individuals was one of the most successful elements of the service and the one most enthusiastically supported by councillors. Early on in post, I was questioned by a severe, grey-haired woman, who was a very senior Conservative councillor in the authority, about the benefits of the youth service. She had been put onto the grants panel and wanted to know all about the budget and how it was spent. Fearing the worst, I explained the position. She took it all in, paused, then looked me in the eye and whispered conspiratorially, 'Well, for heaven's sake, we need to increase your funds so you can at least have a *whole* peanut instead of only half a one.' Sometimes, help comes from unexpected quarters.

TO THE EDITOR

Scouting for all?

Dear Editor,

In your *Letters* pages over the last few months, it has been disappointing to see a number of disparaging remarks about 'local youth clubs'. I refer to comments like '...this is the Scout Movement and not a youth club' (*Drop the dead wood*, September 1992) and 'if Members are not prepared to wear the uniform correctly and smartly, might I respectfully suggest that they transfer to the local youth club', (*Are standards dropping?*, November 1992).

Well, yes — the young people who participate in youth centres and projects run by the local authorities, who are in contact with detached youth workers in rural villages and urban estates, who make use of youth counselling and advice agencies or join the thousands of part time voluntary church or community youth clubs, may not be the same young people as those who join the Scouts, but surely none of us has a monopoly on serving the different needs of young people? Reinforcing stereotyped prejudices about youth clubs being suitable only for those apathetic young people who can't cope with the discipline of Scouting, is hardly a helpful or forward looking attitude.

Last week, I had the unusual privilege of presenting some Chief Scout Awards to over 40 young people (including one girl!) in Basingstoke. Talking with them, I was impressed by their commitment and the range of skills and activities they had experienced in completing their awards, and the support they had received from their adult Leaders.

The following evening, I was on a different housing estate in Basingstoke spending a night with our team of part time detached youth workers, using a double decker bus as a mobile youth club to meet and talk with a dozen local teenagers. I was equally impressed by their views and their willingness to share their experiences in using alcohol and experimenting with drugs and by their ideas on a programme of activities the bus might offer them in the future.

In Hampshire, we are trying hard to 'build bridges' between local youth workers and the local Scout Districts to break down the stereotypes and to work together in the best interests of all those young people we jointly seek to serve.

Tim Caley, County Youth Officer, Hampshire

Letter to Scouting News, 1995.

My support for the voluntary sector was not just a false or artificial political strategy adopted as part of my officer role. I seriously held the view that if partnership meant anything, we as 'the council' had to acknowledge genuinely that the Scouts and Guides, the Boys' Brigade, the Duke of Edinburgh's Award Scheme, church and faith organisations and all the others really did deliver important and high-quality youth work with a vast range of young people in the county. While always conscious of the need to protect and be an advocate for the local authority's work and for my staff, I was also proactive in reminding both councillors and the general public of this wider constituency of service providers for young people. Two examples stick in my mind from this time. Writing in response to some disparaging comments about youth clubs and their members published in *Scouting News*, I tried to take an even-handed and gentle view of our different styles, approaches and target groups and to break down the stereotypes that inevitably went with them. I often found myself asserting in public meetings that 'none of us has a monopoly on serving young people', and I believed it. My letter was published and received many warm responses, including one from the Chief Scout himself and from many local commissioners and Scout groups in Hampshire.

The other example was a Saturday-evening 'family night out' with a Boys' Brigade group in northern Hampshire; one of many regular invitations I received. Initially, I wasn't really keen to go: it felt like just another evening's duty flying the youth service flag – and a weekend evening at that. The venue was a corrugated tin hut somewhere up in the most rural and remote north-eastern part of the county: it took some finding and longer than I thought to drive there. But as the evening progressed, I was suddenly transported back to my youth club experiences in Sheffield twenty years earlier. There was a profound sense of commitment, of sharing, of common endeavour and of enjoyment amongst all those taking part. And the hut was packed out – here indeed were extended families, children of all ages, enjoying an evening of fun, activities, competitions, challenges – organised by the brigade volunteers to thank everyone for their participation in the section's work this year. I sat outside with a large group as the leaders organised the barbecue and burgers on the field and cakes and drinks were made ready in the hut. No one took much notice of me. I had planned to spend an hour and then leave. But this one simple example of youth work in practice – a celebration of young people and a chance for them to be together and enjoy the company of their peers and adults – was a rare experience which affected me powerfully and I decided to stay on longer.

Now with my academic background I was perfectly capable of using posh phrases like 'social capital', 'joint ownership' and 'shared values'. I had often addressed audiences and waxed lyrical about community spirit and the concepts of loyalty and membership. But tonight – up here in a hut in Highclere – the Boys' Brigade were delivering a superb model of it in action, and right in front of my eyes. It was after 11pm when it all finished and I stayed to the end, wanting to soak up the atmosphere to the full, helping them to sweep up afterwards. Reflecting on the experience later, I realised that being a county officer – 'numero uno', as a committee member once embarrassingly introduced me at a youth club evening – meant you rarely had the chance to spend a night in a youth centre, to get to know a staff group or a bunch of young people any more.

One enjoyable route which did let me meet individual young people was through my membership of the Prince's Trust Committee. Every month we met to consider grant applications from a vast range of teenagers who wanted to go on expeditions; produce music, plays or dance; pursue athletic and sporting dreams; undertake training or just do something weird, wonderful and different. I loved being on the committee, because the Prince's Trust was always willing to take a risk with young people who applied, and because no one else seemed prepared to help them. Each of us had a 'caseload' we went to visit and interview each month, and we would then write up a report with a recommendation for financial help. One month, I'd be watching a majorette group marching and twirling their batons in sparkly, sequinned costumes; the next I would be interviewing a *James Bond* film fan, dressed for my visit in a dinner jacket and bow tie, seeking a grant to produce a personal homage to the genre on DVD. Another time it was a young gymnast, needing help with travel costs to her early-morning coaching sessions. I met some amazing youngsters, including a talented artist who sold me one of his vibrant oil paintings of Rowlands Castle, which I still possess.

But this agreeable role was only a temporary oasis amidst the more pressing bureaucratic demands of the day job. I'd managed in my lesser officer roles to keep a fragile toehold on practice by forming links with one or two clubs or key workers: youth exchanges in Reading or detached work in Portsmouth, for example. But now, the price it seemed I had to pay for the top job was accepting that this was no longer possible. So yes, I was a real supporter of voluntary youth organisations.

County Youth Officer, Tim Caley, with Councillors Woodhall, Street and members of "Breakout", Southampton, on a Gliding Day at Lasham Gliding Club, April 1995

Photo: Southampton Echo, April 1995.

PUBLICITY AND PRACTICE

In 1993, a reporter from the *Times Educational Supplement* visited us to write an article about local authority youth services. This he entitled, tellingly, *The Youth Disservice*, and his subtext spoke of the logic of investing in the service at a time of high unemployment and rising juvenile crime – and the fact that politicians didn't see it that way. In the article, my comments that youth services were often easily defined by what they weren't – *not* the soft end of policing, *not* like social workers and police officers – were accurately recorded. Having to define and justify youth work as being opposed to other forms of social intervention has been a continuing theme in my experience. The article linked youth provision to crime reduction and reflected many of the then-national issues about budget cuts, lack of government interest in the service and the vital nature of local support from the Director of Education.

Times Educational Supplement, May 1993.

The other critical point the article made, at my request, was that youth work was a very 'brittle' entity as it could not demonstrate the academic credibility or intellectual rigour of some other professions. Not to mention its public standing and perception. Youth workers, in other words, often possessed a limited arsenal of tools in their work with young people – energy, enthusiasm, empathy, certainly, and credibility with the clients – but not much in the way of public support or resources to do the job. In my view, the impact of this article's publication was positive and heartening. It raised the profile of all local authority youth services and the pressures they were under nationally, and reflected correctly the concerns of my fellow heads of youth services. It certainly raised my credibility and standing locally: colleagues from other parts of the Education Department who wouldn't normally acknowledge my existence suddenly accosted me in the corridors of The Castle and congratulated me on my new-found fame.

As in my previous experiences, spelling out what makes good youth work practice was best served by highlighting and writing up my visits to the best examples I could find. Amidst all this activity and deliberation, I was conscious of the fact that it was my own personal struggle to arrive at an acceptable definition of youth work and its benefits that seemed at stake. The task was to trace a coherent line in the evolution of my youth work philosophy from practitioner to local officer and now to head of service. There were certainly some common threads in defining good practice. Here is one from Southampton, at a project called Beyond Graffiti, which used the special skills of two detached youth workers to create a shining example of good work. I encouraged the project team to publish a report and stamped it with my approval in the foreword.

Beyond Graffiti, Southampton. Project report foreword, 1992.

The same year, in our annual Hampshire Youth Service report, I made another stab at defining youth work practice, writing:

> ...readers will find little reference to 'ping-pong, darts and discos' in these pages, or to other outdated stereotypes of youth club practice. Rather, the evidence here demonstrates a service working closely with the voluntary sector and with colleagues in other agencies, Health authorities, Probation and Social Services, with schools and with District and Town Councils to respond pro-actively to the issues currently facing adolescent young people in Hampshire.

Later, I honed this to the two key characteristics that made the youth service worthy of support. One was about partnerships and their cost-effectiveness, but the other was what I called the very distinctive, perhaps unique, role of youth work:

> *Youth workers are not teachers, parents, police officers or social workers. Their role as adults has no statutory authority or official power. Youth workers operate on young people's terms: the nature of the relationship is entirely voluntary. The best practice includes that ability to engage with many young people – especially those most marginalised or alienated or at risk – to gain their confidence and work alongside them. It is that unique approach that can give a skilled youth worker tremendous strength in developing relationships with young people, which other professionals may not be able to adopt.*

The target audience for this definition was not simply youth work staff, but the officers and elected members who funded the service – coming, as it was, under increasing scrutiny on effectiveness and value for money. I felt the need to focus on a role targeted at those young people at risk or on the margins. And I couldn't help but spell out the political risks of one of youth work's unique characteristics, reminding readers that the paradox or dilemma is that it is that same lack of official status or power that also makes youth services vulnerable in times of political or financial constraint.

THE SEARCH FOR THE HOLY GRAIL: THE 'CORE CURRICULUM' CONFERENCES

The challenges and experiences I was facing in Hampshire were being mirrored across the country, particularly the development of a 'core curriculum'. The government seemed keen to ensure that every local authority youth service had one. The use of the word 'curriculum' was probably a mistake: it was a term that sat uncomfortably with most youth workers, with its overtones of the school classroom and examinations. Not that this was a problem from my perspective – establishing a new county service had engaged us all in thinking hard about policy, programmes and practice. Nevertheless, the national debate about curriculum took over much of my time in the early and mid 1990s. There was much general pessimism, uncertainty and confusion in the field. It seemed that the youth service was beginning to lose its way: battered and bruised by many of the perceived bigger players in the field of youth, it became less sure of its purpose.

The Conservative administration of John Major had displayed no evident interest in the youth service during its whole five years of office. With the falling numbers of teenagers, with the curriculum debates, with the regular 'revolving door' changes in government ministers responsible for youth work and with continuing funding cuts, it was hard to sustain morale at times. A general sense of malaise was on the increase. Notably absent, too, was a sense of leadership or calming of nerves from the National Youth Agency; no sense of a steadying hand on the good ship *Youth Service* as she sailed through these turbulent waters. There was far too much complaining and navel-gazing and not nearly enough getting on with the job. The Community and Youth Work Union continued its predictable and unending mantra demanding an end to budget cuts. Local councillors in some London boroughs repeated their simplistic arguments that those cuts led to riots in the streets.

Analysing the major themes of the youth work press, primarily *Young People Now*, during the early 1990s reinforces that lack of a clear sense of youth service function and purpose. The pages are an odd mixture of local news and politics, Youth Work Week, international exchanges, competitions to win trips to the theatre or to the US, skiing and mountain-biking articles, profiles of TV soap actors, tattooing, the occult, youth work in America and China – in fact, a range of topics that left most practitioners exhausted and perplexed as to how this was helping them respond to real local issues or deliver services at the grass roots.

So the core curriculum bandwagon rolled ever onwards. It is hard to erase the vivid memories of these dire curriculum conference events. Every few months we met to discuss the latest developments or share our new draft documents. Consider the timeline of national interest in youth services. The Albemarle, Fairbairn-Milson and Thompson Reports all came pretty quickly upon each other – within a twenty-year timescale. Since Sir Keith Joseph and Margaret Thatcher had ignored Thompson in 1982, there had been a drought, a vacuum of government engagement with the service for almost fifteen years: a long time. That interregnum had consequences for the latest initiative about developing a core curriculum.

There remained some suspicion about the motivation of ministers in respect of the whole curriculum agenda. Our concerns were that the initiative was more about focusing and controlling youth work priorities than developing programmes for young people. It was not assuaged by the then-minister, Alan Howarth, declaring in 1991 that there was 'no central government plot to dictate a curriculum and stifle the expression of dissent'. Nor by his successor, Nigel Foreman, referring to youth workers as the 'unsung heroes of our time'. It felt more like a sound bite written by one of his sympathetic officials than any real reflection of government policy.[34] Much of this anxiety seemed to come to a head at the second Ministerial Conference held in Birmingham.

Crammed together in the hotel's vast auditorium, we all watched a larger-than-life video of the minister intoning his advice to us from the big screen. He was too busy to attend in person, so had produced this technological substitute. It was something of a surreal experience, and it became obvious that a groundswell of grumbling and dissent was forming and growing louder in the audience. The frustrations of many years were coming to a head. The perceived snub of the minister in failing to attend was reinforcing the suspicions of many about the whole curriculum agenda. At this point the natural 'disputatious' nature of youth workers took hold of the audience and the conference. Egged on by the peer pressure and the inherent 'passion and panic' that sometimes affect a large group of youth service personnel when meeting en masse, a tone of rebellion and resistance was set.[35]

In one sense, this partly explains the hugely unrealistic and overambitious nature of the statement of purpose which was finally hammered out by delegates at the event. With its preamble confirming the service's function as 'redressing all forms of inequality,' it led inevitably to the minister almost immediately repudiating it publicly and ensuring that mutual prejudices and suspicions were reconfirmed all round. Maybe it was just that these Ministerial Conferences had been badly managed and delegates ill prepared. Certainly by the third and last conference, held in a Gothic, mock-crenellated hotel on the seafront in Blackpool in 1992, things were equally uninspiring, at least from my perspective.

But there is no argument about my own highlight of that particular event. Getting on the tram outside our hotel, I travelled all the way to the terminus at Fleetwood, having bagged the front seat upstairs in order to get a driver's-eye view of the line. It was partly nostalgia – I went to secondary school on a tram right up until 1960 when Sheffield finally relinquished its trams, and the chance to recreate the experience was too good to miss. After a long day in the conference hall, searching for the Holy Grail of an agreed curriculum, it was a wonderful relief to rattle and sway back down the promenade on one of Blackpool's finest double-deckers. But on the return journey I did make a mental note to consider how we would start redressing all forms of inequality – just as soon as I got back to my office in Winchester.

BACK AT THE RANCH: PRESSING CONCERNS

After three Ministerial Conferences, the service was no further forward than when it had started the curricular journey. Most authorities were happy to support the statement of purpose, but we all knew that the minister was unhappy about it. It was clear that the government wasn't really interested in youth work and was never likely to interfere or intervene. This allowed for local diversity (or postcode lottery) to widen. On the national scene, Tony Jeffs and Mark Smith bluntly summed up the position as they saw it in 1993: 'central government has no desire to impose a national curriculum on the various warring factions that comprise the Yugoslavia that once was the youth service.'[36]

There was a perceptible shift to a harder edge in government policy on the purposes and functions of youth work. Arguing for universal provision or open-access youth centres or an entitlement for all young people was beginning to sound old-fashioned and idealistic. Now the emphasis had moved to focusing on the problems, on troublemakers, on offenders, on hotspots and on crime prevention. As my new boss, the deputy education officer, instructed me, 'Tim – you're in charge of all the "bad boys" in Hampshire now.' There was nothing inherently wrong with this purpose as one product of good practice. But it was apparent by the mid 1990s that this was to be a *primary* aim of youth work, as far as the government was concerned. 'Curriculum' was simply a handy term, a helpful nudge for the policymakers to move youth services along the targeted and interventionist route to deal with social nuisance.

At a local level, like other colleagues, I had other pressing and urgent issues to deal with as well as core curriculum statements. That list included the continued threat of budget reductions, the impact of local management of schools, the pressure for workers to focus on targeted groups of young people to meet the social exclusion and antisocial behaviour agendas, the growth of commissioning and outsourcing of services to other agencies and voluntary youth groups, the challenge of external funding replacing core council budgets, of analysing and providing reams of bureaucratic details and returns – participation rates and value-for-money calculations of youth contact hours – and many more.

One policy change created particular stress for us in Hampshire: the impact of local government reorganisation. This process, driven by both national policy and local ambition, seemed to drag on for years – causing major planning blight in the process. The two major cities – Southampton and Portsmouth – had always wanted to achieve their political independence from the county council and this seemed their chance to break free of the 'dead hand' of Winchester, as they put it. The 'downsizing' implications of losing the cities forced the county council to reconfigure and restructure its staffing and responsibilities. The youth service was not able to escape these dilemmas; even for county staff based in the urban areas, transferring to their new councils was an uncertain business and a worrying time, especially for part-timers. I took many phone calls from staff in tears or choked with frustration and anger as a result of local government reorganisation and its impact on their jobs. The real difficulty was with those colleagues whose roles included county-wide responsibilities, for example for the Duke of Edinburgh's Award, for outdoor education and for youth service training programmes. How would we reconfigure their jobs – indeed, could we still afford to employ them all? Hours of meetings and acres of paperwork were spent tackling these problems, most of which required the advice of the personnel department on redeployments, reorganisation and redundancies. Not to mention resolving the ownership of youth club buildings, offices, vehicles and equipment – all of which had to be equitably divided up. It was not a happy couple of years, but there was the occasional light-hearted moment. Meeting my personnel officer one afternoon, I found her deep in perplexed conversation with someone from the legal department.

'Having problems?' I enquired.

'Yes,' she said; 'we can't work out who owns the cattle and sheep at Sparsholt College of Agriculture and how many should be transferred to the cities.'

Ceremonial duties at West End Youth Centre, 1996.
Photo: Hampshire Chronicle.

YOUTH WORK CUTS CRIME

In 1994, the government commissioned a report by consultants Coopers & Lybrand to look at value for money and youth service performance indicators. One of the report's findings was that the average cost of a youth crime was £2,800 – and moreover, if a youth work project prevents just one single crime, the immediate saving is £2,300.[37] This was one of the best bits of news I'd had for ages. At once, we moved to use these figures as a useful bargaining chip in supporting good youth work as a valuable means to deter and prevent youth crime. Repeatedly, I reminded councillors that £2,800 would buy them a part-time youth club for two nights per week for a year in their ward. The link between the delivery of youth work and crime reduction was difficult to prove, but there were plenty of local police commanders and district councils who were willing to support my argument. I acknowledge that this was inevitably echoing that 'keeping them off the streets' rationale, but – once again – the assessment tools and the reliability of the evidence we had at our disposal in this arena were limited. This was as good a case as we had and, as head of service, I decided we should use it relentlessly. So in all our annual reports, our Youth Work Week publicity, my committee reports to the grants panel, press releases, letters to the *Hampshire Chronicle* – everywhere that might make an impact and leave an impression – we hammered home the same message. And I was partly reassured by Bernard Davies' later reminder that 'for all its highfalutin aspirations, dealing with the idea that youth work is actually about soft policing is something that just goes with the territory.'[38]

The policy risk to the service of the 'youth work cuts crime' agenda was twofold. First, it was always difficult to provide hard evidence of causality; and second, the increasing dangers of associating the main function of the service with controlling antisocial and criminal behaviour by the young. The risk was especially high for open-access club-based work which, inevitably, began to assume a lower priority in both funding and delivery. Chasing external funding and developing new partnerships reinforced these risks. The irony was that the very particular skill it was agreed youth workers seemed to possess – getting alongside difficult and recalcitrant teenagers – was most in demand by all these other agencies. Courted by the police, youth offending teams, school PSHE teachers, sexual health and teenage pregnancy workers, parish, town and district councils – all keen to solicit my help and that of all my youth workers in sorting out troublesome youth in their patches – what was I to do?

I took a pragmatic line balancing risks and benefits – protecting the youth budget, limiting the dangers to 'core business' and continuing to sustain quality and morale within the workforce. We encouraged local youth officers to work with all their partners in setting up holiday schemes, after-school clubs, crime diversion projects, extending detached work teams to housing estates, parks

Hampshire Youth Conference, 1997. Photo: Tim Caley.

and shopping areas – anything that showed we were taking a proactive line in reducing 'crime and the causes of crime', as the new Leader of the Opposition, Tony Blair, was beginning to call his policy initiative in this arena.

A CHANGE IN DIRECTION

The professional burden of all this was now taking a serious personal toll. I'd been handling the 'Northern Ireland portfolio' for more than eight years. The initial energy and enthusiasm that had gone into setting up a new county service had inevitably dissipated and weakened. Maintenance and repairs are never as exciting as creation and new developments. Working three or four nights a week visiting clubs or attending meetings, the ceremonial duties at the weekend Scouts Jamboree or Guides Festival, writing the grants committee reports on the dining-room table on Sunday evenings – it was all becoming exhausting to maintain. And Hampshire is a large county – living in one corner and driving round it every day put a lot of mileage on me as well as my car. I had two young sons at home now as well: they saw me at teatime and (sometimes) bedtime, but not much more, it seemed. It was around this time that my hair rapidly accelerated its colour change from mainly black to mainly grey.

Since my appointment, when I had inherited a demoralised patchwork of youth provision as a low-priority adjunct within thirteen institutes of adult education, things had certainly improved. At the start, the youth budget was £2 million and there were thirty-five staff. Now, some eight years later, there was a £4 million budget and sixty-seven staff. There was also much more confidence and credibility for youth work from both officers and elected members. We had put in place planning and evaluation systems using Ofsted criteria and we had effective budget controls. High-quality publications describing effective youth work practice were produced regularly. The health of the organisation and standards of work seemed immeasurably higher than when I began the job.

That last paragraph reads rather like a job application – it wasn't quite as simple a decision as 'time for a change'. Certainly, my experiences as an Ofsted additional inspector (see later) had made me contemplate future career directions, as had my various exposures to regional initiatives and work with other youth services in the south-east region. Of course, there was always the perpetual draining nature of the many downsides of the job. The annual fight to protect the youth service budget got harder and harder, the production of committee papers and the management of demanding councillors was constant, the lobbying for grants from district councils and voluntary groups was relentless, and managing and 'refereeing' my four divisional youth officers was cumulatively draining. I had always felt it important to sustain high professional standards in all my work and I was finding this harder and harder to achieve.

But sometimes, it is the little things that trigger action. At my annual appraisal meeting that summer, my manager had referred to me as 'approaching the twilight of my career'. It was probably meant as a harmless, throwaway remark but I rather took umbrage at his premature judgement. But he made me realise that I'd gone as far as I could go in the job: it was time to move on. The director showed me the reference he'd written for me. It's probably the nearest thing to reading your own obituary you're likely to experience. 'The County Council would miss him greatly,' it said. 'I don't want to lose him but he deserves the best possible commendation.' My team leader in Aldershot took a slightly different line. I'd only just circulated the news of my departure to staff when her email reply ricocheted back into my inbox. 'Congratulations on your escape,' it read; 'do you need an assistant?'

Part 3

SUPPORTING GOOD YOUTH WORK

CHAPTER 6

OFSTED: AN INSPECTOR CALLS

It was in 1987 that HMI (Her Majesty's Inspectors) published a report called *Effective Youth Work*. It was one of the first examples of externally observed youth work that sought to isolate and identify the elements of good practice. I was much taken by this little booklet – it seemed to highlight many of the things I was trying to capture in my own attempts to evaluate practice and measure quality in youth service provision. It was full of really good examples of youth work, written up simply but concisely, which provided ideas and signposts for ordinary practitioners. It also noted some important themes. For example, the importance of planning the youth work process (not in a way that denied spontaneity and intuition, but that reflected the complexity and purpose of the interventions), that young people should be active and willing partners in the process, and finally that the workers were aware of their own roles and responsibilities.

It didn't pull any punches in describing the characteristics of less effective youth work either. It noted that, depressingly, workers often worked in relative isolation and had insufficient access to adequate professional supervision. Yet, with inadequate resources, little support and no recognition for what they did, some excellent youth work staff nevertheless seemed to produce outstanding outcomes and successes for the young people they worked with. This was something that I was beginning to see in many places in my youth officer roles: that good youth work often flourished *despite* the management or structure of a service, rather than *because* of it. *Effective Youth Work* ended by saying that, for those responsible for managing the youth and community service, the identification of good practice is of crucial significance. And that the task of explaining youth work to lay people may often be accomplished better by use of examples than by enunciation of broad aims in abstract terms. This was indeed an early confirmation of my own embryonic philosophy as a manager and officer.

When, in 1996, the newly established Ofsted (Office for Standards in Education) sought out candidates from the ranks of heads of youth services to become 'additional inspectors', I was more than willing to put my name forward. The need for experienced, serving youth officers to join the inspectorate was due to the increased cycle of inspections being undertaken in schools, adult education and youth services (and later in Connexions partnerships) from the mid 1990s. It was also aimed at enlivening

Ofsted identity badge, 2000.

and energising the process for the more experienced HMIs in a way that brought new ideas and a more down-to-earth management and operational viewpoint to bear on the process.

As an organisation, Ofsted had a poor reputation at that time, especially among schoolteachers, for whom inspection had become a byword for stress, 'box-ticking' bureaucracy and general intrusion by outsiders who had little experience of the realities of the classroom. The youth service inspections, although equally rigorous, were never seen in such a threatening and negative light. In my view, the involvement of additional inspectors from the field, bringing with them contemporary experience of grassroots and management issues, helped to improve this more positive perception. But then, if people at parties ever asked you what you did for a living, you probably wouldn't tell them you were an Ofsted inspector. (Then again, you might also hesitate to tell them you were a youth worker, knowing that this would involve a glazed response and the need for further elucidation.)

To do justice to Ofsted's intervention in the quality and practice of youth work merits a book in itself rather than a mention in passing – the additional inspector programme alone was a significant improvement initiative. Certainly, the interviews and training programmes were focused and demanding. My abiding memory was being repeatedly told that we must always make judgements only on the basis of observed evidence of practice. Simple advice, but very hard to do, especially on that archetypal freezing Monday night in the youth club. Also that we needed to have some quality indicators in order to 'benchmark' the practice we were seeing; otherwise how could we decide what was excellent, good, average or poor? Our judgements, too, always needed to focus on young people and the outcomes they were receiving at the hands of the youth workers. And finally, that it was easy to be critical or negative: we must also always properly celebrate and grade highly examples of good and excellent work.

Some of this was not entirely new: I had already produced a set of inspection visit protocols for Hampshire and tested them out in some 'practice' inspections in the county.

Sometimes the realities of fieldwork experience in the county clashed with my new-found fervour for inspection and quality. A warm summer's night in 1996 found me, on one of my practice inspections at a youth club in Basingstoke, desperate to impart to my harassed-looking part-time colleague the importance of identifying good and bad work. As the evening session hummed with the sounds of teenagers relaxing, chatting and sometimes shouting, I expounded at length while we sat on the grass, half-watching the young people around us. I came to an end and he looked at me quizzically for a moment, paused and asked, 'Do you know if our new five-a-side goalposts have come yet?' I also experienced the importance of clarifying the ground rules if you're going to 'inspect' something. It is a word that strikes fear and anxiety in the hearts of some staff – unless everyone knows what to expect (and what's going to happen afterwards), the process will be flawed.

Inspection was not completely new to me. I had already acted as an external consultant in roles involving the inspection of youth work practice: as a team member for the evaluation of the Isle of Wight detached youth work project, and with regional colleagues inspecting aspects of youth work in Jersey, Channel Islands. So I was not without some 'inspection' expertise before beginning my stint with Ofsted, but my part-time role began in 1997 and continued for another eleven years – I was a team member in fourteen local authority youth service inspections over this period. It was a thoroughly enjoyable, exhausting, demanding and professionally rewarding period.

As usual in my work, I had a baptism of fire. In March 1997, I undertook my first role as an additional inspector in the Midlands. It was a difficult week involving critical judgements on the service's performance. At that time, additional inspectors were also responsible for drafting whole chapters of the inspection report, which made a tremendous extra demand on my judgement-making and writing skills. Unusually, I was also asked to accompany the lead inspectors in the feedback session to the authority after the inspection had finished. I knew that elected members, officers and young people had been prompted, indeed coached, to use the opportunity to try to challenge and dilute HMI's verdicts. It was a hot and uncomfortable session for all concerned. The feedback meeting needed a cool head as well as resilience in supporting HMI and adhering to those verdicts. The audience – pumped up and irritated – found them unpalatable and wanted them changed; it was quite an early challenge for a rookie recruit on his first outing. The inspection had certainly taken me out of my comfort zone and had made new demands on my ability to bring a 'youth officer' role to the regular inspection team.

ADDITIONAL INSPECTING: A BREATHLESS EXPERIENCE

The experience of being an additional inspector, at least in the early days, was often a breathless one. With minimal preparation, you were parachuted into an authority on a Monday afternoon to start work. You drove to the team hotel (having picked up your hire car) and booked yourself in. You were then given your programme of ten or eleven youth club or project visits, which started in about an hour's time. In the days before satnavs, you used road maps and hastily drawn location notes to find your venues, often needing a torch. Getting lost in the dark in a rural county while looking for the part-time youth club behind the village hall was always an interesting challenge. Having completed your two visits for the night, you would return to the hotel, grab something to eat (if you were lucky – it was 10pm by now) and then write up your EFs (evidence forms). You made sure your grades followed the Ofsted grade descriptors, you checked that your judgements were fair and based on the evidence of what you'd seen, and you tried hard to write coherent sentences and paragraphs. Being fair and impartial in recording the good, bad and ugly sometimes took longer than you hoped. It was often midnight or beyond before you finished. Next morning, at the breakfast meeting with the lead inspector you shared notes, handed in your EFs, moderated the team's verdicts and planned to start all over again. It was a breathtaking, relentless and ruthless pace of operation for four days and four nights.

You soon learnt that there was an Ofsted 'approved' language that you needed to learn and to follow. Judgements had to be 'secure', evidence needed to be 'robust' and weaknesses had to be described as 'areas for development'. In fact, our additional inspector's handbook provided a whole raft of guidance and definitions to help us write our reports. There was even a crib sheet of useful verbs and adjectives that might be used to illustrate youth work achievement, practice or management. This was not as prescriptive as you might imagine, because (as we soon discovered) there are only so many ways you can describe a project as being adequate or satisfactory. In any case, these are not epithets conducive to lifting a youth worker's heart and making their spirits sing. But the process occasionally felt like a straitjacket that hampered our ability to paint the full picture – in either all its technicolour glory or its grimy, grey awfulness. Sometimes, you longed to launch into a paean of joy and rejoicing when you'd witnessed some brilliant practice; conversely, there were moments you'd have loved to lambast some lethargic staff, bereft of imagination, commitment or energy, just going through the motions of working with young people. Neither option was permitted, of course: on inspection duty, your job was to keep your emotions and feelings under control.

Some ten years before, Neil Ritchie, in an analysis of various inspection reports written under the pre-Ofsted regime in the 1980s, had commented on the inconsistency, contradictions, blandness, oversimplification, unhelpful suggestions and avoidance of controversial issues within them.[39] He was pretty scornful too of the notion of 'balance' – much beloved by HMI – concluding that inspectors were no more competent at assessing youth work than any other team of informed or experienced workers would be. Further, he argued that 'the notion of a neutral, independent and apolitical observer of youth work is misguided, because judgments or decisions about practice and policy are ultimately informed by values.' Ritchie also found that much youth work 'is not very exciting, done by people who are entirely well-meaning but who are in need of a much tighter set of guidelines and controls in order to give of their best.' Inspectors were often disappointed by the dismal, tatty environments in which youth work takes place. Given the lack of policies, aims and objectives and criteria for evaluation, it comes as no particular surprise that youth club programmes everywhere were often characterised by 'ad hoc recreational activity'.

My experience as an additional inspector echoed some of Ritchie's analysis both of inconsistencies and of the variation in the strengths and weaknesses of what we were seeing. Certainly there was also some unpredictability in the style and attention to detail of lead HMIs. On one occasion, finding ourselves in a London authority, our lead inspector informed us we needed to complete a 'quick and dirty' job. Most prepared and coached their team members dutifully and in detail: challenging grades, offering feedback and involving themselves in the minutiae of the inspection process. Some were much less 'hands-on', encouraging us to complete the job as efficiently and promptly as possible. Most simply left us to get on with the work and deliver them the numbers.

There was a marvellous camaraderie that developed amongst us additional inspector 'foot soldiers' during the week. Often, bleary-eyed from lack of sleep and slaving over our hot laptops honing our approved Ofsted phrases, we sought comfort and solace in each other's opinions. My first inspection was in a pre-digital age: evidence forms were on paper and had to be completed in triplicate using carbon paper. You had to press really hard with your pen to make sure the bottom copy was legible. Sometimes, it only took a day or so to come to a consensus about the quality of a youth service and its staff. In a few cases, the introductory meeting with the principal youth officer was sufficient. But in others, where there was a mixture of good and bad, or conflicting assessments, or just no overall clarity on programmes and staffing, it was more difficult to come to a secure verdict and we needed time for debate amongst ourselves. It was always encouraging when your emerging viewpoint and your grades were confirmed and cemented by your peers on the team.

Once in a while, you might be discreetly lobbied by officers of the authority where you were inspecting. I understand the technical term is being 'nobbled'. It didn't happen very often because we additional inspectors were fairly low down the food chain in the assessment process. But one icy-cold winter's night, after a session at a school youth wing in the Midlands, I was looking forward to a warm drink back at the hotel when I was accosted by a man in the murky light of the car park. 'Had a good evening?' he enquired. Alerted and a little disconcerted, I agreed it had been a useful visit. Without further ado or introduction, he launched into an attack on his managers, the organisation of the school and the lack of notice and unfairness of the inspection as a whole. I gathered he was an unhappy member of staff. Further, he demanded that his comments be reflected in full in our Ofsted report. Moving swiftly into my official conciliatory and non-committal mode, I muttered some anodyne responses and made my escape. But I reported him to the lead inspector at breakfast time the next morning.

The process whereby our grades and evidence became official inspection verdicts was something of a 'secret garden'. In some cases, it seemed a mathematical formula was used to translate scores into overall judgements. At other times, team meetings debated these issues for hours, particularly in the early inspections. These processes were linked to the changing role of HMI in youth inspections, the ever-evolving frameworks of inspection and the gradual erosion of engagement that was primarily driven by budget reductions and a lower priority for youth services. Originally, youth inspections might visit seventy or eighty sites and our workload as additional inspectors was correspondingly high. Gradually, as the size of inspection teams was reduced the scale of visits dropped to around twenty or thirty clubs and projects. When inspections became an adjunct to the delivery of children's services, the focus on youth work was even more diluted. Then the inspection experience became for me and other colleagues much more mechanistic and ritual – and a much less enjoyable experience.

Even on inspection duty, capturing the themes and isolating the characteristics of really good youth work is not always easy. There is neither an agreed formula nor a handy guidebook. Good performance depends on a number of variables – human and otherwise. There were certainly some Ofsted grade descriptors which helped to define the characteristics of good and bad work. Many such qualities are unsurprising and easy to recognise: when young people show a powerful loyalty and a sense of ownership to their club or their project, it's likely to be good. When they display friendliness, courtesy and good humour as well, it's probably good too. When a service culture reflects sound leadership, when clear direction and effective training are allied to energetic, enthusiastic youth work staff, things are likely to be even better. When youth workers have high levels of expectation and standards for their work and show an energy, empathy and enthusiasm in their relationships with young people, it's a good sign. When the energy levels seem to be buzzing, when confidence and excitement are commonplace, when young people seem to be in charge, that's good too. When youth workers just seem simply to like teenagers and enjoy being with them, that's an uncomplicated, positive culture in which good work flourishes.

VIGNETTES OF GOOD PRACTICE

It's a warm early-spring evening when I drop into a club in commuter territory in West Berkshire. The place clearly provides an oasis of activity, support and challenge for young people. A group of young women are rehearsing and choreographing a dance routine for a tsunami appeal event to be held at the local college. They show concentration and focus in learning the dance and supporting each other – the more skilled helping the less adept. Staff allow the young people to take the lead, only helping when necessary to bolster morale. Their sensitivity and support are appreciated by the members.

I have a word with one of the part-timers at the end. Without any prompting from me, she provides a remarkably mature definition of her role in the centre: 'The club provides a safe environment for young people,' she tells me firmly; 'it challenges them, it provides adult role models for them, it allows them to share confidential and personal information, it offers them new skills and it gives them time and people who are just "around" for them.'

On the same patch, on a bitterly cold night, I come across a mobile youth trailer session. Only five boys have turned up, but the staff work hard to involve them in the programme. They are apparently using mini Go-Ped machines, whose legality on the streets is uncertain. As a result the team is arranging some scooter training using an off-road site and helping sort out the legal issues. The full-timer is a trainee and has only been in post five months. She tells me she 'love[s] every minute of youth work'.

In the West Country now, I walk past the corner takeaway, open early tonight, and spot groups of teenagers congregating outside the club. They shout a friendly 'hello' as I arrive: a good omen. The club has an airy, spacious environment with a warm, welcoming feeling to the visitor. This early-evening session was planned to tackle behaviour issues and to agree membership fees. Members had worked out that you could put 1p in the snooker table and get games (almost) for free, so staff needed to decide on a response.

A small group convenes and a notice is prepared giving members three options on charges. One young woman writes this up, insisting they have to sign their names against their choices (no hiding place here). The work is diverted as a member of staff unwraps the centre's new 'bionic baby'. This has just arrived and is to be part of their programme on sexual health and baby-minding. This takes away the attention of some young people and makes it harder to keep them on task. Members are going to Lundy Island for a fishing trip soon and new tents have been purchased. Tonight is a chance to practise erecting and dismantling them in the outside play area. The members participate with gusto in setting up the tents and trying them out (much hilarity ensues). Both boys and girls take part and staff encourage and cajole them well – including engaging one deaf young man. There are some difficult individuals in membership, with a number currently subject to ASBOs.

Here the snooker table, table tennis and music system are all routinely used as 'vehicles' for youth work – to establish relationships, to pursue issues, to enquire about school, home and holiday plans, or to chat with members. The building gives a sense of being very young-people-friendly, fit for purpose and with a comfortable, lived-in atmosphere and many colourful posters, displays and protocols of behaviour written by young people. It is clearly 'owned' by its membership and this culture has not happened by accident. It is down to the good youth work skills of the staff team.

It's a summer's evening in Staffordshire and I'm strolling towards a centre located in an attractive rural setting close to a park. I can see knots of teenagers playing in the park and suddenly have that worrying feeling that the youth club might well be empty tonight. And if it is, what am I going to say to the staff team, doubtless even now awaiting my arrival with some trepidation?

I walk in and see the club is completely deserted. The staff are standing around, manning the empty coffee bar, patrolling the vacant hall and generally looking sheepish. I try to be positive and supportive: asking whether they have a Plan B for warm weather, and might they consider closing the centre and going out 'detached' to work with their members in the park and on the estate tonight? They are relieved at my response, but also annoyed that they did not take the initiative themselves, before my arrival.

Next, I'm listening to a group of Year 9 and 10 school pupils talking about their youth club and its staff. (They're all from Bristol, so adopting a strong West Country accent is helpful.)

> *They don't treat us like we are ten. Ju and Si are just normal and they actually helps us with stuff that we will never do in school! It is class. [Not literally a class.] (Bev, 14)*
>
> *I loves this group and I recone [sic] that everyone here is just great and if we had to separate I would die/cry; the group leaders are amazing and I just loves them to bits — well not really but they are great. (Charlotte, 14)*
>
> *The youth workers have helped us so much. We can't thank them enough. The group itself is a real help, working with*

personal and life skills. It's great – to put it in one word. Julie, Simon, Nick and Amy are 5 by 5. We love them. (Lindsey, 14)

Well, I have had a great time manz its crazy in this club, Ju and Si is quality they helps us become more independent. I loves it. Normsky, pure livo, mental, snazzie, sherazzy, dandy! (Roxie, 16)

Their language snaps and crackles like a shorting electrical circuit; their laughter is infectious, their energy refreshing. They describe the way their youth workers support them with accuracy and eloquence. They are 'one of the gang', 'like, on our level', 'give us respect and we give them back', 'got patience with us', 'understand us better', 'more relaxed atmosphere – give you more time', 'treat you like adults', and 'explain things in a different way'.

I'm in Enfield, North London, tonight, watching sixteen young people take part in a rehearsal for their Christmas *Stars in Their Eyes* show, due to be performed next week. The group have various special needs and disabilities, some explicit, some not. Volunteer helpers, parents and friends arrive during the session, bringing consent forms and ensuring their children are settled – each is greeted warmly and by name. The team, under skilled leadership, shows great care in responding to the different needs of the members – some passive, some disruptive, some anxious, tearful or in need of reassurance. They clearly know these young people well and engage appropriately, offering advice, help, comfort and guidance when needed. At least two staff use basic sign language to communicate more effectively with the hard-of-hearing members.

The rehearsal demonstrates great commitment, energy and achievement for the youngsters: each completes their 'turn', cheered on by the audience who focus hard on every individual performance. Staff encourage them to join in when needed.

There is a sense of fun and enjoyment throughout the session, and of achievement and outcomes for those performing. Led by Jo's example, the youth workers keep a watchful eye on things, calming down carefully, cajoling participation when required – each one aware of their cumulative, collaborative efforts.

I've always found it hard not to be engaged and absorbed by clubs that support young people with disabilities or special needs. To me, they always seem to be *special* clubs. They manage to combine strong professional experience with family and volunteer involvement that enhances and multiplies the benefits for the young people taking part. A wonderful night and a privilege to watch such high-quality work.

POSITIVE FEEDBACK

Another great joy was providing positive feedback to staff at the end of an inspection session, telling them what a good job they were doing and how their interventions with young people demonstrated high levels of skill and expertise. This was such a simple task to perform – yet evidently it seemed to be a rare and extraordinary experience for many of those receiving my encouraging comments. More than once, I had workers in tears – because it was the first time anyone had ever recognised and praised their work and acknowledged their ability.

And the converse is unsurprising as well, naturally. When not many are attending, when the staff are propping up the coffee bar or don't know their members' names, when they are simply in policing roles, with little or no intervention with young people, that's bad news. Or even when what's going on is likely to end up being assigned that dreaded Ofsted verdict – low-level recreational activity. Or when a service confuses leadership with management: I met dozens of youth service managers in my 150 inspection visits, but I could count on the fingers of one hand those who could demonstrate clear leadership and how it supports good youth work. I met some youth officers who failed even to grasp the concept of being responsible for measuring the quality of the youth work they managed. There were plenty more who were remote from the grassroots, knew little of the issues facing their staff and remained complacent about addressing that gap.

Sadly, the overall quality of practice observed on most inspections rarely reached the highest, 'excellent' standards. Indeed, my vignette examples are the exceptions, not the rule. More often inspection teams saw a raft of what we had to classify as average or adequate or satisfactory youth work – all pretty unhelpful terms as their definition and impact varied depending on who received them. Much of this practice was often bereft of ideas, enthusiasm, planning, programme content, challenge, excitement, enjoyment or achievement – for staff or young people. But there were also regrettably far too many examples of poor practice. What were the characteristics of such work? Ofsted never used the phrase 'bad' youth work, but the descriptors were not difficult to determine. In fact, a number of published reports, mainly in the earlier phase of inspections, deployed some pretty stark and severe language. Even a preliminary trawl of some of my own team experiences reveals some explicit examples, where the key ingredients of unsatisfactory work were spelt out in language that left little to the imagination:

> *It was difficult to discern any achievement by young people as a result of their contact with youth workers. Many of the sessions were of a social, recreational nature and lacked educational focus.*
>
> *Unsatisfactory or poor work was often found where staff were acting solely in a policing role or containing role. Sometimes there was a 'take it or leave it' attitude. Names of members were not known and much of the work was unplanned and unstructured.*

In some cases, staff were not always clear about what differentiated youth work from childminding or policing.

Staff have low levels of expectation, both of their own performance and of the young people they work with. Too many young people were wandering about aimlessly. Such is the level of inadequacy that good work is much more likely to be attributable to the resourcefulness of individual staff than the result of effective management.[40]

Cartoons by Colin Reeder from Youth Service Scene, 1982, and Sebastian Buccheri from Youth in Society, 1999.

My analysis here focuses on the quality of youth work practice and the individual styles of practitioners. For me, these were always the most important factors in determining quality, although the framework also looks at achievement, curriculum, leadership and management. What's more, the inspection process, with all its human flaws and failings, remains the only recognised external evaluation of performance and practice for youth work. There will always be those who complain about inspections and judgements, but the descriptors that guide inspectors to grade work from outstanding to inadequate remain transparent and widely published. While some might argue that the categories are formulaic or historic, they remain the only set of criteria and standards to judge the quality of youth work and youth services that have ever been established and utilised. Over the years, many have sought to reinvent or redefine them, to label 'youth work that works', to write model youth charters and codes, to codify voices from practice and other similar guidelines to working with teenagers. None of them alters, improves or replaces the Ofsted quality assurance and inspection framework – its application is as potentially valuable now as it always has been.

It was during my inspection travels that I recollected an instructive article I'd found in *Youth Service Scene*. This was entitled *My First Visit to a Youth Club*, and it portrayed a picture of a youth club night written by a student on a youth leadership course. His assignment was simply to visit the centre, talk to workers and members about youth club rules, and ask the leader how much face-to-face contact work he or she does. The picture that emerged was not an uncommon experience for some of us additional inspectors on our Ofsted travels. It's a wonderfully honest – and skilfully written – picture of the occasional realities of life in the archetypal youth club:

I arrived at the club ten minutes early and was shown to the warden's office which was already full of people. 'Hello, it's

'Adrian isn't it? I'll be with you in a minute.' That minute was to stretch into many minutes as the events of the evening unfolded. It went something like this.

Member of staff enters and says 'Tucker has beaten up someone' – warden to the rescue. Office empties, phone rings. There is talk of minibuses and football. Various people in and out of the office; at one point the warden quite unconsciously is on the telephone, talking to a member of staff and simultaneously trying to be polite to me. In bursts the caretaker, 'I'll kill the little bastards.' Warden, 'What's the trouble?' Caretaker explains that someone has left the door to the top of the building open and members have set off a fire hose upstairs, aimed it at the lights and fused them. 'I chased them but they got away in the dark.' Warden, 'Did you recognise any of them?' Nothing definite – case closed.

I talk with the warden for a short while... until the caretaker returns to explain that some members have called his daughter a 'slag' and have run off. The enquiry continues – and eventually subsides. In comes a member of staff and argument follows with caretaker about leaving building unattended. Warden acts as referee and situation is resolved. Caretaker's wife now comes in to complain about accusations about her husband's competence and demanding justice about her daughter. Once again the warden presides over events.

When the office finally empties he explains that it is, in fact, his night off! He only came in because of me, but not to be concerned because the events of the night were 'nothing out of the ordinary'. At last the warden takes me to the 'club proper'. My chance to meet some of the club members? He scans the room to look for a responsible member, but is forced to admit '...There aren't many responsible ones in tonight.'[41]

GOOD YOUTH WORKERS: BORN OR MADE?

There has always been a debate about whether good youth workers are born or made. There are plenty of long-held tenets and customs attaching to youth work: over the years it has developed its own culture and mystique. Voluntary relationships, starting on young people's terms, treating everyone equally, being on their side – all that stuff. Is their closeness to their clients an essential component of youth workers' make-up? Do they need to *feel* like teenagers – with a degree of adolescent angst and testosterone that might not be acceptable in other professions? Do they have to adopt childlike behaviour and language to demonstrate their empathy? Has there always been a touch of 'free spirit' in the youth work DNA? Is there an instinctive rebelliousness that sees rules and laws as *available* for interpretation? Are youth work relationships subtly different: genuine, authentic and passionate – but often located confusingly in that undefined area between friendship and client-worker interaction? Is it the informality and responsiveness of youth work that make it special? Do good youth workers always go the extra mile, without reward or recognition? Is the work especially stressful and can it often lead to 'burnout' and exhaustion? Does training help to improve skills and ability, or are some just born with a natural gift in relating to teenagers? Are they really a 'special breed'?

There can be a political edge to some of these questions and characteristics, too. Are most good youth workers naturally idiosyncratic or inclined to 'disputation'? Are 'passion' and 'resistance' natural bedfellows, and is it a myth that they all need an enemy to blame? Are they conspiracy theorists at heart and do they all share a radical, Marxist analysis of history and class struggle? Are there grassroots heroes and capitalist villains still? Did they all read *Pedagogy of the Oppressed* when they were at college and assume Freire was talking about them? Were many of them chanting anti-Thatcher slogans in the 1980s, and are they still angry about neo-liberalism now? Would many of them have absolutely no idea what to do if peace broke out? And are they all hopeless at administration, paperwork and punctuality?

There can be a structural and institutional component as well. Do youth workers hold self-evident the truth that all provision delivered by local authority youth services is good and should be re-funded and re-established as it used to be in the 'good old days'? And – to that end – should funds be removed from all the centralist, top-down, government-sponsored and exorbitantly expensive schemes (take your pick: Connexions, National Citizen Service, Duke of Edinburgh's Award)?

And, finally, there is an issue of quality in the debate. Presumably the number of really good youth workers (born or made) is small, because unfortunately it is an unpalatable fact that even in the years after the publication of the *Transforming Youth Work* report in 2001, the quality of youth work delivered by local authority services was not very good. Ofsted reported that the number of services judged inadequate or to be giving unsatisfactory value for money was high in proportion to the number inspected.[42] Nuggets of youth work gold are hard to find, and the good old days are not, perhaps, so good after all. Analysing why some youth services were targeted for budget cuts must at least acknowledge the perceived lack of quality, value for money and benefits to the young people allegedly being served. Not to mention being in competition with nurses, police officers, teachers, sports centre staff and librarians for council funds.

AND MOMENTS WHEN THINGS JUST 'CLICK'...

But for all these negative connotations, you can't beat the rewarding feeling you get when things do go right. When, for whatever reason, and often in the most unexpected situations, your relationship with an individual or a group of young people suddenly comes good. That moment when you 'get' what youth work is really about, and you recall happily why you chose this line of work in the first place: it's the moment when things just click.

As one seasoned practitioner put it: 'Every shop floor youth worker can describe that satisfying feeling when, faced with a challenging situation, their response hits the precise note and seems exactly spot on. The crisis is defused, the young people seem content, a rightful glow of well-earned satisfaction (natural professional skills and abilities having been displayed) permeates the air.'

Another echoed a similar emotion: 'All youth workers love that moment when everything seems to just click between themselves and a young person – that moment of conversation, moment of trust, moment of significance. And all of them hate it when young people are misrepresented, judged unfairly and not listened to. And, mostly, they love the variety of every day, of every week and every moment with young people.'

There is a timelessness in these views. The paragraphs above are taken from two sources: Sydney Bunt's article *Youth Workers, Born or Made?*, part of the BBC TV *Working with Youth* series, published in 1972; and James Ballantyne's description of 'moments that click', taken from his entertaining blog *I wonder, does every Youthworker…?* published in January 2017. Forty-five years apart, but making exactly the same point.

Moments when things just click are the ones you remember most vividly – they remain clear years after the failures and disappointments have long faded from memory. Working in a 'last chance saloon' for pupils excluded from schools, Marilyn – an experienced youth worker in Hampshire – recalls her time on a secondment that was supposed to last six months but in fact went on for seven years. Her memory of one particular experience remains vivid:

I was sitting on Southsea beach one morning with one of my students – thirteen-year-old Alim – enjoying the sunshine, both alone with our own thoughts; an odd couple maybe, but not an uncomfortable or awkward silence. Suddenly Alim said out of nowhere, 'Marilyn, look at the light dancing on the sea; it looks like jewels on the water.' It made me look more carefully and, yes, I could see them as well. I still think [of] that now when I see the light sparkling on the sea: it reminds me of that day and that moment.

Taking Alim back to the children's home that afternoon, another young man approaches us and asks who I am. 'Her name's Marilyn,' says Alim.

'Is she your social worker?'

'No,' he replies.

'So who is she, then?'

Alim replies shortly, 'I dunno, she's just someone who takes me out for tea and cake and listens to me.'

There is a pause. Looking directly at me, he asks, 'Can you take me out for tea and cake as well?'[43]

My own exceptional moment was during a piece of consultancy work in London. It was a foul evening, cold and pouring with rain. Jumping onto the train at Woolwich Dockyard, I realised I'd left my umbrella behind and only had my long, grey coat and a beanie to protect me. There were two planned visits tonight: the first to a youth council meeting at Greenwich Town Hall, and then on to a youth club in a tower block somewhere nearby. I'd been given a paper map and had been assured it was within walking distance from the Town Hall. The youngsters at the council were well organised and fully engaged in their work: I didn't need long to form a judgement. Setting out to find the second appointment, the rain was coming down even harder; it was quite a long walk, hilly, dark and very wet. I made a few false turns and the map began to disintegrate in my hands as I tried to find the tower block. My woollen coat was getting heavier as it soaked up the rain: I was thoroughly drenched and getting more and more miserable by the minute.

At last I found the place: on the ground floor of a tall tower block, it reminded me a little of my own Kelvin Youth Centre. I was booked to interview a group of members about the issues they faced in their local patch. My first instinct was relief at getting out of the rain, as I peeled off my coat and beanie and put them on a radiator to dry out. I sat around the table with the teenagers and just let them talk at me: they were expecting me and had prepared well. We hit it off from the outset, or maybe they just took pity on my predicament. As I slowly warmed up, steam rose gently around me. But etched into my consciousness is one powerful memory of an incident at the end of the session.

Finishing a lively dialogue with a particularly thoughtful fifteen-year-old black young man, we seemed suddenly to reach a shared understanding. Responding to one of his points, I replied, 'Well, that all depends on your ambition and your personal philosophy.' He got up, walked over to me, smiled his agreement and shook my hand wordlessly. It was one of those moments when things do indeed click: my damp discomfort was forgotten. I'd obviously got through to him somehow; that brief, simple exchange alone had made tonight's visit worthwhile and rewarding. As I headed back to the station, I realised it had stopped raining.

CHAPTER 7

'NEW LABOUR', CONNEXIONS AND WEST SUSSEX

In 1994, Tony Blair became the new leader of the Labour Party. It was his youthfulness, his wide appeal and electability that had led him to the leadership. Politically, his success had been based on the recognition that Labour needed to win over those voters who had traditionally been alienated by the party, so he set about rebranding it as 'New Labour' with a vengeance. Abandoning all references to 'socialism', weakening the power of the trade unions and generally jettisoning the party's left-wing image, Blair developed the concept of a 'third way'. 'Tough on crime, tough on the causes of crime,' was one of his sound bites, and another mantra was his policy priority on 'education, education, education'. Blair's popularity and that of his party swelled, as the Tories, bogged down in problems over Europe and sleaze, plummeted. In May 1997, Blair's tactics were vindicated as he won the election, ending eighteen years of Conservative government. His victory certainly felt like a sea change in both political and social terms for a generation that had grown up under Mrs Thatcher.

YOUTH WORK IN THE SUNSHINE?

Like many people, I sat up most of the night watching the election results on television. There was a feeling that we were at a watershed: a new dawn of political optimism and opportunity. What's more, for someone working in local government and with young people, it seemed that at last we might be getting some political and social recognition for our efforts. Perhaps all those years of invective about 'municipal socialism' had been worth it: things were about to take a turn for the better. Across the country, colleagues shared the same new-found hopefulness – with the prospects of a higher priority and increased funding for our efforts. The really confident hoped that we might finally achieve formal, maybe even legal, recognition for local authority youth services. As Tom Wylie summed up eloquently, for many youth workers the election of a Labour government in 1997 marked the hope that at last 'the sun was about to shine on youth work after long years in the shadows.'[44] The new Secretary of State for Education, David Blunkett, evoked high hopes too. After all, he had made it clear that in his view:

> Youth work changes lives… it helps young people to develop the personal skills they need to make a success of their lives. It allows them to influence and shape their lives and the services available to them. There are few better ways… of delivering change than through good youth work.[45]

And on a personal level, I recalled his groundbreaking invitation to a group of us detached youth workers in Sheffield some twenty years before to come along to his council committee and describe our work. It seemed that the fallow years of fruitless core curriculum debates in the early 1990s were to be a fading memory. We all felt a new momentum and an unusual spring in our steps. Things seemed to be looking up.

Young People Now cover, June 1997.

PASTURES NEW

By now, I'd left Hampshire and taken on another county youth officer post, this time in West Sussex. The post of head of service was an attractive one. The previous incumbent had been headhunted to take up a job as chief executive to the Guides, a prestigious national appointment with an office in Buckingham Palace Road. Her reputation and that of youth work in the county were well respected. At my interview I was quizzed on what the distinctive contribution of youth work was to 'disaffection' and other social problems amongst the young. I felt on confident ground: my philosophy on defining youth work policy was pretty well established. 'The paradox of the youth work approach,' I answered, 'was that although without statutory authority and with ambivalent professional credibility, youth workers have a distinctive approach that gains the trust and confidence of young people, operating as they do on their terms and developing relationships that other professionals might not be able to achieve. The youth service might be politically vulnerable,' I acknowledged, 'but that distinctive role – that very lack of authority – gives a skilled worker an advantage and a unique strength.' I added 'that the job of the principal youth officer was to ensure that role is understood and to protect it from being confused or subsumed by other roles, especially the ones being driven by the agendas of other agencies or partners.' That must have sounded acceptable because they offered me the job.

On my first day I was shown into my new office at County Hall in Chichester. The room was fairly unprepossessing: small, cramped and with grubby, grey carpet tiles. But it was the atmosphere and possessions that caught my attention at once: entering the office was a bit like discovering the deserted wreck of the *Marie Celeste*. For whatever reason, the room had been left untouched for months – nothing had been moved since my predecessor had left for her new job in London. Her notebooks and pens, her laptop and conference slides, her library of books – even the potted plant quietly expiring on the window ledge – were all undisturbed. And there, left open on the desk – as though she was just checking up on an idea for running the Guides before she left – was a copy of *How to Lie with Statistics*.

Moving into my second term of office as a head of service was a fascinating comparative journey – and one not afforded to many colleagues. Until I left Hampshire, I thought it was a good youth service. Only when I arrived in West Sussex did I realise that the quality of practice, the commitment of staff and the expertise of managers were way, *way* higher in my new authority. And what does that say about inconsistency or benchmarking of youth services? What immediately impressed me was the sheer professionalism and positive, proactive culture of staff; by which I mean the high quality, high standards and high expectations that youth workers, both full- and part-time, had of themselves and the young people they worked with. Also, the very comforting experience, competence and capacity for hard work of my three senior managers. I dubbed them 'The Keeper of the Flame', 'The Defender of the Faith' and 'The Conscience of the Department' in recognition of the critical roles they each performed in helping me do the job. A strong officer team and inspiring and competent youth workers on the ground make life so much easier for any boss. One could delegate with security and confidence. This was in marked and eye-opening contrast to my previous experiences where relying on managers and senior staff was sometimes a lottery. It wasn't a surprise to me that the National Youth Agency had already recognised West Sussex as one of eleven 'higher performing' authorities in England.

The security and capability of my managers gave me the confidence to concentrate on strategy and policy, rather than having to 'fire-fight' the day-to-day problems and issues. For example, I was already the chair of the South-East Region Principal Youth Officers' Group and a member of the National Youth Agency's advisory board. I had taken on the rewarding role of external examiner for the youth and community work course at John Moores University in Liverpool, and brought a group of students on an 'exchange visit' to West Sussex to help them experience the comparative social and cultural norms between Liverpool and the south coast. It also allowed me the luxury of establishing a personal goal – that of visiting all the youth centres and projects across the county: almost two hundred of them. This was a task that took me two years to accomplish. Not only was I able to speak personally to club staff during their night-time sessions, but I religiously wrote a personal note to each of them the next morning, on personalised county youth officer note cards that I had found in my desk drawer, thanking them for their commitment. I am convinced that this style of personal visit, of 'management by walking about', of a handwritten thank-you letter, contributes immeasurably to the good health and morale of any organisation. These things matter.

NEW LABOUR AND YOUTH POLICY

The new Blair government adopted some different processes in policy and decision-making. Parliament, the Cabinet and civil servants were relegated to a minor role: in their place came an inner circle of advisers, press officers, 'spin doctors' and various other unelected officials and hangers-on. This was a very centralised form of operation, with all the inherent dangers of micromanagement and control freakery that implies. It was to be an important feature of much policymaking in the New Labour years, and it had worrying implications for those of us in services for children and young people. In its youth work policies, New Labour had something of a mixed economy. While supportive of children and young people, it sought 'joined-up' solutions to problems like social exclusion and it felt the need to target interventions at those in need, especially the NEET group (not in employment, education or training). It flirted early on with different forms of delivery including commissioning and outsourcing. It was keen on systems that gathered evidence, adopted targets and could demonstrate measurable outcomes. Inspection regimes began to adopt Labour's processes to collect such data from local authorities. It soon became obsessed with these 'targets' and 'charters', creating a massive statistical reporting infrastructure that bogged down many local authorities in a constant round of data collection.

For us, this meant providing a whole new raft of attendance records and age ranges, and details on teenage pregnancy, drug addiction, school leavers, youth unemployment figures and more. Many of us knew full well that this attempt to gather data and measure productivity in youth work was of limited value, but we had little choice but to comply. Linked to this process was the creation of a new kind of government language. New Labour came to specialise in management jargon, forever referring to 'accessing', 'passporting' and 'rolling out' things, as well as setting up 'pilots', 'beacons' and 'pathfinders', not to mention engaging its 'stakeholders' in best value and 'joined-up' thinking and partnerships.

Soon, these new systems started to take the edge off the hopefulness with which New Labour had been initially welcomed by most of us in the local government arena. For example, the new Youth Minister, Kim Howells, raised expectations amongst the workforce when he confirmed his clear view – in a conference speech to the Standing Conference of Principal Youth Officers in 1997 – that the youth service must not 'be reduced to a mechanistic system for getting kids off the streets'. However, he had soon changed his tune, noting later the same year that the youth service was now in his view:

> ...the patchiest, most unsatisfactory of all the services I've come across. I've never met such down-at-heart, 'can't do' representatives as I've met of youth services throughout Britain.

It was an off-the-cuff comment, prompted (probably justifiably) by the variability of both the quantity and quality of youth provision across the country that he was visiting.[46] But the undertones of negativity and resistance in his language caused concern to many, and the speed with which he had apparently changed his mind was worrying. It was a little reminiscent of the confusion and dizzy turnover in Youth Service Ministers that was a characteristic of the early 1990s' curriculum conference days. The adrenalin rush of optimism about youth services at the Labour election victory was soon to be tempered by concerns over the plethora of initiatives, statistical returns, projects and funding streams which started to clog up our desks and divert our attention from management and delivery.

Moreover, attitudes to teenagers were hardening and becoming more negative and punitive. In 1998, the Crime and Disorder Act required local authorities to publish 'crime and disorder strategies' and introduced Antisocial Behaviour Orders (ASBOs), child curfews and the removal of school truants from the streets to their homes or to designated safe places. The ASBO soon became a new symbol of the social policy landscape. It dealt with disruptive individuals through a magistrate's banning order which circumscribed behaviour or placed a curfew and restriction on activities. From being the preserve of gang members or working-class 'juvenile delinquents', such behaviour now described the kinds of activity almost any young person might choose to adopt. Much of this policy, as Bernard Davies accurately puts it, 'was shaped by deficiency rather than potentiality models of the young.'[47]

From my perspective, the biggest threat from these policy shifts was to open-access youth club work. Universal provision was being squeezed out in favour of work with targeted, disadvantaged and hard-to-reach groups; the threat to the work's core values (and its budgets) was obvious. Funding was skewed to NEET reduction, teenage pregnancy, drug use, crime reduction and antisocial behaviour. Not much was left for running the local youth club, sustaining street work or keeping our range of information shops open. But I was single-minded in the need to retain our core provision, located in our traditional youth centre programmes across the county. Sometimes the rationale to defend such work now had to be couched in more pragmatic terms than I would have preferred. We adopted a number of arguments: the benefits of early intervention, the value of the non-stigmatising approach, the refusal to stereotype or categorise young people as they came through the club door, the benefits of providing positive alternatives rather than punitive ones, the need for local facilities for local youngsters. These were arguments that I knew found favour with almost every local councillor in the county. All of them came into play to ward off the selective targeting of 'troublemakers', 'problem families', or those 'antisocial and disruptive' teenagers who seemed now to be in the spotlight.

But I remained anxious: we needed to be very careful that we did not endanger the critical voluntary nature of youth workers' relationships with young people. In a familiar vein, I reinforced the point that the youth service is not the 'soft' arm of the police, probation or youth justice services. Many grassroots youth workers were reporting to me that the use of ASBOs was effectively criminalising young people. Curfews, naming and shaming, zero tolerance campaigns, the appointment of 'ASBO coordinators', police community support officers, park patrols, neighbourhood wardens – a new multiplicity of initiatives and employees was being deployed in this crime reduction arena. All sought to target and control young people's activities and behaviour. Being moved on from their usual meeting places became a common experience. One night, on Ofsted inspection duty in Cheshire, the detached work team complained to me that there were now so many categories of civic employee whose role included 'youth', many with titles emblazoned on the back of their high-vis jackets, that young people were confused about who to talk to, who to trust and who to avoid.

On one occasion, I experienced for myself how it must have felt for young people. Walking through a London borough high street one afternoon, I was stopped by two Metropolitan Police officers, one inspector (male) and one constable (female). I'd been taking some photos of the Victorian shop fronts with their elaborate stone doorways and window facades, clearly at risk from the luxury flats redevelopment going on all around them.

'Can I ask what you're doing?' demanded the inspector.

I explained.

'Do you have any identification?' he continued.

I pulled out a letter, ironically from the borough council where he was based, confirming my current employment in the authority. His female colleague was beginning to look slightly embarrassed. He studied the letter, thinking hard as to whether I was worth pursuing any further. He decided I wasn't.

'Just checking up,' he concluded, and they strode off towards the Thames.

All of this was shifting youth work's principles of voluntary association in a big way. Implicit in many of these new posts was a coercive, non-negotiable element – backed up potentially by police and criminal records. Voluntary association and group work were being subtly replaced by individual programmes and a case management approach, informal relationships by formal and bureaucratic ones. More and more, youth workers were pressed into servicing the needs of other agencies. Ironically, their contribution was highly prized because they seemed able to 'reach the youths other agencies couldn't reach'. Detached workers in particular were asked to visit the parks and precincts where the police had received complaints of 'youths gathering' and see if they could defuse and remove such young people elsewhere. Many detached projects began to portray themselves (in a form of black humour peculiar to the breed) as wearing flashing blue lights on their heads as they brought their minibus to round up the teenagers at the latest hotspot. Indeed, some services formalised the process – creating their own 'mobile' or 'hotspot' response teams, with badged minibuses to match, in order to undertake just such work.

REGIONAL GOVERNMENT, TARGETS AND FUNDING BIDS

Another challenge was the growth of regional government. In our patch, the Government Office of the Southeast was ever more influential, impinging directly on functions previously carried out by the county council. We were having to live, too, with the new regional boundaries – Hampshire had been rejoined with the cities of Southampton and Portsmouth, unhappy bedfellows historically, along with the Isle of Wight. The new 'Pan-Sussex' reality encompassed West and East Sussex with its political polar opposite, Brighton and Hove. Much new money was short-term, targeted and achieved only through difficult, competitive and time-consuming bidding processes. The constant pressure to audit, map, consult, plan, target-set and evaluate continued. This was genuinely all a worry and a threat. Some of these new arrangements put at risk both the engagement of elected councillors in supporting our work, and our accountability to them through elected committees at County Hall. They also ran the risk of generating much activity (and paper) but little real outcome; of producing no tangible added value or benefits to the young people on the ground they are supposed to help. It was tough work being vigilant in keeping our core services focused on young people and not diverted into these other arenas and agencies.

As an experienced head of service, my growing frustration was that the pursuit of targets was starting to dominate all my work and that of my senior colleagues. In West Sussex, we had to take on a new project officer to cope with both the new administrative demands and the funding application workload. Luckily for us, Peter brought a particular and successful talent to writing funding bids. His technique seemed to be based on his strategy for playing the National Lottery – 'You have to be in it to win it, Tim,' he kept on reminding me. This role easily filled thirty-seven hours' worth of activity every week.

With hindsight, I might have recognised that proving you were being successful was not a new phenomenon. Twenty years earlier, my Berkshire boss had regularly complained that, if only people would let him get on with running the youth service, he would probably make a good job of it. But the incessant demands for facts and figures about what he was doing, why he was doing it and how he might do it better, were a constant interruption in effective management. 'It's like my allotment,' he told me. 'If I dug up the roots every other day to see if the plants were growing all right, they would be ruined.'

It was beginning to feel like Tony Blair mistrusted local government every bit as much as Margaret Thatcher had done. The risk of valuing only what could be measured as opposed to measuring what was valued was a key complaint. In effect, as workers and managers we were asking, 'How do you count confidence, compassion, citizenship and the other outcomes on which youth workers put such emphasis? How can you value good relationships?' Targets prescribed the flexibility and freedom of professionals to implement their craft with young people. One of youth work's salient features – the discretion of the practitioner in a face-to-face relationship with the young person – was under serious threat.[48] Around this time, Howard Williamson, a respected youth policy commentator, recalled how an HMI colleague of his had mused:

> *When youth work has been absorbed into a number of new initiatives trying to do all this targeted and focused work, somebody is going to come to me in twenty years' time and ask what 'youth work' was. And when I tell them they will say: we need it back.*

Williamson warned that there were dangers in youth work being seduced into the 'warm, fuzzy' notion of integrated services, the primary risk being the loss of youth work's distinctive educational focus.[49]

THE SMILE: A TRIUMPH OF GOOD YOUTH WORK

In response to these challenges came an instinctive reaction amongst many staff against the whole panoply of targets, recorded outcomes, products and 'deliverables'. Determining the percentage balance between open-access and targeted work became seen as an exercise not dissimilar to counting the number of angels dancing on a pinhead. As Jeremy Brent, an experienced youth centre practitioner in Bristol, mused – 'who claims the success anyway in measuring good work: is it the youth worker or the young person?'

Relating one of his young members' transformation as an example of good practice, Brent described what happened, entitling the piece *The Smile*:

Southmead Youth Centre, Bristol – home of The Smile.
Photo: Young People Now, November 2005.

A 15-year-old girl attends the youth centre. She comes not in her own right but as a shadowy appendage of her boyfriend. She looks miserable and unhappy and takes no part in any activities. Staff note her presence and are friendly and welcoming, but no plans or goals are made for her – there is no initial interview and no assessment procedure. Gradually she gets to talk a bit, we find out her name – we'll call her Kelly. Then she starts confiding to one staff member. She chooses to do this – the youth worker does not 'intervene' with her, though he is ready and able to respond. Over a number of conversations she tells him how miserable she is, how her father dislikes her, how she is not going to school, how she wants to move out, how she has eating problems. Problems for which we possess no solutions. We do organise a meeting for her with a housing worker.

Then, one session after Kelly had been coming to the youth centre for about six months, she smiles. She even smiles at me, though my contact with her has been minimal. Now Kelly throws herself into the life of the centre. She plans a display of photos of all the club members. She plans a trip to a theme park. She is active, articulate; she enters into social relations with young people and adults. She is part of something. She looks well. How can we measure this success? There has been no product, no target met, no plan completed, yet all the evidence points to there being an important personal outcome for Kelly. It is the sort of episode that is the bread and butter of youth work yet it is nothing we can give a certificate for, nothing to gain public recognition by. There may be outcomes for her in years to come – but these we do not and cannot know. Still, that smile is so important: a real achievement, a triumph of good youth work.

This is a long quotation, but it is an important and representative example – most youth workers can identify a 'Kelly' they've known and worked with, and recognise the smile as a triumph of good youth work. Like the author, they would never seek to overvalue or claim some specialist skill or expertise in describing the development that led to Kelly's change of spirit. They too would accept the danger of becoming pious about the nature of the youth work relationship, claiming mystical or romantic attributes of some kind of a pure and unmediated understanding between workers and young people. The much-vaunted voluntary relationship is not a panacea, nor does it exempt us from responsibilities and difficulties. There is a strain in being on the receiving end of managerial pressures and demands that often conflict with our direct work with members. We are a kind of 'kink in the chain of command,' as Brent rather eloquently describes it. Or put more simply: youth work can be a messy, ambiguous and complex activity. His commentary in *The Smile* was a welcome antidote to the targets and outcomes debate, and widely read and applauded by practitioners and managers alike.[50]

CONNEXIONS: A DIVERSION FROM TASK

Early on in my time as head of the West Sussex service, we were all anxiously awaiting the launch of Connexions. It is difficult to capture now the suspicion and concerns about the establishment of the government's 'much-heralded' new Connexions service in 2000; not least whether it was the harbinger of the demise of youth work and youth services. Some feared a Connexions 'takeover' in which developmental youth work was to be abandoned in favour of this new rigid, bureaucratic regime. Predictions of the imminent fall of youth services were redoubled.

The government's decision to set up Connexions arose from its dissatisfaction with the effectiveness of careers service advice and

connexi ns

The best start in life for every young person

Photo montage: Chris Nash, 2006.

information offered to teenagers, particularly those at risk of social exclusion or those who fell into the NEET category of 'not in education, employment or training'. Allied to this concern was the perceived lack of collaboration and information-sharing between the many agencies which sometimes dealt with young people. Certainly there were high ambitions for Connexions: every thirteen to nineteen-year-old in the country was to have their own personal adviser. It would provide every young person with 'the best start in life'. The adviser would act as triage nurse, mentor, advocate, careers officer and social worker, and would link up all the agencies already involved in supporting young people. The concept of a personal adviser rendered the role of the youth worker potentially redundant, especially as the government appeared keen to establish a national structure, training programme and professional qualifications to go with the Connexions brand.

A great deal of money was spent on setting up the forty-seven Connexions partnerships across the country. Chief executives, finance officers and quality managers were appointed – all on generous salaries – office accommodation was rented in expensive city-centre premises, furniture and equipment were lavishly deployed – all in a fetching mix of the corporate orange and purple colours. Visiting the West Midlands Connexions office in central Birmingham some years later, I was amazed to discover that in the chief executive's colossal office, his new, polished walnut oval table could seat over thirty people. The Connexions logo was designed and marketed relentlessly – along with branded mugs, baseball caps, mobile phone covers and even a Connexions paperclip, whose design meant it was hopeless at holding papers together. A vast empire of training courses, certification and accreditation programmes, handbooks and student material was hastily and expensively produced by the Connexions Service National Unit. Diploma courses for personal advisers were put in place and, later, management programmes for senior officers. Everything was printed and produced on the heaviest, glossiest paper I had ever encountered. Some of my colleagues were tempted by the huge salaries on offer for Connexions chief executive jobs – and some made the transition successfully and effortlessly into their new, larger empires. Not all were motivated by mercenary ambition, I hasten to add. Some doubtless saw the benefits of greater integration and control of careers services and supported this new, ambitious venture. Others, tempted maybe but racked by doubts over principles and the sustainability of the new project, just bided their time and waited to see which way the wind blew. That was me.

I was often characterised in my times as a principal youth officer as being a pragmatist. To me that was a compliment: it acknowledged my practical, down-to-earth and realistic approach to policy, practice and management. In my line of business, realism and pragmatism were synonyms. Being suspicious of those who promised certainty, who peddled simplistic solutions and who were always convinced they were right was a default position for me. That probably owes something to my training in history, with its constant reminder that problems are complex and their resolution frequently difficult. This has influenced my occasionally hesitant leadership style – although some might have seen this as indecision or weakness. Speaking at a joint conference of Connexions and youth workers in the early stages of the 'brand', I realised that caution and pragmatism were out of favour; in fact these had turned into virulent terms of abuse. Some of the delegates, spurred on by a keynote speech from a university academic, denounced any strategy that might dilute or weaken the purist approach to youth work practice in the then-turbulent times. My counterargument about living in the real world, working alongside those who disagreed with me and remembering my responsibilities for the jobs and salaries of my full-time staff cut little ice. For them, being a pragmatist was only one step removed from treachery and betrayal of the long and hallowed history of youth work. Reeling a little from their verbal attacks, in my head were the eerie echoes of that long-gone curriculum conference manifesto – the role of youth work 'is to redress all forms of inequality'.

In our neck of the woods, most of us held our breath and our professional nerve about Connexions and waited to see what happened. We needed to take a pragmatic line – at least in public. While we did not know all the consequences for our service, what was certain was that the government was committed to Connexions happening. Thus, I was convinced that a positive response was the right one. I was fortunate that in West Sussex our relationships with our careers service colleagues were excellent and we both made an early pact to stick together in sorting out policy and practice for our staff teams. Singing from the same hymn sheet, we called it.

Both Steven, my careers adviser colleague, and I were long enough in the tooth, professionally speaking, to know that a realistic and down-to-earth line was the best bet. One day in his car, driving together to a Pan-Sussex Connexions meeting in Brighton, he admitted, 'We're never going to find all these "disappeared", Tim; are your lot?'

'I doubt it,' I replied.

But it was a distracting and time-consuming exercise: in my annual West Sussex review report in 2001, my diary showed that I attended 1.3 Connexions meetings every week. And the professionalisation of Connexions was well underway too – diplomas for personal advisers, training programmes for careers staff, joint multi-agency meetings with Youth Offending Teams and health and police, alongside publications pouring out of the newly created Connexions Service National Unit. There was a whole industry developing for yet more joined-up approaches that were to create another 'step change' in culture and practice for all those involved.

Around this time I was invited to attend a national think-tank event to be held in Windsor Castle to discuss the national policy development and roll-out of Connexions. How my name was chosen remains a mystery to me; probably the chair of the Association of Principal Youth Officers had a spare place and offered me up. It was quite a high-powered gathering, with government special advisers (SpADs), national school head representatives, departmental officials and 'movers and shakers' from the Connexions Service National Unit and other national bodies. Our task seemed to be to work out how Connexions could fit into the government's policy development for children and young people overall. What would these triage-nurse-type personal advisers actually do? How could you transform 'bog-standard' careers officers into them? How best could the structure and management of the forty-seven Connexions partnerships succeed amidst the maelstrom of local authorities who, sometimes unwillingly, had been coerced into their creation? We were accommodated in rather monastic, cold and sparsely furnished single-bed guest rooms within the castle precincts. Which was probably all part of the Spartan plan – to force us to concentrate our minds and determine how Connexions was going to work. Like electing a Pope, we were locked in until the puff of white smoke signified that we had come up with an acceptable answer. Obviously, we failed in the end, but I recall some stimulating and argumentative group discussions – mainly at an intellectual level that was more rarefied than I was used to. But the views from the top of the castle and the chance of a private evening visit to St. George's Chapel were unmissable.

Particular concern was raised about the job of the personal advisers whose roles and responsibilities seemed still unclear. Would their relationships with young people remain voluntary, and how realistic were the proposed ratios and caseloads of advisers? Much talk was made about the establishment of a 'new profession' with training courses and diplomas for personal advisers proliferating. Most youth workers and heads of service remained unpersuaded of these developments. We knew well that most Connexions staff were drawn from the ranks of the careers service advisers who essentially continued to operate a 9am-to-5pm office-based routine. They had no aspirations to become youth workers or change their professional approach. A new professionalism amongst existing staff and agencies would be fine, but a new profession was not needed. We were much helped in this view by the similar public position taken on Connexions by Tom Wylie, the director of the National Youth Agency.

Not all Connexions PAs worked 9am to 5pm, nor were they incapable of delivering good youth work practice. Inspecting a South London authority in early 2008, in one of the last tranches of youth service inspections, I came across Aisha. Aisha was called a Connexions specialist personal adviser, and worked in a large secondary school with much of her work focused on asylum seekers. Watching her interview a sixteen-year-old who had arrived from Eastern Europe the year before, and was privately fostered, living in unsuitable council housing and working in his uncle's pizza shop was a joy to behold. Her style was helpful and persuasive, offering encouragement and good support in equal measure, which was clearly valued and appreciated.

Aisha had a borough-wide role, and worked in six schools, the youth offending team and the local one-stop shop. Her current clients were mainly Somali and Afghan boys, but she covered a wide range of issues including work with single mums, self-harming, depression, family support and language barriers, as well as writing funding bids for the many groups who fell through the net of council support.

Aisha was an ex-social worker who understood the law and could advocate with some force with local authority welfare systems. She was highly committed and constantly engaged on behalf of her client group. She loved her work, she told me: 'When you read the backgrounds of some of these young people, you are humbled; I'm impressed when they just get up in the morning – many make progress very quickly, becoming school prefects, for example.' Clearly, Aisha was a very unusual and exceptional example of a Connexions personal adviser.

Good work like Aisha's helped to improve and cement the links between Connexions and the youth service – particularly in the field of advice, information and youth counselling centres that local authorities supported, many of which involved youth workers. There was obviously a valuable synergy between the role of Connexions advice on jobs and training, and youth work advice on personal and social issues. I visited a good example, the Two-E Centre in North London, handily placed at a busy street corner and on a school bus route, which provided an airy setting, furnished with a plentiful supply of colourful material aimed at young people.

The centre provided a range of services including condoms, STI tests and legal advice. The Connexions PA was based here, successfully using it as a contact point for her work. The annual reports showed Two-E reached 333 young people, mainly in the seventeen to nineteen-years age range, with 1,621 contacts. Of these, 214 were female and 119 male, with a significant number of Greek, Turkish, Kurdish and Kosovan attendees. They kept excellent management information and analysis of their clients, even detailing both 'hard' and 'soft' outcomes of the centre's achievements. A strength of its work was the committed young staff team who (while not all youth-work trained or qualified) provided a friendly and caring welcome to everyone who walked through the door.

Nevertheless, the national picture was not nearly as positive as these examples of good practice. Probably when it saw the scale of resources necessary for all the Connexions partnerships to deliver the ambitious programmes it had promised thirteen to nineteen-year-olds, the government rather lost interest in what had been its flagship youth policy. And the reason for youth services' survival was partly linked to this corresponding decline of Connexions. In the end, youth work and youth services survived in much better shape than their careers service counterparts. Youth work, which had always been much cheaper, re-emerged into the policy spotlight and on its own terms. In fact, Connexions failed partly because of the protectionist stances of a number of national government departments. The Home Office wouldn't let Connexions have youth offending teams and the Local Government Association resisted any attempt to transfer local authority youth services into the pot. So, in the end, all they got were the careers service companies. Although, in some ways, Connexions might be seen as a first trial – a precursor to the later Every Child Matters initiative with its similar focus on partnership integration and joined-up working among a multitude of agencies working with children and young people.

INSPECTED IN WEST SUSSEX

In late 2000, West Sussex Youth Service was inspected by Ofsted. There were a number of my colleagues who relished the anticipation of the 'tables being turned' on me at last. As I had visited many of their youth services as an additional inspector, they were looking forward to me being on the receiving end for a change. Just desserts, I suppose. My inspection preparation work plan was almost blown off course around this time by a very determined woman from Bognor Regis – Mrs B, I shall call her. Complaints about youths and youth clubs were a regular feature of my life and I should have known better in dealing with this particular one. Mrs B lived next door to a local youth club, and footballs, or worse, often ended up in her back garden. Normally this was an issue I would have left to the local youth officer to resolve as amicably as possible. However, I found myself in Bognor one summer afternoon and decided to pop in for a chat. Big mistake. After being harangued for about two hours on the ghastliness of youth and the incompetence of the council and all its staff, I finally escaped back to the calm of my office in Chichester. In my keenness to be seen as responsive and helpful, though, I had given Mrs B my direct-line telephone number. Second big mistake. For the next two weeks, every morning on the dot at 8.30am she rang me to update me on the list of items currently nestling amongst her geraniums in Bognor. Every morning, Tina, my secretary, buzzed me apologetically to tell me she was on the line again. Eventually, we both gave up on each other and I delegated the matter to the local team. And the lesson learnt – never, ever give anyone your direct number. Also, as King George V so admirably put it, 'Bugger Bognor'!

Preparing for the inspection had monopolised our attention for weeks: in those days you had some months' notice of your ordeal, and we had worked incredibly hard at preparing all our teams and ensuring all our policies and paperwork were up to date. Bluntly, I became obsessive about the whole thing. My demands for meticulous attention to detail and painstaking levels of planning became legendary. We bought fifty new folders, colour-coded them with all our logos and crammed them full of every policy document, committee report, curriculum file, training portfolio, press cutting, project report, youth exchange – everything I could think of that might impress the inspection team. They filled two tables and shelves at the inspector's HQ. I required every worker, especially the part-time leaders whose clubs were often located in impenetrable parts of deepest West Sussex, to produce two location maps: one to get the inspector to within a mile of the club, and the other of a scale detailed enough to show them where to park their car. I was leaving nothing to chance.

At that time, Ofsted asked every club to produce a unit plan, providing basic information which would give an idea of what to expect on the night. In our case, this meant over two hundred plans; I scrutinised every single one personally. One bright spark described his club layout as 'four walls and a roof.' It was probably a surprise for him when he received it back from me with a terse personal instruction ordering it to be rewritten. We set up an Ofsted 'project group' and convened numerous staff meetings to prepare for the ordeal. The trick was to balance sound preparation (loads of Plan Bs to cover every eventuality) without frightening everyone off the whole procedure. One youth worker whose detached team were likely to be visited on the first Monday evening asked me if he should organise four or five young people to be ready to appear on the streets that night. Pausing only a second, I replied, 'Could you make it eight or ten?' In reality, having 'insider' information about the inspection process was of limited use. You could not pull the wool over the eyes of experienced lead inspectors, nor try to hide your service's imperfections and weaknesses. Honesty is the best policy, I had always argued, and, now it was my turn, I had to accept that approach in my own service.

It was well worth it: the verdict of the inspection team was a powerful one. 'West Sussex is a high-performing youth service. Its work with its target age group of young people is impressive.

Young People Now and The Buzz
(West Sussex staff magazine)
reports on Ofsted inspection,
April 2001.

The service is well led and managed. Significantly it achieves these results with only an average level of funding. It therefore provides excellent value for money.' One of the proudest elements for me as head of service was reading this extract from the West Sussex inspection report:

> *Young people displayed pride in their centres and took pleasure in showing people round and in explaining the breadth of provision on offer. What was of particular note was the tolerance and sensitivity they showed to one another. The youth service cannot take sole credit for the attitudes of those young people involved with it, but the ethos of trust and generosity which it has fostered has certainly had an important contribution to*

make to the way in which they interact.

The inspection awarded West Sussex the best set of grades ever to be achieved by a youth service up to that time. The team of six inspectors spent more than a week visiting seventy-two youth work sessions and over 75% of our work was graded excellent, very good or good. My first reaction was to congratulate everyone who had worked so hard, and to publicly confirm that they should be 'rightly proud of their work – they have earned the inspectors' judgements'. There was an important wider significance for me in the report's verdict – that it reinforced the benefits of a generic and universal youth service and not one focused solely on difficulty or disadvantage. That broader vision of youth work had been out of favour for many years – it was felt that old-fashioned youth clubs could not deliver the goods. Our Ofsted verdict firmly dispelled that myth: indeed its findings reinforced exactly the opposite. And it was one strongly in line with the wishes of our elected members, too.

The verdict also helped strengthen a growing national consensus about the need to sustain a youth service separate and distinct from Connexions. Indeed, the report seemed to recognise such a need, for if local youth services became subsumed into Connexions there was a risk that the variety of provision which Ofsted praised so highly would simply disappear. If youth workers all become personal advisers, who would deliver the infrastructure we currently provided? If the focus was on the top 10% of those most disadvantaged, what would the service offer the other 90% equally entitled to a service? If the key value base of youth work, namely the voluntary nature of relationships, was lost, what would distinguish the youth service from the raft of other statutory professionals dealing with the thirteen to nineteen-years age range?

I was able to bask in the glory of all of this for some considerable time. The NYA sent *Young People Now* to find out how we'd done it. As their analysis put it, *Ofsted reports have been fairly grim reading* over the past two years. *So it makes a pleasant change to be able to write about a service which has been deemed to provide work of a very high quality and offer excellent value for money.*[51] Unfortunately, as the *YPN* report also presaged, our experience in West Sussex was unrepresentative and 'against the tide' in terms of developments in youth services nationally.

TRANSFORMING YOUTH WORK: RESOURCING EXCELLENT YOUTH SERVICES

In 2001, the Department for Education and Science, helped immeasurably by Tom Wylie's policy-drafting skills at the National Youth Agency, produced a new policy agenda heralded in a vivid green, glossy document entitled *Transforming Youth Work: Resourcing Excellent Youth Services.* Launched on a bright, sunny March morning at the Design Centre in Islington, *Transforming Youth Work*, or '*REYS*', as we affectionately came to know it, seemed at last to be the answer to all our prayers. There was much good-humoured banter about the new 'reys' of sunshine in which we might henceforth be able to bask. The policy undoubtedly reflected and ushered in a second 'golden age' of youth work for me. Inaugurated by the then-Youth Minister, Ivan Lewis, it contained ring-fenced budgets for youth services, common planning, targets and performance indicators, and management training. The launch was attended by all the key dramatis personae of the youth work world, from national government and youth work agencies, to senior Ofsted inspectors, managers and practitioners of all kinds – everyone was keen to be present at this milestone event. It was, as Tom Wylie, the NYA's chief executive, later described it, 'a bold new architecture for youth work with a national framework establishing the basis for local co-ordination and delivery.'[52]

This was an unsurprising comment, as most of us recognised

that Tom himself had played a significant role in writing the documents in the first place. In fact, his drafting reflected an ingenious tactical manoeuvre by bringing together in one document a mixture of youth work values, unique service targets, a pledge on standards for young people and a list of leadership requirements for authorities. This was an intelligent compilation that killed at least two birds with one stone. It soothed the anxious breasts of ministers in the department by providing the requisite 'toughness' to improve quality and comply with the continuing demands for quantitative and qualitative measurement, outcomes and targets. And it spoke to the hearts of practitioners through the adoption of the (long pre-existing) NYA values statement, and through its subtle, but calculated, distancing of the youth service from Connexions. It was also, as commentators noted, the first government statement on the youth service since the Albemarle Report of 1960.

REYS was part of a broader plan to invest in and reform the public sector, one aim of which was to make services more efficient, effective and accountable. This made funding from the taxpayer increasingly dependent on public services demonstrating a positive impact on service users and on other stakeholders. For youth work this meant demonstrating that young people were achieving positive outcomes as defined by higher levels of educational achievement, reduced antisocial behaviour and teenage pregnancy, and positive contributions to their communities. It also required services to become much more joined up (again) – either through partnership working or, in due course, through actual mergers. For some workers and service managers this meant they worked more closely with professionals whose values and approaches might be different from their own.

More ominously, though it didn't appear so at the time, *REYS* also introduced youth work to some of the more tangible results culture in the format of best-value performance indicators on reach, participation, and recorded and accredited outcomes. Later, Every Child Matters (2003) introduced the five outcomes of all children's services to which youth work now had to contribute – being safe, staying healthy, enjoying and achieving, making a positive contribution, and achieving economic well-being. Again, this seemed a reasonable requirement for most heads of youth services to deliver. But there was a longer-term sting in the tail. Youth work was seen as one of the services required to integrate into the planned local authority 'youth support' partnerships. Although it sounded innocuous at the time, this requirement began to cause some serious policy problems. Youth service managers now had to balance much more critically resources spent on 'targeted' youth support work, required under the new regimes, against the more traditional open-access, 'universal' service of entitlement to all young people in their areas. Squaring this particular circle was a continuing dilemma for managers and practitioners alike.

THE SUN SETS ON NEW LABOUR

If New Labour had begun with an apparent commitment to young people and, hopefully, by extension, to youth work, by the time of the last Blair government in 2006 the sun had begun to set and the shine was being to look a bit tired and tarnished. The early commitment and optimism had become diluted and dissipated by the continuing launch of new initiatives and programmes. *Youth* work was no longer much talked about – *children* loomed much larger in the public consciousness than teenagers did. No surprise there, really: my report on children and play on Kelvin Flats twenty years before had identified that the under-thirteens, the junior club age range, were always going to be more popular than teenagers. And easier to work with: as one of my Sheffield detached work colleagues once angrily responded to a complaint about the low numbers of teenagers he was working with, 'If I had a hundred lollipops to give away outside the Town Hall on a Saturday morning, I could easily attract that number of youngsters.'

The primacy of the youth work methodology and its availability to all young people was inexorably being replaced by work that focused on the most deprived or vulnerable. True, there had been additional money through the *Transforming Youth Work* development fund; true, there had been the concept of a 'youth offer' with places to go and things to do for young people; and true, there had been the new Myplace state-of-the-art youth centres – though no funding for the staff to run them. But overall the landscape was moving inexorably into 'integrated youth support services' and to youth workers *contributing* to the overall role of local authority children's services. Connexions partnerships all but disappeared as they were subsumed back into local councils. The Director of Children's Services in Essex was quoted in *Young People Now* as saying, 'I expect to see people who currently work in a youth service with youth work skills belonging to a multidisciplinary team. Over time,' she added, 'there will not be a youth service.' [53] The posts of principal youth officer began to disappear around this time, replaced by strategic managers, or generic heads of children's services or lifelong learning. Integrating services was reinforced by the commissioning of some responsibilities and by devolution to locality teams or area managers, often grouped around schools. The worry, obviously, was that the quality of youth work delivery would suffer if its management was transferred from those embedded in its practice to managers with no youth work experience and little understanding of its potential. Reinforcing these structural changes was the continuing focus on young people with the greatest need, the most disadvantaged, those who were vulnerable or at risk. What price funding for the local youth club as a priority over such individual youngsters?

Towards the end of my time in West Sussex, I was seconded

to the Government Office of the South East (GoSE) to develop links between youth services and Connexions partnerships in the region. My job was to try and 'translate' how the youth work contribution might be engaged in Connexions delivery at a grassroots level. This secondment was much to the annoyance of the county council's chief executive, who accosted me in the staff car park one afternoon demanding to know why I had agreed to join 'that lot in Guildford'. The role with GoSE widened my brief even further, including 'bespoke support', as the Government Office jargon put it, to the Milton Keynes, Oxfordshire and Buckinghamshire partnerships, and helping with post-Ofsted-inspection plans in a number of local youth services in the region. One of my clear memories of working in the rather palatial GoSE offices in the centre of Guildford was how unusually quiet it was. It took me a while to work out why this was so. Simply, it was because the phones never rang; everyone communicated by email, even with colleagues a few yards away. Compared to the noisy maelstrom of the average youth office that I had been used to, this was a relative mausoleum of a workplace. But they seemed to welcome my presence and the positive impact of my youth service expertise. Later on, reading my staff appraisal report, I discovered that my boss had enjoyed my 'professionalism and wicked sense of humour.' At the time, I simply relished this new challenge and the chance to work with lots more youth services on a wider, regional scale.

I was less conscious of how the secondment role was altering my career ambitions and prospects. Increasingly, my focus and interest in youth work strategy had widened beyond simply heading up a local authority. After all, I had been at it for some twelve years already. The taste I had been allowed thus far of a regional and national perspective had whetted my appetite for more; for both greater freedom and the chance to test out my new skills at different levels. Having completed my secondment to Government Office, I really did not want to return to my old job in West Sussex. Luckily, the opportunity for a change soon presented itself. But I have always kept the farewell card sent to me from Sandra and her staff at the Quayside Youth Centre. In it she wrote, 'it always felt safe knowing you were in post.' Surely, that was as kind and generous an epitaph as anyone could ever ask for.

CHAPTER 8

THE PRIVATE SECTOR: THE FINAL CURTAIN

It was 2003 and there was a 'post-*REYS*' golden glow about youth work and youth services. Personally, I was still benefiting from the glamour of the West Sussex inspection verdict with its highest set of grades awarded to a youth service: I was the 'blue-eyed boy', as a colleague from Birmingham reminded me sometime later. I had some credibility, too, as an experienced Ofsted additional inspector with a reputation for clear thinking and firm judgements. Also, I had recent experience of secondments – to the Sussex Connexions partnership and to the Government Office of the South East, both of which gave me experience and a taste for a wider, more challenging brief. Then, out of the blue, I was headhunted by a private consultancy company called Libre Consulting, who offered me a new job in their education division.

Leaving the security of the local authority to join the private sector was both a relief and a risk. It was flattering to feel I had been chosen from a potentially wide national field, but there were some downsides. Or rather, new experiences to get used to within a new culture. To begin with, there was the relentless pace and demands of chasing 'business'. You were responsible for finding your work, you needed to market and seek out clients continually, and when you had them you needed to attend to 'billing' equally relentlessly. Performance mattered: you were only as good as your last job. If you made a mistake and the client complained, you lost money. If you weren't up to the job, you were simply given notice. The travel was particularly wearing: in my first two years I was in York, Redcar and Rotherham at one end of the country and Hackney, Hounslow and Surrey at the other. My life was spent on train journeys, rolling suitcases and laptops up and down the land. I became immensely familiar with London's Waterloo and Euston stations and with the uniformity of Premier Inns, Travelodges and Ibises. But, if truth be told, I couldn't complain because I enjoyed the high pressure and the 'payment by results' culture. There's nothing wrong with competition and the need to prove the quality of your product: heavens, I'd spent long enough trying to explain that to youth workers. What sharpened the message in the private sector was that if you failed, you were sacked – a fate which rarely if ever befell local government employees. Too many youth workers felt they were owed a living by the council – whatever their level of competence or ability.

Nevertheless, my new situation gave rise to some moral dilemmas and scruples. These involved concerns about the levels of compromise I was willing to accept in this new role. The private sector generally and the company employing me in particular were both profit-making enterprises. The surpluses accruing from my consultancy day work rate ended up ultimately in the pockets of the company directors. Was this an acceptable state of affairs? Was it right that council budgets – taxpayers' hard-earned income, at the end of the day – were being used to buy in expensive external consultants, when the council already employed a panoply of officers and staff to do the job? Should I have thought harder about the consequences of leaving the state sector? How was my conscience feeling: could I still sleep soundly at night in this new environment?

At first, I tried to make light of this dilemma, joking with clients that, like Florence Nightingale, consultancy was really a vocation for me and, normally, I would be doing it for nothing, only my private sector bosses wouldn't let me operate under such a liberal regime. Even for me, that didn't sound very convincing. Later on, as my skin thickened in my consultancy roles, I took a harder line with clients, knowing that my expertise had a market value and, usually, that I was negotiating a reasonable price for the job they wanted done. I knew that my work was valued by the fieldwork staff I encountered because most of them told me so. Helping them gain the confidence to do their best work, enabling expensive resources to be used more effectively, focusing clearly on the client outcomes, offering a choice of policy options for consideration, leaving a raft of bespoke 'products' for the client to use after I'd gone – all these provided value for money as a consultant.

But I still had some pangs of guilt about the process, particularly if my appearance in an authority coincided with budget cuts, staff reductions or closures. Indeed, there were some circumstances when I felt that employing consultants like me was an abdication of responsibility by the officers concerned. After all, they were already being employed to deliver management and leadership functions – they were paid to take difficult decisions. They shouldn't really need external help, however skilled it might be. On one occasion, revealing some of these viewpoints nearly lost me a very lucrative contract. During the interview for the role, I began to raise one or two awkward moral and ethical questions for the authority, until I realised I was annoying my interviewers. I got the job and completed it to their satisfaction, but the question marks still remained.

It turned out I was good at this new job – my billable days each month soon became the highest in the education section. I was bringing a big chunk of income to the company off my own bat. Indeed, I soon realised that the company were 'charging me out' at a very high rate, but the proportion of that rate I saw in my salary was a lot smaller. Combined with the fact that many of our clients asked for me personally to handle their contracts, gave me some pause for thought. After two years in my new role and some significant consideration, I told my boss I was leaving. He was not happy and tempted me with an even more lucrative part-time contract. But I turned him down and, in late 2005, I became '*tim caley consulting*'.

I had learnt something new and significant in my first private sector consulting post: that I had an array of experience, skills and abilities that organisations were willing to pay good money for. This was an eye-opener – immersed, as I had been for so long, in the public sector where everyone earned the same irrespective of their ability or insight. Local youth services up and down the country actually wanted *me* to come and talk to their staff, to help them improve their services, to prepare for inspections, to go out and visit practice, encourage the troops, write it all up with judgements based on observed evidence of practice, and provide them with a report and recommendations. You forget sometimes, when you're in the middle of things, that your own credibility and expertise are not as commonplace as you might imagine. Back in my Hampshire days, I often spoke at conferences and events held by other agencies. After one session with a group of probation officers, I received a kind letter from the seminar's organiser. 'After listening to you speak to us,' she said, 'we knew that you had 'mud on your boots.' When I used to present my credentials in front of my various youth work audiences on my consultancy travels, I felt a tinge of pride and satisfaction in telling them that I had 'come up through the ranks' – part-timer, full-timer, detached worker, youth officer, and head of service (in two places). Even the most recalcitrant amongst the youth work staff teams that I faced were willing to give me the benefit of the doubt with that pedigree.

TRANSLATION SKILLS AND HEALTH CHECKS

In my early consultancy days, I spent much time trying to help workers and managers 'translate' their youth work into the language of government targets and requirements. Mainly this meant the five key Every Child Matters themes and how good youth work practice contributed to them.[54] Most part-time staff worked conscientiously in their own centres, on their own projects or out on the streets in detached work. But some had been in the job a long time and had slipped into comfortable habits. Being stretched or pulled out of their youth work practice comfort zones was hard for them. And often their managers – even when they recognised there was a problem – were not able to help them because they were unfamiliar with current levels of practice, or its quality, because they spent little time visiting it. What both workers and managers struggled with was their new responsibilities to explain how youth work contributed to the national agendas.

This was a feature of my very first job: two weeks in Cambridgeshire working to improve the service's curriculum and support the staff. The plan was simple: we'd agree three or four places to concentrate on for my visits. In the first week, I'd spend a night with each of them, write up my judgements and share them with the staff team the next morning – focusing on strengths, weaknesses and ways to improve or develop. Then in the second week, I'd revisit and repeat the process – producing an overall evaluation for the service at the end. For me, this was fairly basic, bread-and-butter youth officer activity – but doing it with new people, in a new authority, with new and different sets of cultures and practices was a wonderful and rewarding challenge. I loved the work. In truth, it didn't feel like work to me; it was something I really enjoyed doing and looked forward to. Getting out at night to spend time in all the youth centres, talking to practitioners, watching their work with young people, providing positive feedback where I could, suggesting areas for improvement where they were listening, writing it up for them afterwards, returning again to look for signs of change or improvement. My client officer in the authority was delighted with the outcome, too. 'You're worth every penny,' she told me afterwards, 'even just for rekindling the enthusiasm of my part-timers, never mind the curriculum stuff.'

It was the word 'curriculum' that seemed the obstacle to progress; many workers seemed wary of this new 'academic' concept that had been parachuted into their Tuesday night senior youth clubs. So I simply told them, 'Curriculum is what you've been doing with your members every night for the last ten years. It need not be an object of fear or trepidation: just think about the Every Child Matters themes and link them to your centre plans and programmes.' In many places, I found that drafting out a template for a 'curriculum story' they could fill in was helpful. My primary targets here were the responsibilities of youth service managers; their job, I argued, was to help workers demystify the label 'curriculum', demonstrate examples of curriculum stories and explain how existing good practice could be translated to meet the government's required outcomes. To do this properly, I added, they would need to visit practice at night and share challenges from practitioners' viewpoints. Moreover, they must not set impossible targets or produce 'wish lists' – they must only make demands that were achievable by their workers. Most importantly, whatever else they did, they must *never, ever* produce more paper, more forms or more action plans: they had enough of those already.

Linking this kind of external explanation alongside a positive reinforcement of a service's existing strengths bore fruit with workers and managers alike. These may be small gestures but their impact on morale and spirit was important. The point here for me was that good youth workers had nothing to fear from curriculum or inspection as good practice would demonstrate sound impact and outcomes in any of the agendas. Naturally,

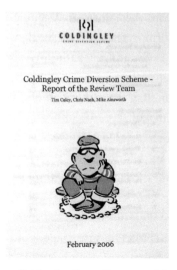

Coldingley Crime Diversion Scheme (Surrey) and Youth Moves (Bristol) project evaluations, 2006.

that assumed a basic familiarity with the Ofsted framework and descriptors of good and inadequate youth work practice. But even the most experienced and able workers sometimes needed help to explain their work in the language that was increasingly required by funders, managers or inspectors. Hence, my development of templates for use by fieldwork staff to show their impact against the new criteria. These tools tried to bridge the disconnection between those people who are perfectly capable of delivering good youth work, but are unaware of – or can't articulate – how they perform such skills. These kinds of checklists and templates were only one small part of the picture, though. They were more about behaviour and 'managing the process' of inspection, especially aimed at part-time staff. The greater focus needed to be on the ability to be *professionally strong* as youth workers. What I meant by this was having the confidence to explain their youth work craft, the range of their programme, the achievements they could evidence and discuss with visitors. Providing this kind of mental confidence seemed as important as writing the guidelines that assisted and supplemented them. Not rocket science, any of this, I freely acknowledge.

Over the next five years I was incredibly busy, working on strategic reviews, health checks, evaluation reports and writing policies and curriculum documents. Preparing for inspection was the most popular project for authorities and the processes involved became familiar practice. I was able to pioneer and develop this model of a 'health check' or 'mock-inspection' programme incredibly successfully. The work reinforced a theme I had proclaimed in my consultancy brochure when I set myself up. My particular interest, I summarised, is in 'delivering pragmatic solutions that engage practitioners at the coal face and in translating theory into the improvement of practice for organisations and their staff.' And for me there was an important bonus – I enjoyed the process from start to finish and was determined to do it thoroughly, professionally and to the highest standards.

Accompanied usually by a small team of three associates, we would arrive in Camden or Wokingham or Liverpool or Staffordshire (and once in Gibraltar), meet with the service and then spend the week visiting some twenty or thirty youth projects – mainly at night – observing the work, grading it and writing up our judgements, and then feeding it back to the management at the end. It was much more informal and helpful than an Ofsted inspection because we were allowed to talk people through the process, explain the meaning of grades, help them to moderate or benchmark their own practice, feed back honestly on the night and, in our final report, prepare a raft of ideas and suggestions for improvements or follow-up. This was something Ofsted never had time for and we were much in demand.

TIM'S TEN COMMANDMENTS

As part of my consultancy package, I had devised a preparation checklist for inspection which I called *Tim's Ten Commandments*. Like Moses, I was very keen that my ten golden rules should be set in stone for practitioners.

It was intended as a light-hearted, but important, reminder aimed at part-time workers, who often bear the brunt of the inspection process and are often the least prepared and confident of all the staff involved. It is incidentally also a truism that part-time youth workers (the majority of whom are women) always do most of the face-to-face work with young people and thus are well placed to know the issues facing them, but are often excluded from the key debates and decisions which inform service policy and delivery. My ten commandments were something I circulated regularly to youth workers: seeing the list adorning the walls of a small youth club in Bracknell Forest one evening where it had been pinned up by the club leader was of great encouragement to me.

However, my best efforts never had much impact on those staff who are skilled at articulacy and rhetoric but quite unable to deliver good practice at a grassroots level – the 'bullshit brigade', as they are sometimes described. I expect they exist in every organisation. It is easy to spot members of this tribe within the youth field. They possess two main hallmarks: first, an ability to talk eloquently and endlessly about the work, allied (second) to the elusive nature of any evidence of actually doing it. Never one to suffer fools gladly in the first place, dealing with these individuals often tried my patience. But I had a tactic that always worked well and gave me great comfort as a manager or inspector. Listening attentively as one of the breed explained the complexities and difficulties of their current workload, I would nod with sympathy and empathy, and then say how much I would like to come out and see them in

TIM'S TEN COMMANDMENTS

1. **Thou shalt be professionally strong**

2. **Thou shalt display a positive, pro-active and "can-do" mentality**

3. **Thou shalt <u>manage</u> the inspection process**

4. **Thou shalt focus on *impact* and *outcomes*, not bang on about content and process**

5. **Thou shalt let young people speak for thee – for they art much better at it than thou art**

6. **Thou shalt remember to tell the story of young people's journeys and achievements**

7. **Thou shalt prepare thy evidence carefully in advance to avoid wasting the inspector's time**

8. **Thou shalt not whinge and moan about thy budget and lack of support from thy managers**

9. **Thou shalt remember that this is only one hour's session – not thy whole youth work life**

10. **Thou shalt smile, be confident and enjoy thyself**

© tim caley consulting 2007

Tim's Ten Commandments, 2007.

action: would 7pm tonight be good, or maybe tomorrow evening? Their faces were a treat to behold.

Less serious, but more common, was the response I often received on arrival at a sparsely populated youth centre. 'You should have been here last night,' I would be told, 'we were packed.' Or its regular variant, 'There's football on the telly tonight, so most of them won't be in till later.' Even in my earliest youth officer jobs, as my staff teams had recognised, I had honed the accuracy of my internal bullshit-ometer. Maybe, too, as some of my interviewees in writing this book acknowledged, youth workers were sometimes their own worst enemies, shooting themselves in the foot by protesting too much, too often and too loudly: over-egging their stories so that ultimately people stopped listening to them.

BUSY TIMES

My busiest years came towards the end of the New Labour government, from 2006 to 2009, when I undertook almost fifty different pieces of consultancy work across the country, including thirteen in London boroughs. As well as a consultant, I was also at various times an interim manager, a teenage pregnancy coordinator, a critical friend and an executive coach. I was covering a lot of ground, too. In Brighton and Poole, I seemed to spend so long working across the council services that I almost become an honorary member of staff. In London, my consultancy jobs spanned Enfield in the north, Merton in the south, Tower Hamlets and Greenwich in the east and Hounslow in the west. Many happy evenings were spent in youth clubs, out with detached work teams and in schools, voluntary organisations and visiting the myriad schemes and projects that worked with teenagers.

Some jobs were brief; others meant I could spend months working alongside youth work staff teams. These were the best times. In Enfield, Ponders End Youth Centre remains a wonderful memory. Indeed, it was here that I came across the Music Project. Run by Mark, a dedicated part-timer and a skilled bass guitarist himself, on three nights per week, the project used state-of-the-art technology and a range of instruments for members to explore different musical cultures. One young woman explained how the project had recently performed at the Barbican to celebrate the Duke of Edinburgh's Award. She went on:

> *We cover and produce all kinds of music. It is down to the young people to decide what song they would like to do. We have many different influences such as Red Hot Chilli Peppers, Jazz, African drumming and more. Our next project is to get involved with local schools and invite them to write music with us.*

Listening to them work together one night on interpreting and rearranging a Beatles number, I became aware of the skilful musicianship of the leader, his ability to get them to explore chords, harmonies and syncopation, and to work together using their different skills – keyboard, guitar, percussion. He had planned this session, preparing music and song sheets for the group, and his interventions were low-key but effective. He encouraged members to play solos and insisted on repeating sections where errors occurred or improvements were needed. The young people present were focused, committed, listened carefully and shared debate with a positive and humorous style. They displayed good mutual respect and tolerance – reflecting well a set of protocols and rules for the Music Project which they themselves had devised. This was one of a number of sessions I highlighted as an example of good practice in the service's new curriculum document, one of a number of 'products' that I created for the service.

ROS AND JULIE: FIRST-CLASS DETACHED WORK

Having a longer time in any patch often led me to discover the more intense and fruitful evidence of great youth work in action.

Like the time I worked in Knowle West, an estate in south Bristol, on an evaluation of a local voluntary project called Youth Moves. One warm summer's evening I was privileged to observe one of the best examples of detached youth work I'd ever seen. Now, visiting and inspecting detached youth work requires some different quality control standards compared to centre-based work. It is the sheer vulnerability of the staff that hits you first, along with the lack of control or boundaries. It is this ability to 'colonise' a space in order to make it safe and youth-work-friendly, and to label yourself as an acceptable, approachable adult figure within it, which seems to me a hard act to pull off.

Enfield Youth Support Service curriculum documents, 2007.

This example shows that skill being deployed by two very clearly experienced detached youth workers in Filwood. What especially impressed me in this observation was the effortless 'stillness' with which the lead worker, Ros, conducted the session. It fully deserves this longer extract:

> *Melvin Square sits in the centre of Filwood – on a warm July evening it is quite a pleasant place: trees and grass provide a small oasis and natural meeting place. But the shutters on Costcutter and the forbidding and run-down appearance of the shops add a certain element of threat. Police cars with their yellow, green and silver-chequered bodywork cruise by on their way to the Broadbury Road pound. Sometimes, their*

drivers glance over to the group of youths playing football and gathering round the two youth workers.

On the grass at the edge of the path, a Calor gas stove is heating up a kettle for making tea. Ros and Julie, the two part-time detached workers, use the tea-making as a contact point to meet and talk to young people in this spot. It's one of a number they use in delivering a detached youth work presence on the estate. The decision on locations is made by the team in response to needs and, sometimes, requests from the police or other agencies. Their work is closely linked to Hengrove School and this partnership brings 'added value'. They are recognised at night in their detached role by pupils they are already working with in school – a valuable and unusual synergy. The work is much appreciated and valued by both the school and the police.

They bring along a large red plastic box – their detached work 'kitbag' – which as well as the stove and tea/coffee supplies, includes mindbender quizzes and other curriculum materials to prompt discussion and use as triggers in their work with young people. Ros uses the upturned red box to sit on for most of tonight. Their presence has attracted quite a large group from the local area by 7pm. Most seem to know them and they know many of the names. They've met before, either at Hengrove School, at Redcatch Park or in other places. The boys kick a football around – against the shops and cars sometimes – but without any malice. There are four new girls tonight – Julie makes a point of talking to them, introducing the detached work team and welcoming them. Without pressure, she explains a little of what they do, how they can be contacted, how they might help. She gives each of them a card with the detached project's contact numbers and information. This card is a good example of its kind.

The session is clearly well-planned and skilfully delivered. Both staff display a natural talent in engaging positively with young people. In the hour-and-a-half-session observed over fifteen teenagers were in contact with them – impressively there were equal numbers of young women as young men. Ros used a quiz game to engage the group in some shared discussion on progress and school achievements. She interposed humour with challenge to reinforce young people's intelligence, sometimes in contrast to their academic exam results, and to point up the problem-solving abilities of group participants. She used examples of littering and the football hitting her car to link environmental awareness, boundaries and mutual respect. And all of this while sitting unmoved on the red box! Julie moved around the group picking up conversations, using the tea-making as a tool for relationship building, supporting Ros when necessary. This was a relatively new group to the team, so the levels of achievement and interaction observed were all the more impressive.

Ros and Julie enjoy their work and treat the young people with respect – in return they have gained the friendship of the young people participating in a natural way. This was very good quality youth work practice.

WORD OF MOUTH

Encouragingly, most of my consultancy work came through personal word-of-mouth recommendation – repeat business, in the jargon. Hearing about how I had helped youth workers sharpen up their practice in Tower Hamlets, the head of Camden invited us into his borough to do a similar job: 'Your reputation precedes you,' he unselfishly informed me. Southwark valued our advice and talked to their peers in Greenwich to invite us to do a similar job for them. Often, within one authority, one job might easily lead to another. In Kensington and Chelsea we started by running a health check, moved on to improve the youth curriculum and finally rewrote the self-assessment review prior to the service's Ofsted inspection. In Enfield, I began one year with 'echo' inspections, curriculum development work, stakeholder consultations and a review of the Duke of Edinburgh's Award Scheme – and I was still there eighteen months later, working on *Transforming Youth Work* and integrated youth support service structures for the council. Likewise, once we'd started in Greenwich, appraisal reports for the youth service were followed by staff conferences, work with the police on Operation Staysafe and evaluating the borough's Youth Card project.

It was in Greenwich that I experienced an instructive, not to mention embarrassing, example of how being in the right place at the right time was often an advantage for a consultant. In the lift at the council offices, working for the head of the youth service, I bumped into a colleague from Kent, now occupying a very elevated directorship role in the council. Catching up briefly, he seemed keen to find out what I was up to these days. 'It's tough here,' he explained to me, 'Government Office London are on our backs all the time about one thing or another. Never a moment's peace, Tim, you're well out of it!' The next morning I had a phone call from my youth officer client. Would I be interested in taking on a temporary role as the borough's teenage pregnancy coordinator? They were very high up the league table of teenage conceptions and their previous coordinator had left a month ago. Government Office were threatening retribution unless they did something quick. Consequently, I added another interesting role to my existing job.

Analysing the lessons learnt from these consultancy projects was not too difficult. I used a simple, rule-of-thumb quality control mechanism to rate the leadership and management of my consultancy authorities. There were the 'smart' ones: these were the services that were up to speed with the latest national policies, were confident and articulate professionally and knew how to deliver good practice using the skills and expertise of their workers. There were not as many of these smart cookies as you might hope. At the opposite end of the spectrum were those I categorised simply as 'not knowing what day it was'. They might be under pressure from their bosses and elected members, they might lack confidence and authority as managers, or they could be living in the past, relying on practices that had long since disappeared. But mainly, and there's no way of sugaring this pill, they were just not as bright nor as capable as they needed to be. The challenge to improve things in these places was therefore much harder than normal.

In London, where I spent the majority of my time, finding good managers and qualified, experienced fieldwork staff was always a problem. The quality of the provision suffered accordingly. The work here was often about setting higher standards, building systems and capacity, or trying to create stability amid the volatility of political contexts and budget allocations. Sometimes, as one of my clients described it to me, the role involved some serious 'spine-stiffening' amongst managers and their teams. Not in a physical sense, but in the need to stay professionally resilient in defending the core business of youth work, as it was constantly buffeted by the winds of change.

One balmy summer evening I arrived at an East London canal-side youth centre around 7pm to find a knot of a dozen or so members waiting to enter the building. 'Isn't it open yet?' I asked. 'Nah,' they all replied, 'she never gets here till about quarter to eight, if we're lucky.' They were right. The part-time worker did arrive to let them in before eight, but the session was due to start at 7.15pm. Inspecting youth work quality is a little difficult when the members cannot even get into their youth club.

In the same London borough, my second visit of the night saw me arrive at a high-street venue at around 8.15pm – to discover the part-time staff closing up the centre, pulling down the steel shutters while the members were milling about in the street, having been told the club was closing early as the staff needed to go home. Things changed when the leader spotted my presence. The shutters were raised and the youngsters invited back in.

Of course, London boroughs were often difficult and turbulent places to work in, with maverick councillors, political extremism, temporary chief executives, and general management confusion and mayhem. These situations must have required levels of personal resilience on the part of beleaguered heads of youth services that not all of them possessed or could sustain. There were times when I heaved a sigh of heartfelt relief when my contract came to an end and I was able to pack up my laptop and leave. Compared to the maelstrom of Hackney and Tower Hamlets, my previous roles in Hampshire and West Sussex appeared oases of tranquillity.

Not all the consultancy support was about local authority youth services. I recall spending a happy few days with the E3 Undercover Gardeners in Bow, East London – tagging along with them as they worked at 'greening' one of the old 1930s Peabody housing estates. Their enthusiasm in combining gardening and horticultural skills, along with the skilled support of their youth workers, made for a joyful experience as an outside 'critical friend' observer. The local residents appreciated the work too, speaking warmly of the project's benefits to the estate and to young people. One spoke of adults 'beaming' as they passed by the youngsters planting shrubs and bulbs. The scheme had improved the look of the estate and had definitely reduced vandalism; young people now 'owned' the communal areas of the estate, she felt, and in addition, they acted as a peer restraint on their friends who might be tempted to damage their work. The testimony of the young people involved told its own positive story:

> *You learn how to garden – digging, watering, and learning
> how plants grow. We learn new skills and looking after the
> environment. We make friends with some new people. They
> [the adults] think we're great – good inspiration and role
> models. It's our area, we've got to look after it.*

Involvement in these kinds of small-scale youth schemes was
important to me in remaining 'grounded' in the reality of the
work – and my ability to measure its benefits and value. In my
experience, it is all too easy to become seduced by the quasi-
academic and intellectual world that sometimes permeates
evaluation, impact and performance measures. This is a debate
that continues to run and run, I acknowledge. But joining the E3
Undercover Gardeners that week over ten years ago reminded me
forcefully of this point. My report on the scheme warned of 'the
difficulties of rigorous assessment of projects that seek to deliver
informal learning and the soft outcomes implicit in work with
young people.' I went on to highlight the dangers of over-reliance
on statistical outputs, inflexible or bureaucratic outcome targets,
and unrealistic performance indicators. My view restated the
importance of judgement, anecdote, stories and common sense
– as long as they are based on a methodology that incorporates a
sound analysis of the evidence of practice, discussions with young
people, observation of the staff's interactions and of residents'
responses. These are just as valuable as the scrutiny of secondary
documentary evidence with its statistical outputs, outcomes and
targets.

'GOING AROUND DOING GOOD'

A regular theme of my consultancy work was the requirement
to deliver the kind of hard-hitting or uncomfortable judgements
that others seemed unwilling or unable to provide. These might

be about the quality of work, about value for money, about the collaboration of partners, about the level of ambition on behalf of young people, or about management and governance competence. Perhaps my northern tendency to call a spade a spade preceded me. Maybe some of my clients were using me as a surrogate to say the things they felt, or wanted to say, but feared they couldn't. In either case, my willingness to provide critical feedback, in every sense of the phrase, appeared welcome, indeed encouraged. I remained confident and comfortable with this task as I knew my process and judgements were sound, based as they were on solid training, standards and the evidence of what I'd seen and heard. So I was more than happy to report and stand by them to councillors and officers in the variety of forums, council chambers and staff conferences involved.

Sometimes clients brought in an external consultant because they disagreed with each other about policy, or there was a split between officers and elected members on the way forward, or, simply, they just didn't know what to do and hoped someone from the outside would 'wave a magic wand' and the problems would all disappear. Here I had to tread more carefully in picking my way through the minefields of policy and personality within an authority. Making robust judgements had to be tempered with a strategy to ensure they might be acceptable and deliverable to the varying factions once I'd gone. Not least to protect and support the youth work staff who are usually left with the job of picking up the pieces in these situations. Occasionally, I accepted that a report might fall on stony ground as its message was too hard to swallow. Then, it would simply be accepted and filed somewhere, and I would be thanked and paid off and not asked back. You win some, you lose some.

From time to time, my consultancy work involved supporting individual colleagues in one-to-one coaching or what I termed 'critical friend' support. Often, I felt on less secure ground in this arena – worrying about what I could offer that would be helpful, new or add value to the individuals or groups that sought my assistance. Maybe I shouldn't have been too anxious. Simply preparing properly, reading all the background documents thoroughly, agreeing the ground rules of engagement, listening hard in the sessions, prompting critically and asking the challenging questions, avoiding collusion or flippancy, setting ambitious targets, treating people seriously and professionally – all of these characteristics seemed to be as much in demand as my other 'health-check' operations were. More than once, colleagues would thank me, saying I had helped them to see things more clearly, or reassured them by 'knowing where they were coming from', or reduced the size of their problems by considering them in a wider context or simply by using the occasional bout of humour or inspired madness to lessen the tension. Half the time I wasn't aware of using all these skills, but was more than happy to accept their verdicts.

This final push to use my youth work experience in helping others was a powerful driver. I enjoyed the challenge of the work, the job satisfaction and that successful feeling of 'making a difference'. It seemed a worthy role to try to improve practice, enthuse staff and celebrate good work and sound leadership. It felt important and rewarding – it was a culmination of my career, building on all the different jobs and experience I'd had in my youth service roles so far. It almost felt like 'going around doing good', as an old-school HMI had once described his role to me back in Winchester in the early 1990s. It was at least trying to give something back 'in the service of youth'.

CLOSING THE CURTAINS

But by late 2009, I was finding it difficult to sustain an optimism about the way youth work was heading nationally. My growing sense of impatience and frustration is reflected in the language adopted in the foreword of a strategic review I undertook in a borough council in the south-west of England. It sounds critical of the local authority and its provision – but in fact the analysis probably reflects what was happening to most services across the country. Youth work was being blown by the competing winds of other agencies' agendas and the government's continuing micromanagement of integrated children's services. I started by noting that, in recent years:

> *...the youth service seems to have 'taken its eye off the youth work ball' – sidetracked by debates on the components of an integrated children's service. It appears to have lost its brand and identity: deliberately re-badging itself with job titles that exclude the words 'youth service' or 'youth work'. Whilst managers chose the titles in an attempt to demonstrate the service's commitment to integration, their adoption was a mistake. Firstly, they are inaccurate because they do not reflect the tasks that managers and workers actually perform. Secondly, they confuse both elected members, who want to support traditional youth work, and youth workers themselves who feel uncertain about what's now expected of them and what the new priorities mean. And thirdly, they create a severe risk of the service being subsumed into and 'disappearing' within the new locality arrangements.*

My suggested solution for the authority was pretty simple. It needed to reassert the fundamental characteristics and values of the youth work contribution to the issues facing young people in the borough:

> *It must be clear on the boundaries and limits of youth workers' roles. It needs to adopt a much tougher line in resisting demands (from councillors, youth centre committees, schools,*

police officers) on work that is not within its ambit. This is especially true on concentrating on work with the target group of 13–19-year-olds. It must move from a re-active and unfocussed style to an articulate, pro-active, policy-led youth service. It needs to be buttressed by much firmer leadership to this end. It needs to have policies that are coherent, pragmatic, fit for local purpose, understood by all, deliverable within budget and whose impact is measurable.

The unreasonable demands being made on the youth service by elected members were a particular cause of anxiety, and I continued in an uncompromising vein, reiterating one of my most oft-repeated themes as a youth work consultant:

The service needs to be much sharper in its use of language – to reflect its clarity of thought; much tougher in the standards it requires – to evidence its impact, outcomes and performance; and much more pro-active in explaining and 'selling' itself to others – instead of just talking to itself. Youth workers need to know what their core business is and when they can say no – and be confident that they will be backed up by their managers when they do. Likewise, elected members need to understand that expecting youth centres to be open every night and youth workers to respond to every social need of teenagers across the Borough is not only unrealistic, it is a dereliction of their duty to set policy priorities for their own authority.

This set of judgements was based on my growing unease about the shifting sands of the youth service landscape nationally. As budget cuts and the austerity agenda gathered momentum and grew sharper for local authorities, the difficulties in sustaining youth work practice and provision became even more acute. Inextricably linked to this was one obvious and ironic consequence: there was little funding available to spend on external consultants either.

ADVISING APYCO

As chance would have it, in one of my closing pieces of consultancy work in late 2010, I was invited to talk to the national committee of APYCO (the Association of Principal Youth and Community Officers) one cold December morning in Birmingham. I'd known the chair from his previous job in a tough authority in the West Midlands. Inviting me along to talk to his new committee on the future scenarios for youth services, he confided that, in his opinion, I was something of an 'éminence grise' in the youth work world. Probably he meant this as a professional compliment.

While my agenda item was about the future, everyone present recognised that the writing was on the wall for the organisation. As budget cuts hit youth work hard, so head of service posts were disappearing, and dwindling membership implied serious loss of income. Not only this, the professional rationale for this experienced leadership group of officers was being swept from under them at the same time. The committee were fully alive to the predicament they were in; there was little I could offer by way of advice or even sympathy. 'Those of you who are currently negotiating your redundancy or pension arrangements,' I suggested firmly, 'need to press for as good a deal as you can get, because things are going to get worse. Those of you who are still too young to retire,' I added more hesitantly, 'may need to revisit your CVs to hone up your transferable skills and to begin some serious networking amongst allied services and professions.'

In order to sweeten the bitter taste of this message, I had composed what I hoped was a humorous series of articles to be circulated in advance to the executive members. It was written in a loose, *Private Eye* style that I thought they might appreciate. This was to be the first issue:

Once upon a time, a long while ago, there was a land of plenty. The roads were paved with gold and flowed with milk and honey. The people were happy and contented. Resourcing Excellent Youth Services had been published for a little while. It was around 2003. Heads of Youth Services across all the regions were joyful and in high spirits. Their budgets were full and some were growing even fuller. There was revenue and capital streams, youth opportunity funds and some hadn't even spent all their Transforming Youth Work budgets yet. The Association of Principal Youth and Community Officers ('Happy Co.' as we all knew it) was bursting with members and subscription income was going through the roof. It was even forming a plan to take over Connexions and maybe Youth Offending and Teenage Pregnancy too. Some Executive members felt they should take over the National Youth Agency.

Everywhere was calm and peaceful. Elected members were tranquil and compliant: they asked no difficult questions. Turbulence was hardly ever felt. But this could not last. People felt it was too good to be true. And, lo, it came to pass they were right. For in 2010, a terrible thing happened. Gordon and New Labour disappeared from the earth. At a stroke, Aiming High turned into a one-year strategy – losing nine years overnight. The new coalition took over and now David and Nick were in charge. They said there was no money left and so everything had to be cut.

And so a terrible time of austerity began. Budgets were slashed. Policy frameworks were broken up and used for firewood. Every Child didn't Matter anymore. Young people weren't important because they were only little. The coalition wanted a Big Society so only big people were important. Heads of Youth Services weren't big enough to join this. It was a tough time and the Board were all frightened at the sight of this new landscape. They liked the old one better. It had budgets, milk, honey and no cuts. The new one had redundancy and redeployment and the National Citizen's Service. This last thing terrified the Board especially, for they had never seen it before. To be continued…

As it happened, this wasn't the last time I acted as a paid consultant or adviser. Some four years later I undertook a brief assignment for the Cabinet Office which marked my one and only claim to being a government 'SpAD' – or special adviser. This involved assisting the Department of Community Affairs by judging local authority applications to the rather awkwardly named *Delivering Differently for Young People* scheme. Travelling up to Whitehall and sitting on panels with two young people representatives and two Treasury staff, I dutifully ploughed through application forms, listened in on telephone conference calls and interviewed officers and members from local councils, all hoping to benefit from the budget available. It was a fairly depressing experience and, while I did my best to bring an experienced practitioner's view to the judgements and decisions, I'm not sure it made much difference to the overall value or benefit of the programmes. There was one powerful application from a project in North Tyneside, though. Unlike some of the other bids, the team from the North East seemed genuinely enthusiastic and keen to change things for young people in their neck of the woods; they had even travelled down to London to speak to the panel personally. We agreed unanimously they should have their £50,000 grant. But ultimately, one of my clearest memories of the experience was the comparison between the imposing external facade of the Treasury buildings and the

Working for Motiv8, Gosport, 2012. Photo: Tim Caley.

tawdry, low-rent office facilities on the inside. And also the fact that each of the Cabinet Office staff carried *two* BlackBerries – one clearly being insufficient to deal with the importance of their information and communication needs.

Part 4

KEEPING THE
YOUTH WORK
FLAME ALIVE

CHAPTER 9

BRINGING THE STORY UP TO DATE

The banking crisis of 2008 marked the beginning of a period of severe financial austerity. The optimism of the ten-year strategy outlined in the *Aiming High for Young People* report published the previous year was kicked into the long grass, along with the Labour Prime Minister, Gordon Brown. With the election of the coalition government in 2010, the signs of austerity and their impact became much clearer.

During the coalition government, a paper entitled *Positive for Youth* was published (in 2011) which sought to develop a cross-government policy for thirteen to nineteen-year-olds. But inevitably it soon disappeared into the multifarious cracks between competing Whitehall departments.[55] Things had always been patchy and inconsistent, but now there was no longer any common national picture or strategy for youth services. Local determination and budget cuts affected authorities and services randomly. The shift from open access (mainly youth centres offering programmes to all) to targeted work (with hard-to-reach, at-risk, detached or other marginalised groups) accelerated. Youth work skills were recognised, but only in supporting social care needs, in early intervention and often on a caseload basis. Some workers took on the job of the old education welfare officers, visiting families at home to track down non-attending pupils. The remaining youth clubs and universal age range provision were commissioned out to the voluntary sector or simply sold off. Some national schemes involved youth work expertise, but many were on a 'payment by results' basis which added complexity and difficulties for local providers, mainly charities and voluntary youth organisations. The government proclaimed its support for the concept of a Big Society, with the private sector, charities and volunteers implementing social policies to help their local communities – thus filling the gap that government support left behind. But the concept proved more rhetoric than reality: an idealistic attempt to urge others to backfill the hole left by the government's withdrawal of state support for young people.

These policy trends should not be seen as new or exceptional – they reflect continuity in the decline of the concept of public service welfare and its replacement by more significant roles for the market and the private sector in service delivery. In her perceptive and persuasive analysis, Tania de St Croix has described this process as the 'marketisation' and 'monetisation' of youth work. Its characteristics include a shift in what youth work and youth organisations look like and how they are constituted: the line between private and public becomes blurred and confused. For example, voluntary youth organisations are now increasingly difficult to distinguish from the business enterprises whose forms and practices they have adopted. They have chief executives, boards, professional website branding and logos; they deliver 'innovative' work with 'vulnerable' groups, providing new 'life chances' for young people. Their officers spend a considerable amount of time writing funding bids and acting as subcontractors and commissioners for national and local government budget streams. They have to demonstrate impact, outcomes, value for money and a measurable social investment return on their work. They are often bidding against other voluntary sector providers, becoming competitors in the contracts marketplace.[56]

In 2013, the government transferred responsibility for the youth service from the Department for Education to the Cabinet Office. This was more than an administrative handover. It represented a symbolic change and an important philosophical rupture with the past. Since the origins of state-supported youth provision, prompted by *Circular 1486: In the Service of Youth*, first published in 1939, youth work had been seen as essentially an educational service. Now, for the first time, it was relegated to a department that looked after all those functions no one else really wanted. Worse was to come. Three years later, in July 2016, the government decided again to move responsibility for the youth service from the Cabinet Office to the Department for Culture, Media and Sport. So youth work's government location and political status had swiftly declined from Education to Cabinet Office to Leisure and Sport. At least one previous Children's Minister, Tim Loughton, was prepared to call this move a mistake which 'takes youth work even further away from education', which he felt was its appropriate location. He added:

> I cannot see how the profile of youth services, which have taken a real battering from local authorities in recent years, can be improved by being absorbed into a department with a very diverse and wide range of responsibilities.[57]

CUTS, CUTS AND MORE CUTS...

But sadly, no one was listening. As early as 2014, a survey of the changing trends in local youth provision, collected from the regional youth work units, recorded the acceleration of youth work decline in national policy and local structures. As the authors of the report depressingly concluded, 'there is little appetite for a statutory youth service.'[58] A similar analysis of London youth services, published by the London Assembly in 2017, showed that since the 2011/12 financial year at least £22 million had been cut from youth budgets, and on average each London council had reduced its funding by nearly £1 million or 36%. More than thirty youth centres have been closed, at least 12,700 places for young people have been lost, youth worker numbers have fallen by 39% and funding to voluntary sector youth work has been reduced by 35%.[59]

Photo: Green Party London Assembly, January 2017.

It was the same elsewhere; from the beginning of the coalition government, Leeds had reduced its spending on youth work by 50%, Sheffield by 57% and Doncaster by 73%, while local authority provision had virtually disappeared from Manchester, Birmingham and Newcastle. In the shire counties in the south of England, the picture was similar. By 2015, Tom Wylie confirmed that over half of all youth service work had disappeared in the last five years. Movingly, he continued:

> *Across the country you will find youth centres shuttered or sold, specialist projects closed or open infrequently with minimal staffing, hundreds of professional youth workers made redundant and their specialist skills lost. David Cameron has closed more youth centres than Harold Macmillan's government built.*

Wylie argued that the years of austerity had shredded local youth services – and these will take decades to rebuild. In many places the sector has returned to the condition it was in during the 1950s. Tony Jeffs, writing at the same time, concurred: 'by the time the process of rolling back public expenditure is completed in 2017, little is likely to remain of the once thriving statutory youth sector… it will become a fast-fading memory.'[60] The omens are not healthy. No white knight is on the horizon. 'Something will turn up' is not a helpful motto to adopt at this point. Deliverance will not be secured by undertaking more evaluations and impact studies – it's too late. And certainly not by demanding that government and business *must* recognise, fund, inspect, deliver and invest in youth work, as the National Youth Agency demanded in 2014.[61]

The outcome of the 2017 general election, which provided a defeat for Theresa May's attempt to obtain a stronger mandate for negotiating Britain's withdrawal from the European Union, gave some commentators renewed optimism, as did the apparent higher turnout of young people voting for hope and change. Public opinion seemed to be swinging away from the Conservatives and their hallmark policy of austerity. It felt, for a while, that there might be a pause – a review, even, of continuing budget cuts to local authority services and a recognition that young people had been suffering disproportionately in jobs, housing and income as a result of austerity policies. Shortly afterwards, the tragedy of the Grenfell Tower fire in Kensington and Chelsea reinforced that shift in opinion. It focused attention on the catastrophic implications of local councils (apparently) subcontracting to builders and contractors, and commissioning out to arm's-length management organisations their civic and social (not to mention moral) responsibilities for the safety and well-being of their own local residents. It remains to be seen whether these events will mark a permanent shift in the political climate. Whether from a youth work perspective, it may lead to greater opportunities to challenge market-led systems and privatised companies in delivering local services to young people. Whether the tide may be turning – or not.

MEASURING THE IMPACT OF YOUTH WORK

Part of youth work's continuing difficulty has been demonstrating the benefits and the outcomes of its work. This has been a regular feature of this story, of course. Measuring 'social impact' is the current terminology, although for the first twenty years of my youth service life it was simply absent or unimportant. As a practitioner in Sheffield – in the youth club, as a detached worker and in the community – no one in authority, certainly none of my managers, ever questioned or challenged the effectiveness or benefits of the work I was doing. It was simply taken for granted that the youth service was generally a 'good thing', part of the council's range of provision like schools, libraries and recreation centres. This was the prevailing culture of local authorities and of the police service, of schools and hospitals in those pre-Thatcher days. No one required evidence of performance or made comparative judgements about the quality or quantity of services. There was no publication of school league tables, hospital waiting lists or police crime-solving rates. The public had no idea about the comparative cost-effectiveness or value for money of these services because no one had ever asked them for the information.

That isn't to say as youth workers we didn't all try hard to deliver a quality service, self-defined usually, or that we were without self-doubt and anxiety about whether we were performing well or making a difference. If you had poor attendances or a bad night in the club, you tended to take it personally, blame yourself and agonise about how to improve your programme for the next session. Out on the streets, when you met no one after two hours in the cold and the rain, you wondered if youth work was the right career choice for you after all.

All this began to change in the early 1990s when youth services firstly had to provide attendance numbers and age ranges, and then begin to justify in more detail the expenditure that they were making in running youth clubs and funding grants to the voluntary sector. At the outset, this was relatively benign and easy to provide. Sometimes, linking the work to crime prevention and social disorder – the 'keeping them off the streets' argument – was a handy way to explain how positive, diversionary activity through youth centres and activities justified the costs. Later, these quantitative explanations had to be supplemented by more sophisticated information about programmes – about what 'issues' the service was tackling and why. This was an early appearance of the curriculum debate. Thus, crime, drugs, alcohol abuse, unemployment, truancy, advice and counselling, after-school and holiday activity, work with girls, arts work, music projects, detached and outreach schemes, rural work – all began to make their appearance in an endless and undifferentiated list of things youth work could deliver. This was dangerous territory because almost nothing could be excluded.

Later, the requirements were extended to include the 'softer' outcomes and achievements that young people gained from their exposure to statutory youth workers. What social skills, what levels of self-confidence, what examples of citizenship and civic engagement could be cited from youth work interventions? Later still, this turned into the need to achieve defined and measurable outcomes – 'recorded and accredited' – against a percentage cohort of the eligible age range. Much statistical effort and analytical gymnastics went into providing these numbers for whoever asked for them. But confidence in their security, their reliability or their usefulness was always limited – especially among the youth workers who had to provide them. What's more, there was always the temptation to put a more positive 'spin' on attendances, successes and outcomes, maybe over-exaggerate the numbers in your monthly returns, secure in the knowledge that there was little interest and even less capacity to verify your data. In my youth work days, that temptation was limited and low-level. Depressingly, there is no doubt that in more recent regimes – where target-driven outcomes are based on statistical returns and/or payment by results – the potential for more systemic manipulation and fabrication of evidence has increased.

Current discussions on evaluating interventions involving young people, especially those at risk, seem to be in a 'revisionist' mode. The challenge to develop robust evidence, collect and analyse relevant data, agree performance indicators and measure social impact and outcomes has been around for many years. Funders and commissioners remain focused on requiring such information from not only statutory providers but, increasingly nowadays, from charities and voluntary organisations working in the field. The inherent difficulty for both groups is that the work is always engaged in 'soft' outcomes and qualitative evidence, which does not always lend itself easily to the harder, 'value-for-money' interpretations that are demanded.

Paul Oginsky, a former advisor to ex-Prime Minister David Cameron, has argued that there is no reliable way of measuring the impact of interventions that seek to assess changes in young people. There is no 'Holy Grail' for measuring character development, motivation, confidence, honesty or other agreed determinants of change, he has said. His alternative is to ask the young people involved themselves to describe if and how they have changed and then to ask for witness verification by those who know them. Being assessed is not as reliable or replicable as being measured, but it is the best approach for this kind of work. It provides strong evidence of change and development in young people and can be conducted in ways which are rigorous, he has asserted.[62]

In similar vein, the Centre for Youth Impact has recently published some new ideas about positive social impact measurements in the field of youth work. The centre has argued that agreeing what constitutes positive social outcomes is the first contentious issue. The second is the assumption that these outcomes are easy to define and evaluate. The third is the hypothesis that 'successful' proof of impact and benefits accruing to the client groups leads to funding or political support. A related characteristic at play here is the reluctance of some of those engaged in programme delivery to 'play the game' of evaluation and impact evidence at all. Some are unconvinced of the impact agenda and processes, others actively resist it – arguing that it is inherently a political exercise linked to the rationing of scarce resources. In these situations, arguments about impact measurement can become essentially a defensive strategy, where impact is confused with quality or philosophy and where publicity or public relations is confused with evidence. The strategy is defensive because there is usually a perceived threat. This threat may be the loss of funding or support if an organisation fails to 'tick all the boxes', demonstrate enough 'robustness' in its evidence, jump high enough over the bars or meet the prescribed external standards.

The assumption that there is only one way to gather quantifiable data, that uses positivist, scientific methods that recognise only what can be 'proven' to be true, linked to a 'theory of change' model which demonstrates a clear cost-benefit analysis and a quantifiable return on social investment, is also open to challenge. Working with troubled teenagers is a practice less suited to the use of such impact tools and logic models, and it is therefore much harder to meet the standards. The challenge is to ensure that our youth work dialogue reflects not defensiveness or threat, but that different cultures and practices can openly share their joint pictures of effects and benefits to young people.[63]

YOUTH WORK STORYTELLING

For many, telling the youth work 'story' has been one response to the dilemma of providing evidence of youth work's benefits – a process particularly associated with the campaign group, *In Defence of Youth Work*. Certainly the range and quality of these stories can be positive and impressive. They often reflect young people's views and voices directly, and they value the process of the work as highly as the outcomes. However, the strategy is hardly a new one and the examples seem identical to the many 'case studies', 'testimonials', 'snapshots of practice', 'voices of youth' and 'youth work that works' examples scattered through the last thirty years of local authority youth service publications – including all those produced by the National Youth Agency, by every national voluntary youth association, and even my own examples produced during my head of service days in the 1990s. These stories have their strengths and their weaknesses. They speak to the committed youth work audience whose willingness to respect and admire them is taken for granted. They are less persuasive to the neutral observer, to the politician, the accountant or the academic researcher and evaluator. They rarely provide accurate quantitative data, nor comparative 'control group' information (a weakness Mary Morse acknowledged in her research fifty years ago), nor are they validated externally by partners, other agencies or academic bodies. Many produce detail and adopt a public relations or lobbying approach in the hope that it will act as a proxy for evidence, impact or value. They only measure what is usually a very short interaction or intervention – normally the youth club weekly sessions – and it is hard to ignore all the other factors which may also be attributed to changing young people's lives. Thus the value of stories in the youth work impact and benefits marketplace is limited.

There has been almost no attempt at longer-term follow-up research that tries to measure the value of youth work intervention over time. Probably the only example of such 'longitudinal' studies of youth work impact is Howard Williamson's *The Milltown Boys Revisited* which was published in 2004, some twenty-five years after his original volume *Five Years*, a study of young people, poverty and crime on a 1970s Cardiff estate. This told the story of a group of over sixty young men – mostly youth club members – with whom he was in contact as the local youth worker. Of this original group, Williamson tracked down half of those remaining and in his later publication he revisited their stories – of personal, family and social relationships, work, and experiences of the criminal justice system. He recorded examples of how his own youth work relationships with them as teenagers had made a lasting and positive impression on many of them through their later lives. Williamson's study is probably unique in that he was able to combine his roles as academic researcher, youth worker, social scientist and policy adviser in telling his story. In that sense, it has a uniqueness and a persuasiveness which other

Howard Williamson, The Milltown Boys Revisited, 2004.

accounts lack. But even Williamson was accused by some of a rather 'rose-tinted' recollection of events and of 'cherry-picking' his examples to suit his arguments. More seriously, it was (and is) still hard to prove attribution, i.e. that it was the impact of his own personal relationships as a youth worker with these teenagers that had made the difference in their lives some thirty years later. We may just have to conclude that the things that make youth work special – its informality and responsiveness – also make it particularly unsuited to pre-planned outcomes, impact assessment or monitoring technologies.

THE ROLE OF THE STATE DECLINES

The idea of youth work as a distinctive means of intervention with young people remains important and accepted still. We know that young people still want places to go, things to do and people to talk to. But the social context that links the responsibility of the state to delivering such interventions is no longer recognised. The national structure and continuing employment of people called 'youth workers', with full- and part-time jobs within local authority 'youth services' – that seems to me to be gone, probably forever. Local authority youth work is no longer a viable career option. And not just because of budget cuts or political opposition; the fact is that the state is no longer willing or able to accept the idea that young people need or want the kinds of intervention provided by such state employees. At one level, this is a crude decision that the country can no longer afford what I've previously described, rather scornfully, as 'ping-pong on the rates'. As youth work jobs disappear, inevitably the number of students on youth work training courses falls as well. To a record low, in fact – in 2015/16 only 673 students were on youth and community work courses across the country – less than half the number (1,277) recruited six years earlier. And of those who graduated, only 3% took up a local council youth services role, according to the National Youth Agency.[64]

What we are seeing now reflects a broader – and harsher – interpretation of the limit of the state's responsibility for children and young people. The current received wisdom runs something like this: children are the responsibility of their parents or carers; if they require out-of-school facilities (leisure, sports, music), these will be provided by private sector companies – at a price. If they have problems, then they can access telephone help lines, counselling and online advice, peer support, charities and voluntary services, or whatever might be available locally. If they break the law or get drunk or do drugs or behave in an antisocial manner, then they become the responsibility of the police. This caustic social nostrum is at the most destructive and negative end of the spectrum conjured up by my title *Keeping Them Off The Streets*.

And so that particular form of distinctive youth work practice – 'open-access' youth work, whose historical home has always been the youth club – is in danger of extinction. Budget cuts have exacerbated the policy shift: a focus on targeted youth support, on formal and structured practice with individual young people, rather than the more universal and flexible forms of youth work intervention, is now the preferred option. And as the pool of open youth work expertise and experience inevitably diminishes, as the knowledge and ability to recognise good practice disappears, as providers are now located in professional backgrounds like housing, social work or the evangelical churches – so youth workers and youth work itself risk becoming a threatened species. The harder it is, therefore, to reach agreement on those coherent and compelling arguments in support of the benefits of youth work, because there is no longer a sufficient 'critical mass' of professional expertise to understand and to put forward the arguments. Or to put it another way, there are not enough people left who know what good youth work looks like.

BUT GOOD YOUTH WORK SURVIVES

Reacting to these critical policy shifts is not easy. Commentators have focused on returning youth work's role to a 'secular, civic responsibility', one that engages with the lives of young people in ways that prioritise their interests, rather than those of the state or corporate sector. Tony Jeffs puts it this way: 'we can only begin rebuilding a battered youth service when that task is linked to the mission of rebuilding the battered public realm.' Tom Wylie echoes this analysis, noting that little is likely to change for the better in many young people's lives, or in what youth work can do to support them, until central and local government rediscover their own enabling and leadership roles. Continuing, he notes that 'young people and their needs will still endure. It is especially incumbent on those in leadership roles in youth work to develop more coherent, consistent and compelling arguments to campaign on their behalf.'[65]

That sentiment would elicit support and applause from most of us. Thankfully, there are positive and encouraging signs amidst the difficulties – places where recognition of the value of youth work remains embedded in local councils and their elected members, and where good practice survives. In Brighton and Hove, for example, where in 2017 a vociferous and well-organised campaign led by young people to resist cuts in the youth budget was successful. In Warwickshire, where the use of stories to raise the profile of youth work's worth has provided a rallying cry to defend provision. In Portsmouth, where the youth service has been happily located in the Housing Department for many years. This arrangement has proved a success: youth centres have stayed open for universal provision, funding has been protected through the use of housing revenue income, and the policy focus on the needs of young people on local council estates has worked well. In Derbyshire and Nottinghamshire a youth work alliance (D2N2) has driven a successful defence of open youth work, and in Nottinghamshire itself the council has protected funding for an open-access youth offer.

In some areas, structural alternatives – the evolution of 'mutual' enterprises, comprising employees and young people, to run youth services – have been trialled, mainly in London but also in Devon and Knowsley. The theory is that mutuals will preserve a public service ethos while attracting private money to supplement dwindling state funds. But the jury is still out on whether these models will last – or, more likely, whether they will ever be sufficiently robust to resist the reality of continuing budget reductions, or long-lasting enough to provide continuity of employment for their employees and high-quality services for their young people. In Knowsley, youth worker Sandra Richardson transferred her team from the council into a mutual in 2014, but she admits they are struggling to secure new revenue streams. 'It's a flawed assumption that if youth services were to spin out they would flourish in the open market,' she says. 'It's a really difficult market and, at the end of the day, we're not businesswomen; we're youth workers trying to run a business.'[66]

Also on an optimistic note, while there may no longer be full-time jobs for 'youth workers', there are plenty of opportunities for those with youth work training, qualifications and skills to find work with young people: work in a wide range of projects with children and young people, within the voluntary and charitable sectors, in some schools and some parts of Children's Services Departments. In the youth and community work course at the University of Brighton and at similar institutions nationally, some 98% of the graduates found employment in 2016. Youth work skills are still valued and sought after – but the work may simply be with different agencies and in different settings than in the past. It is encouraging that the voluntary sector is stepping into the breach left by the decline in local authority services in such a big way. Our analysis of 'doom and gloom' needs to be mitigated by the impact of their positive efforts across the country – sustaining open-access youth clubs, maintaining local detached work and counselling projects, providing employment to trained and qualified youth workers, and working valiantly to continue a high-quality 'youth offer' in local communities.

KIRSTY IN GOSPORT

For Kirsty, working for Motiv8, a voluntary youth charity in Gosport, south-east Hampshire, selling the benefits of youth work is not a problem. The charity's building is located amidst an industrial estate of second-hand car dealers, garages, tyre fitters, welders and recycling units close to Gosport town centre. It is a modern, brightly coloured and open-door oasis amidst an otherwise bleak landscape. Expanded last year with capital savings and a 'Buy a Brick' fundraising campaign, the centre means the world to its users, staff and their partners in Gosport. Kirsty is especially proud that young people come through the door all the time, to share their problems, their successes and their worries. Her office walls are adorned with her personal awards and certificates, but it is the displays of quotes from young people she likes the best.

Her staff team are much in demand from local secondary schools: 'They're crying out for our help and support,' she says. The charity provides one-to-one and group sessions working with Year 10 pupils affected by issues such as depression and mental health, bullying and sexual exploitation (especially online), and anger management. Kirsty explains that many of these pupils – especially the young women – seem vulnerable and lacking in emotional intelligence: they struggle to recognise or establish healthy relationships with their peers and with adults. The charity regularly receives referrals of teenage and even primary school pupils, permanently excluded because of behaviour problems. In previous times, such vulnerable young people would have been supported in-house by the school's inclusion department, but budget cuts mean many of these no longer exist. Coupled with a two-year waiting time for Child Adolescent Mental Health Service referrals and similar long delays for implementing Education Health Care plans for these youngsters, turning to Motiv8 for help is an attractive option.

The staff possess both relevant expertise and effective skills, their interventions work well, and it is cheaper and more cost-effective than the alternatives. Her team have developed programmes that mix both hard and soft social skills (accredited by Ofqual) which head teachers lap up. There is a waiting list for the charity's services in these arenas. Here, youth work can certainly still provide a marketable commodity and a set of particular skills that are recognised and in demand by other professionals.

Kirsty acknowledges that the financial climate is more difficult now and she needs to work to 'repackage' the programmes on offer to meet the exacting needs of her varying client organisations. There are 'translation' skills in play here. Just as the secondary schools have pooled their budgets to allow them to afford a full-time youth worker, so Kirsty notes that sometimes she needs to 'change my language depending on the person in front of me'. Here, both partners reflect the new pragmatism in sustaining services to meet young people's needs. Even more encouragingly, Kirsty is running three 'open-access' youth centres in her patch. They're only open one night a week and staff are only employed for three hours each. The funding comes from a variety of sources – the county council, the Police and Crime Commissioner, the borough council mayor's fund – and it all involves significant administrative bureaucracy, from the annual funding applications to the different outcome and reporting requirements. Needless to say, all this makes life brittle and long-term stability a problem. But the clubs are popular and well attended, and the members benefit from links with the charity's range of other youth provision through their part-time staff. There is a cost to Kirsty as the manager, though. Every year, she confesses that, 'I have to go through the budget and see if I can afford my team for another twelve months.'

But Kirsty is not fazed by the impact and evaluation agendas. Her organisation has impressive and long-established monitoring and quality control systems in place to handle the hard statistics.

Kirsty and young people at Leesland skateboard park, Gosport.
Photo: Matt Stevens, November 2017.

The 'soft' outcomes and achievement requirements are supplied through a 'case study' approach, again well embedded in the practice of her staff teams. Her only frustration is the problem of capturing the external data from other agencies – schools, police, councils – all of whom seem strapped for the staff resources to supply them. And she does worry that the youth work role is threatened by the focus on the 'sharp end', the 'heavy-duty' cases, the most vulnerable. 'Sometimes, it feels like youth workers have turned into social workers,' she says. 'We're involved in family plans, team around the family meetings, and we act as lead professionals for ensuring all the agencies do what they say they're doing. It's a positive engagement in raising the credibility of the charity's capacity, but the downside is that it's a diversion from the main role and function of youth work.' Sighing, she concludes, 'But you have to be in it to keep the staff employed in the first place.'

As to the longer term, she remains optimistic and upbeat for youth work's future. Eventually, she feels, 'the circle will come around again – and I'll still be here to see it.' In the meantime, she is packaging her youth work in bite-sized chunks for different providers, plugging the gaps perhaps, but as Kirsty succinctly puts it, 'the needs haven't gone away – just some of the youth workers.'

One of her young volunteers, Steph, would agree wholeheartedly with that verdict. Steph first got involved with Kirsty and her team when she was thirteen. Now, five years later, she is a volunteer youth worker at one of the junior clubs on the Rowner estate and completing her Level 3 health and social care qualification. Along that journey, she took part in one of the charity's many music events, this one called *Breathe – Legal High Project*. Recording that experience, she described it as 'hands down one of my best achievements.' Kirsty shows me the Facebook message Steph sent her recently:

> *Motiv8 is so much more than just a charity to me. They've non-stop helped me since I was 13. Now being 18 and working with them is me giving back to them all the time and effort they gave me. So I just want to thank all of the team for everything over the last 5 years. Shoutout to Sarah for the harmonies...*

Smiling, Kirsty reflects on these words. 'Steph was one of those who came back after five years for a cup of tea,' she recalls. 'I guess she's one of my rewards in doing this job.'

CHAPTER 10

CONCLUSION: WHITHER A FRAGILE OCCUPATION?

Working with young people remains a rewarding but fragile occupation. Insecurity continues to be a key element of the job description. Predictions of the demise of the youth service remain a constant. The earliest reference to youth work as a 'Cinderella' service was recorded in the 1980s – or maybe it was ten, or even twenty years earlier. It has been in a state of crisis or 'at the crossroads' for as long as I've been involved with it. Even one of the service's foremost writers, Howard Williamson, concluded almost twenty years ago that:

> ...the youth service may be a Cinderella service which has never reached the ball... its history is a complex one of political detachment, indifference and disinterest, role ambiguity and rudderless direction.[67]

Yet youth work has many rewards: moments of rare pleasure and elation, potent examples of good practice, stories of significant successes and achievements for young people. In youth work practice, it would seem, the height of the 'highs' is matched only by the depth of the 'lows'. But it never seems as stable or satisfying as other, more 'normal' jobs. That sense of insecurity related to youth work is comparable to other roles that require a similar investment of personal adrenalin and vulnerability – acting or writing, perhaps. We know there is a shared and enduring ethos or philosophy underpinning youth work. We know that there is a body of expertise – values, knowledge, skills – owned by professional youth workers. For some these are innately present; for others they have to be learnt through training, practice and experience: that expertise is the 'light' that practitioners bring to their practice. From time to time, gifted individuals demonstrate additional happy attitudes and inspiration that add to the mix – bringing 'light upon light', so to speak.

But it is still true that youth work has rarely been seen or treated as a wholly professional activity. On the contrary, many youth workers continue to encounter deeply embedded dismissive perceptions of their work, fed in part by the informal style, the hazy public understanding of its function and the continued lack of a legal basis for the work. The self-image of youth workers themselves sometimes reinforces these views. Rarely looked on as a profession, youth work is perceived by others as simply the provision of recreation and activities: 'playing table tennis', 'youth clubs', 'trips and residentials'.

Even where youth work is accorded a valid and valuable role, workers sometimes feel they are treated merely as a subset of other practices – a relatively low-cost substitute for other professionals. 'I just feel as though I'm a cheap teacher,' as one recalled. Another concluded, 'We've become a reactive service, always fitting into something else… never recognised for what we are.' Anguished cries of this kind are far from new, though some might argue they also represent another, less attractive youth work trait – that of professional protectionism in the face of legitimate challenges to demonstrate impact and effect.

Even the most powerful examples of recent youth work practice have suffered from this same syndrome. Jayne Senior recalls, in her 2016 account of the work of the project *Risky Business* – which tirelessly supported young people suffering from sexual abuse in Rotherham over many years – that the staff were routinely discounted as 'just youth workers: clueless amateurs…'[68] The subsequent report on Rotherham Council corroborated the accuracy of her perception, but repudiated it with vigour, celebrating the benefits of the youth work contribution she and her colleagues had made:

> *…the contribution that youth workers made was not properly appreciated or valued. They were not accorded the professional respect given to social workers. Too often the information they gleaned was ignored and not acted upon. They spoke uncomfortable truths that no-one wanted to hear. They undertook critical work that is now missing from the Council.*[69]

VALUED PROFESSIONALS OR CLUELESS AMATEURS?

The youth workers in Rotherham who, against the odds, spoke those uncomfortable truths on behalf of young people did indeed display an instinctive set of professional standards and values. Not to mention bravery. Some observers may not have accorded them professional status and their arsenal of skills and expertise may have seemed limited, but 'clueless amateurs' they certainly weren't.

Yet it is a revealing phrase, and one that resonates with my own youth work experience (and the themes of this story) over the decades. I have often felt some discomfort, a sense of anxiety and insecurity, ambiguity even, in many of my different youth work roles, especially at times of crisis, threat or bleak doubt. To begin with, my lack of initial qualification as a youth worker and the feeling of being something of a fraud, an amateur indeed, compared to my more academic and well-trained colleagues. Allied to that was a clinging fear of suddenly being 'found out' or 'exposed'. The uneasiness of my early transition from youth worker to manager, and the apparent consequential loss of my street credibility with the workforce. The realisation that as a new county officer, my role had shifted irreversibly from 'lobbyist' to 'lobbied' and, ever afterwards, everyone I dealt with saw my job title first and their perceived stereotypes about it, rather than seeing me. Plus my chances of engaging directly with young people had narrowed exponentially. And finally, the sense of 'poacher turned gamekeeper' which accompanied my work as an Ofsted inspector and consultant, and the invariable doubts and moral dilemmas that went with those duties.

Conceivably, it is simply that my various posts have unavoidably meant playing different roles – wearing different hats for different audiences – and switching regularly and seamlessly from one to the other, often on the same day, but trying all the time to be on the side of young people and to treat them as adults. Hobnobbing with royalty and the aristocracy one minute, chairing public conferences and meetings the next; plotting tactics to persuade councillors to increase our budget one day, spending a night with teenagers on the Basingstoke detached work bus the next; writing learned articles for *Young People Now* and the *Times Educational Supplement* one month, serving behind the coffee bar at the school youth wing the next. More than once, these shifting roles caused me the occasional bout of dizziness or worse – 'cognitive dissonance' is the official term. Often they involved a degree of public performance and presentation – of playing a part – in front of a variety of audiences and interest groups. This contained an element of artifice, certainly, but not, I would argue, artificiality.

Learning to adapt to each new audience involved finding the appropriate toolkit and techniques to utilise. Some were easier than others, some became second nature, some proved more difficult or impossible to achieve. Especially when there is an innate suspicion about those adults, particularly in leadership positions, who seem to be on the side of young people. So straddling different cultural boundaries and professional groupings, adapting flexibly to the demands of all those diverse 'constituencies' that Liz Hoggarth described so impressively in the 1990s, has been a decisive and vital feature in all my jobs. I've always been a bit suspicious of people who are constantly *certain* about things – convinced of the efficacy of their simple solutions; especially when they express those convictions with an unshaken or messianic fervour. Sometimes, perhaps, I was just sitting on the intellectual or policy fence, stuck in an uncomfortable no man's land betwixt and between sets of competing cultural assumptions about 'youth' and their place in the world. In these circumstances, operating in a way that tried to keep faith with young people seemed the simplest and most natural way to behave: an unconscious role-modelling of good youth work practice, perhaps. And I always needed to feel able to sleep at night, satisfied that whatever had happened during the day, my conscience was clear.

There is a kernel of significance about youth work and its advocacy that I'm wrestling with here. In this context of professional ambiguity and uncertainty, how best to become accepted as valued professionals welcomed to the policy table, rather than dismissed as clueless amateurs with nothing to contribute? It may be the case that defending youth work's fragile contribution needs more than just the voices of practitioners. Strong leadership and optimistic, agile and 'switched-on' managers are a valuable part of the picture, too. Their contribution to providing sound and persuasive evidence of the benefits of youth work is vital. Sometimes, to be plain, practitioners themselves are not the best candidates for that advocacy role. The strength of their arguments needs to be aided, buttressed through a form of benign interpretation and translation.

It reminds me of those photo calls that global leaders hold during conferences, when each brings along a self-effacing official sitting behind their right ear, translating the mutual language of diplomacy. My role as a youth service manager was often like that: capturing from the youth workers the issues, the challenges, the positives and the possibilities of their work, and then rewriting, re-explaining and translating it all (in my head or on paper) for a different audience that didn't speak the youth work language. It might often be a demanding audience: one that required explanation, accountability and evidence. But equally, it was often a more sympathetic one – keen to help but unsure how to respond, unclear as to what they were backing and needing reassurance about how it might improve things. Either way, the translation normally required a 'filtration' process, the avoidance of misunderstandings, separating the wheat from the chaff, sieving out the bits of belligerence so that the clear nectar of youth work liquor gleamed more brightly.

STRATEGIES FOR A STRONGER FUTURE

Like many, I remain saddened that youth work's potential role seems to have been deleted from consideration as part of the state's repertoire of provision for young people. That seems to me wrong and mistaken, for good youth work can always play a valued and valuable part in the jigsaw that makes up the national picture of services for young people and their communities. Manifestly, too, I still endorse David Blunkett's view, expressed fifteen years ago as Secretary of State, that youth workers:

…help young people to develop the personal skills they need to make a success of their lives; there are few better ways of delivering change than through good youth work.

But I am not downhearted: like Kirsty, I'm convinced the circle will come around again. Our shared set of youth work values, expertise and principles is more important and influential than we think. Through applying the same ethos and ideals we cherish with young people – our willingness to listen, our focus on help and support, our lack of 'side' or agenda, our advocacy role on behalf of young people, our neutrality and our compassion – we may be better able to shape our contribution at the current political and strategic tables. It is by using our service's history of vulnerability, by capturing our ethos of fragility, that we may be able to bring more influence to bear on the current debates. Paralleling our youth work skills in our tactics in the current arenas may serve us well. This may appear at first sight a counter-intuitive strategy, but it is based on tried and tested experience and success in defending and growing youth work practice across the country.

The paradox of the youth service is that without statutory authority, and often with ambivalent professional credibility, it provides a distinctive and successful approach in its work with young people that other agencies cannot achieve. That distinctive role – that very *lack* of authority – gives it an advantage and a unique strength. Using that vulnerability adroitly allows the best youth workers to be accepted and recognised by young people in an unusual, personal and idiosyncratic way. There is some subtle process at play here: one that involves mutual approval and an endorsement of parity. As Ray Gosling reminded us, the youth leader must be simultaneously *an accomplice on the inside and a witness on the outside.* Accomplished youth practitioners learn to handle that duality spontaneously, enabling them to 'reach the parts that others cannot reach' in gaining young people's trust and establishing positive relationships with them. These concepts are not simply slogans or sound bites: they are intrinsic to our craft. This is not merely about running youth clubs, delivering leisure-time activities, reducing crime and antisocial behaviour, keeping them off the streets – important though all those are. These are critical ideas that reflect our philosophy, our credibility, our underpinning values, our expertise and our techniques. We must try and harness them more consciously and effectively to demonstrate how powerful they can be; powerful not just in improving the lives of young people, but also in adding social capital, value and cohesion to the communities in which they live. That is what the best youth work does – that is what youth services can deliver. Here is one strategic key that may help to unlock our influence and advocacy for its benefits in the future.

If our task is to agree a way forward in reimagining and restructuring (as some writers have described it) youth work delivery, then it needs to be realistic, pragmatic and to demonstrate hard-headed thinking. To begin with, 'reimagining' is a rather warm, fluffy, youth work kind of word whose meaning is pleasantly opaque. 'Warm words butter no parsnips,' as the saying goes. And what does restructuring mean? Are we proposing a return to local council funding and control, or not? Where would the money come from? How would it be allocated, managed and governed? And would anyone left in the 'youth services' field agree on how to spend it, anyway? I've already argued that a return to historical arrangements for direct national or local authority funding for youth services remains unlikely. Turning the clock back seems an implausible option.

Our responses must build on current hopes and positive momentum. At present, practitioners and commentators alike are keen to capture harbingers of better times for youth services. Some argue that a policy of more than ten years of austerity is ripe for review and reversal. Others point to the social consequences of the decimation of local youth provision across the country –

the increases in gangs, in knife crime, in alienation and in the absence of positive provision for teenagers and their families. This impetus has already prompted some harder and more astute thinking by commentators on youth policy. Bernard Davies has acknowledged that the current structure of local youth provision will have completely disappeared by 2020, and accepts the need to 'break out of the neo-liberal mind set to re-imagine more appropriate state responses for youth work.'[70] That marks an important step change in opinion. The language of simple, but often politicised phrases and slogans, like the 'welfare state', the 'neo-liberal state' or the 'austerity state', no longer seems helpful to us in this discussion. Life has become more complex than that. Commentators acknowledge the new challenges facing the 'youth sector' – although they are not agreed on the membership of such a sector, or indeed if it still exists at all. We are now in a climate that requires proof from service providers that they can deliver quantifiable yields in terms of 'well-being' or 'welfare improvement' to justify the investment of social capital provided by the government directly or (more likely) by subcontracted government agencies, networks and commissioners.

The marketplace in which youth provision needs to compete to attract funding or investment requires high-quality and successful programmes that engage young people, have discernible outcomes and reduce the cost to the state in terms of service or welfare.[71] Those imperatives will need to drive the context of any future consensus for a way forward. But, as I have argued relentlessly at conferences with youth staff, policymakers and others, this is not such a difficult task. We are perfectly capable of providing the evidence of our profession's achievements and successes in all these arenas. We already have the skill sets and capability, the leaders and managers, the practitioners with expertise and experience, the people with the passion and energy to make a difference to all these social issues and in all these marketplaces.

The scope of those arguments needs to include all the extensive, hard-won and well-written evidence of good practice of the kind recounted in the pages of my story. It will need to incorporate all the skilful, tactical and pragmatic advocacy that explains the benefits and outcomes of youth work practice to policymakers and funders alike, using their culture, their language and their expectations. Delivering that advocacy needs a tenacious ability to function professionally and credibly with myriad different audiences, along with a resilience and repertoire to manage consistent performances. Not an easy remit, but mastering the art and handling the interpretations adeptly can bring a powerful cachet and credibility to our cause. Driving our strategy, we need to be much shrewder, much tougher, much more tactically astute.

My inclination (in this story and elsewhere) has always been to adopt a non-political approach. Party-political rhetoric or protest deliver precious little impact in the task of winning friends and influencing people. Our advocacy for our craft needs to reflect a much smarter approach: one that avoids overtly politicised polemic, but argues compellingly – on the basis of evidence, confidence and strength – for the benefits of good youth work. Granted, all this takes time and effort: it requires collaboration and consensus, it must eschew factionalism, empire-building, over-exaggeration or deluded romanticism. Building credibility and political influence for your professional expertise is a painstaking, laborious and demanding task – and often a long-term one – but it is a necessary requirement if youth work is to play a role in the future marketplaces and within the new arenas.

KEEPING THEM OFF THE STREETS: REPRISE

Of course, in writing this story it is inevitable that some current issues are missing. My fieldwork experience and most of my management roles predated the internet, the digital world and social media. It is fruitless for me to pretend that I can fully understand, far less incorporate into this volume, any cogent analysis of the impact of these technological changes on young people's lives, based on my own experience of practice. (I'm conscious, too, that this story is focused on England: youth work in Wales, Scotland and Northern Ireland is also outside my scope and experience.) But some things are probably still the same. There are enduring issues for young people which impact just as powerfully in today's world of WhatsApp, Twitter, Instagram, Facebook and Snapchat as they did in my world of schools, homework and *Top of the Pops* back at Greenhill-Bradway Youth Centre in 1971. The language, the definitions, the means of communication, the pressure, the speed and the immediacy are all different now – driven by the online world which predominates in young people's social interactions and lifestyles.

But at heart, young people's needs, hopes, ambitions, feelings, challenges and experiences are not dissimilar. That growing-up process, that transition from adolescence to adulthood, remains a potentially fraught journey for all of them. Remarkably, young people are certainly more open, more honest, more aware, more sensitive, more ambitious, more generous and more confident now. And in parallel with those strengths there are (probably interrelated) difficulties; they are more vulnerable, more at risk, more under pressure to achieve or conform, more open to abuse (emotional, physical and sexual), more likely to be unhappy or disappointed, more prone to mental and physical illnesses. And more of these issues exhibit themselves through the online world as well as in the real one. Moreover, the gap between success and failure may have widened for many young people, reflecting the wider social and cultural divisions in our society.

More than twenty years ago, I summarised my own personal credo, or at least the 'stuttering steps' towards it described earlier, about the benefits of youth work. I still like these words (and I certainly still stand by them), although they may have to serve as a form of epitaph or finale:

> *Youth work complements the formal education system by aiming to support the personal development of young people through programmes of informal or social education. Uniquely, it works with young people on their terms to help them face and respond to issues in their own lives. It is an educational process – it gives young people access to learning. It works positively with many partners to enhance the range and variety of services for young people. It can act as an advocate for young people, but prefers to enable them to speak for themselves. It starts from the position that developing the abilities and confidence of young people as an investment in the future should be a cornerstone in the development of a national youth policy.*

Keeping Them Off The Streets, I have argued in this book, is not simply a stereotyped pejorative response by adults and governments to dealing with the perennial 'problem of youth'. It reflects a more affirmative concern about youngsters, about their needs and about the hard process of growing up that is a commendable trait in a sometimes-unsympathetic adult world. That may be a reflection of the eternal optimism that lies in the heart of every youth worker. But my story reflects another truism – young people still provoke the same stereotypes amongst some adults and they all still have the same needs; at least throughout the decades of my experience, whether it was Pete, Ian and Plug at Kelvin Youth Centre in 1973; the 'Emmer Greenies' young women in 1983; the Highclere Boys' Brigade troop in 1993; the Undercover Gardeners in 2003; or the Motiv8 young people on the streets of Leigh Park in 2013. And there are plenty of youth centres still available and plenty of teenagers who need them and might fill them. What's more – amazingly

– grassroots youth workers are still surviving and still passionate about their work; especially those idiosyncratic and committed part-timers and volunteers whose work populates the pages of this story, although, regrettably, sometimes invisibly so. Many of those part-timers are women, and they have played a leading role in my story as well. All my exemplars of good youth work have been heroines – Detta in Emmer Green, Marilyn in Portsea, Ros and Julie in Knowle West and Kirsty in Gosport. Many others may be nameless, but their clubs, projects and detached work have been a constant memory and inspiration for this narrative. I salute them, one and all: they have been the bedrock of so much high-quality provision for young people. Their enduring commitment and engagement increase my confidence and hope for the future.

CINDERELLA AT THE CROSSROADS AGAIN

Through the decades, we have constantly been anxious about youth work as a profession and the intellectual tradition and academic rigour that underpin our craft. We have had to acknowledge that our arsenal of skills may be limited. Often, quality and achievement are dependent solely on the personality and ability of individuals, not organisations. We may not yet have cracked the dilemma of measuring impact and outcomes effectively. But we need to recall and rehearse Tom Wylie's adaptation of some words of Robert Kennedy in reinforcing our youth work mission:

> *…it is the great task of youth work to see injustice and try to end it, to see prejudice and strive to overcome it, to see potential and seek to nurture it.*[72]

The best youth work has always been both unique and dynamic. Unique in that it sustains that distinctive stance of trying to work with young people on their own terms and from their viewpoint;

dynamic in that it must constantly adapt to the changing needs of the young people it seeks to attract and serve. The highs can certainly be powerful and addictive: this book is partly written to salute and rejoice in those, wherever I have found them. We need to hold on to those feelings, especially at times of despondency, political volatility and an unappealing outlook. As this book is written, Cinderella is once again at another set of crossroads. We need to accept that – fragile an occupation youth work might be, but it is still an investment in young people that is sorely needed. We all need to play a role in keeping the youth work flame alive and burning brightly.

EPILOGUE

It's February 2014 and a cold night out on the Leigh Park estate, north of Portsmouth. I'm standing outside The Original Place, a youth club built in the 1980s to serve local teenagers. The building is next to Off the Record – a youth counselling agency that's also been around for thirty years or so in the area. They're both in some jeopardy now as budget cuts are threatening closure. The council has commissioned out the youth work to a voluntary organisation – Motiv8 – which is doing its best to keep projects going for local youngsters.

I'm waiting for Mark – he's the Motiv8 detached team leader for tonight's session. He's sorting out his kitbag of torch, leaflets, condoms and other stuff. There are six or seven teenagers sitting on the low brick wall outside the club, coming and going, chatting to each other, cadging fags and sipping out of Coke cans, as teenagers do. They seem like regulars, and know Mark and each other. They're not so sure of me – unsurprisingly, as I'm tagging along tonight with the detached team as part of a consultancy job with Motiv8. My role is evaluating their 'youth hub' contract with the council. At nearly sixty-seven, I'm rather old for winter detached work, but they're willing to accept me happily enough.

We set off up the road and spend half an hour walking the streets: too bitter for many to be around, but Mark exchanges hellos with one or two we pass by. Soon we find ourselves in the play park; it's almost pitch-dark here, the street lights seem to be turned off once you're out of the main roads. Mark meets a group he's seen before. He talks to them about current concerns: job interviews, school, anything they could do with. He needs his torch to show them some programmes of local activities they might be interested in. It's very cold and I'm freezing now. I'm seriously impressed with Mark's perseverance and tenacity in following up leads, gently interrogating the young people and offering advice and encouragement where appropriate. He clearly has excellent relationships with these teenagers.

They plan to carry on along another part of the estate for half an hour more. I decide I've seen enough, thank them, say goodbye and head back to my car at the youth club. Later, I write a brief judgement of the session for my report:

> ...*in less than an hour out with the Havant detached team, over 20 young people were contacted outside The Original Place club and in Warren Park; most were already known and greeted by name by staff; advice on employment, apprenticeships, sexual health and promotion of youth hubs was given: a very positive and impressive session.*

This was probably my last session on the streets in detached mode, almost forty years after I started out myself way back in 1975. I still enjoyed the night and the buzz it gave me in meeting new young people, listening to the things that concerned them and seeing the staff offering their unreserved help and support. Even though I was strictly in 'observer' mode, it was good to see that some things never change.

A NOTE ON HISTORY AND SOURCES

My first two degrees were in history, so I should know that anyone who writes a historical and autobiographical story needs to be held to account on a number of fronts. They must be willing to declare their interests, provide their evidence and explain the reasons for their judgements. They need to acknowledge their sources, and they should be as honest as they can about the origins of their own thinking and values. They need to be ready for the challenges of bias, selection, concealment, overemphasis and the glossing over of mistakes, problems or embarrassments. The benefit of hindsight is a wonderful tool for the revisionist historian – especially in an account that spans over forty years. So I hope, as all authors would contend, that I have done my best to acknowledge these requirements and that the text meets such standards. The errors and weaknesses that remain are mine alone.

As my introduction makes clear, this narrative was never intended purely as a scholarly study, nor does it have academic pretensions other than to recall youth service policy and practice through the lens of my own personal experience and viewpoint. I have tried to keep the number of references and footnotes to a minimum, and to eschew a formal bibliography at the end. In his marvellous study *Underground London*, Stephen Smith warns of the kind of volumes that 'recline on a luxurious bedding of plump footnotes.' Of course, I wish now that I had kept all my supervision notes from Kelvin Youth Centre in the early 1970s, and a diary of my time as a head of service in Hampshire and West Sussex, or my well-thumbed copy of the Connexions logo merchandise catalogue. At the end of the day, with primary sources, evidence is often simply that which survives. In respect of Ofsted, I should add that I am aware of the responsibilities of the Official Secrets Act which I signed at the time, and have tried to take special care in recording accurately and fairly my account of my work for the inspectorate.

As also noted in the introduction, it has been evident that there are very few similar personal accounts that connect government youth policies with local experiences in youth and community work. There are histories of youth work, numerous project reports, many examples of good practice, and a library of academic essays and journals, many of which reflect the intellectual or idealistic tradition of youth work. But I found little in my own research and reading that connects policy to personal fieldwork experience and, indeed, to managerial and inspection experience in my case. I hope my small efforts help to fill this space. Not so small, maybe: I've been surprised at how panoramic this narrative seems to have stretched. It was Charles Dickens who exclaimed how much he was looking forward to 'taking up his big brushes again' as he began work on *Little Dorrit* – a book with a much larger canvas and broader historical scope than many of his earlier works.

There have been some influential texts that have seemed important to me, both during my youth work practitioner days and subsequently, which I record here as part of my own explanation of roots and thinking. I have always been a big fan of Richard Hoggart, ever since I listened to him lecturing at Birmingham University way back in 1966. It is one of the very few lectures (on Stendhal's *The Red and the Black*) I can still remember from my student days. Reading and rereading *The Uses of Literacy*, first published in 1957, remains a joy. As a northern boy myself, Hoggart's ability to capture the social and cultural habits of working-class communities, in his case in Leeds, resonates with my own experiences in Sheffield. I had no idea at the time that he had been such an influential witness at the *Lady Chatterley's Lover* trial, nor – more important in this story – that he was a key member of the Albemarle Committee on the youth service. I did know that he had been the first head of the Centre for Contemporary Cultural Studies at Birmingham University, but unfortunately my student courses did not allow me to get involved with the new, exciting work with which the centre seemed to be engaged.

Hoggart's description of his writer's 'craft' also feels important to me. He spoke of the strong impulse to '…bring the different kinds of experience together, the abstract and the sensuous, the public and the private, the large and the small, the big issues and the small habits, the large ideas and the petty smells.' And he also recognised that to do this effectively, writing a simple chronology would be insufficient: 'you are at all moments the boy, the elderly man, the middle-aged man, the youth just setting out, you constantly shuttle between them all as events stir memory.'[73] If I can claim any closeness to these skills in my own account, I would be delighted.

Anyone writing about the youth service owes a huge debt of gratitude to Bernard Davies, whose magisterial three-volume *History of the Youth Service* is the definitive work. 'Chronology – with attitude' is how Davies himself described it, accurately reflecting the powerful mix of history, analysis, critique, rhetoric, emotion and humour that he paints on his extensive canvas. I suppose for those of us who lived and worked through most of Davies' record and recognise many of the characters, the impact is even more intense. In fact, my first, rather uncomfortable brush with Davies was his *In Whose Interests?* published in 1979: a powerful polemic challenging those of us involved in taking the Manpower Services Commission's 'shilling' on job creation and youth employment schemes as to who benefited from such activities. This text also reasserted the historic principles of social education which Davies had first defined with Alan Gibson in their seminal *The Social Education of the Adolescent,* in 1967. Much later, his research project with Bryan Merton, *Squaring the Circle,* published in 2009, accurately and eloquently reflected the dilemmas of many youth work staff and managers in trying to reconcile both open-access and targeted youth support – while maintaining all the other facets of their traditional range of 'joined-up' provision during the New Labour years. Luckily, Davies continues to write for *Youth and Policy, In Defence of Youth Work* and elsewhere, with unrelenting passion and to the great benefit of youth work.

Rereading Ray Gosling's *Lady Albemarle's Boys,* an early pamphlet about his experience as a youth worker in Leicester, was also a revelation. He described the youth club he established as catering for the 'unclubbables', teenage prostitutes, young shoplifters, gamblers and thieves. He provided a pioneering and perceptive analysis of the core voluntary relationship between young people and youth workers, and of the value of both youth clubs and outreach and detached work. He was a groundbreaking youth work theorist and practitioner: 'I was for the underdog, for the seedy and the left behind,' he explained. He was perhaps best known as a radio and television broadcaster; his work always focused on the ordinary, the idiosyncratic and the minutiae of social life and cultures, including the 'accents of the scruffy and secondary modern children,' as he put it. The little things of life, he once said, are more important than the big things. Gosling is the kind of man you would have loved to meet and talk to if you were a youth worker. Sadly, he wrote very little after *Lady Albemarle's Boys* in 1961, but many of his radio and TV broadcasts have been preserved at Nottingham Trent University.

The reader will be aware of my reliance on the many significant contributions of Tom Wylie, director of the National Youth Agency for over ten years from 1995. Tom was not a prolific author of books, preferring to use his considerable influence and experience in a wide range of articles, pamphlets and policy drafts that spanned the whole expanse of youth work, youth services, government and social policy. His continuous 'behind the scenes' presence, allied to his national credibility, knowledge and expertise with ministers, civil servants, departmental officials and others, was instrumental in keeping a high profile for youth work and sustaining its success nationally and locally for almost ten years at the National Youth Agency. Certainly, *Transforming Youth Work: Resourcing Excellent Youth Services* and *Aiming High: A Ten-Year Strategy for Young People* might not have had his name on their covers, but they would never have appeared without him.

More important for the likes of me and my peers, Tom was also always willing to travel up and down the country to talk to staff groups, address conferences, appear on panels and generally spread the youth work word and sow the youth work seed wherever he felt he might be on fertile ground – or stony, for that matter. Like many a head of service, I was very grateful for this kind of support, especially when he lent his considerable clout to challenging those less sympathetic councillors or Directors of Education and Children's Services who needed extra persuasion on the value of their youth services, or when, in the early 2000s, he took a firm and critical policy line on Connexions.

The National Youth Agency's archive collection is held at De Montfort University in Leicester, where I spent two weeks trawling through both the exceptional and the commonplace. My main target was to read all the back issues of the magazine *Youth in Society* (renamed *Young People Now* from 1989) and the newspaper format *Youth Service Scene* and its predecessors, dating back to 1963. I also diligently read my way through *Youth and Policy* from 1982 to 2006: a task which would have earned me a lifetime of indulgences in medieval English society. Dispiritingly, finding nuggets of youth work gold amongst the overwhelming

mass of very average writing in all these sources was rare. Most of
the articles in *Youth and Policy* are nowadays simply unreadable –
or at least couched in such abstruse, academic language as to be
unfathomable to the average reader. At least *YiS-YPN* and *YSS*
target a more general readership, including practitioners, which
helps. There are useful examples of good practice, helpful book
reviews and ideas for programmes, and keeping up to speed
with national policy developments is a valuable element of both
publications. But there is still a lot of depressing repetition about
the service's failure to define youth work, agonising about whether
the youth service is a profession, arguments about salary scales
and budget cuts, and relentless carping about government failure
to recognise the value of youth work and to fund it properly.
On a more positive note, two recent publications I have found
illuminating and hopeful are Jayne Senior's powerful and moving
account of her work with young women in the Risky Business
project in Rotherham (*Broken and Betrayed*, 2016) and Tania de
St Croix's story of the enduring passion and commitment of part-
time workers and volunteers (*Grassroots Youth Work: Policy, Passion
and Resistance in Practice*, 2016).

For social history in the 1970s, I have used Dominic
Sandbrook's books *State of Emergency: The Way We Were: Britain,
1970–1974* and *Seasons in the Sun: The Battle for Britain, 1974–
1979*, and have also relied on Alwyn Turner's *Crisis? What Crisis?
Britain in the 1970s*. Both these authors manage to combine
a broad analysis of policy and strategy with a stunning eye for
illuminating social and cultural detail in fashion, films and
television, music and newspapers. For background in the 1980s
and 1990s I have also relied on Turner's *Rejoice! Rejoice! Britain in
the 1980s* and his equally excellent *A Classless Society: Britain in
the 1990s*, along with Simon Jenkins' *Thatcher & Sons*, an analysis
that convincingly confirms the direct political lineage of John
Major, Tony Blair and Gordon Brown from the Iron Lady herself.

It seems too early to find similarly objective accounts of New Labour and the Blair years – or indeed of English social history from 2000 to the present. There are a number of political tracts and hastily written stories by journalists, some linked to television programmes, as well as autobiographies by the main characters. Maybe Turner or Sandbrook, or another of my favourites, David Kynaston, will turn their attention to this period in due course.

Albeit incidental to my primary focus, I have used Selina Todd's fascinating book *The People: The Rise and Fall of the Working Class* (2014) to illustrate some important themes regarding young people stretching from the Albemarle Report to New Labour. On youth crime, James Sharpe's *A Fiery and Furious People* (2016), a detailed history of violence in England from the Middle Ages to the present, reinforces succinctly how class differences were at the heart of the historical responses of both the authorities and the public to youth violence and crime. Upper-class hooliganism was simply 'boisterousness' or an excess of high spirits, whilst working-class violence was a serious criminal matter. On this issue, it is salutary to be reminded – by Geoffrey Pearson in his *Hooligan: A History of Respectable Fears* (1983), written at the height of the Thatcherite 'law and order' debate – that, amidst the cobwebs of historical myth, there is really no such thing as a golden age. There is only a 'seamless tapestry of fears and complaints about the deteriorated present,' where each generation 'has been sure of the truthfulness of its claim that things were getting steadily worse and equally confident of the tranquility of the past.' And, like James Butterworth forty-five years before him (in *Clubland*, 1932), Pearson concludes that 'hooligan continuities' are inescapably the result of economic and material poverty, disadvantage and inequality.

NOTES TO CHAPTERS

Prologue
1) Bernard Davies, *Young People Now*, November 1999.

Chapter 1: Kelvin Youth Club: Starting Out
2) Jonathan Raban, *Soft City*, quoted in Dominic Sandbrook, *Seasons in the Sun: The Battle for Britain, 1974–1979*, p.79.
3) Geoffrey Pearson, *Hooligan: A History of Respectable Fears*, Macmillan, 1983, pp.74 and 221.
4) This analysis owes much to Mark Smith, *Developing Youth Work*, 1988.
5) Ray Gosling, *Lady Albemarle's Boys*, Fabian Society pamphlet, 1961.
6) Ray Gosling, ibid. p.vi. Gosling's fuller description (in his early autobiography, *Sum Total*, published in 1963) was that *I was for the working class, for the underdog, for the seedy and the left behind.*
7) Selina Todd, *The People: The Rise and Fall of the Working Class*, 2014, p.240.
8) Richard Hoggart, *The Way We Live Now*, 1995, p.288.
9) Quoted by Howard Williamson, *Young People Now*, August 2005.

Chapter 2: Kelvin: The Life and Death of a Youth Centre
10) Reported in Pawson and Brailsford's *Illustrated Sheffield Guide*, 1862. Allegedly, Liquorice Allsorts were created by accident in 1899 when a clumsy salesman working for George Bassett tripped up, jumbling all the different samples he was carrying, creating an almost psychedelic mix of sweets. Quoted in *The North (And Almost Everything In It)*, Paul Morley, 2013, p.63.

11) Richard Hoggart, *The Uses of Literacy*, 1957.
12) Posted on the Sheffield Forum website by user davewhits, November 2011.
13) Stanley Cohen, *Folk Devils and Moral Panics*, 1972.
14) David Marsland, *Youth Service Scene* Special No. 4, Summer 1976.
15) Fred Milson, *Growing Older in the Service of Youth; Youth Service Scene*, September 1977.

Chapter 3: Detached Youth Work
16) Ray Gosling, ibid., p.ix.
17) H. J. Marchant and M. R. Farrant, *Making Contact: A Stage in the Detached Work Process*, Manchester Youth Development Trust, 1971.
18) Mary Morse, *The Unattached*, Penguin, 1965, pp.194–196.
19) The historians can't decide if it was Socrates, Plato or Aristotle who penned this familiar complaint around 400 BC.
20) Tania de St Croix, *Grassroots Youth Work: Policy, Passion and Resistance in Practice*, 2016, p.118.
21) Jeremy Seabrook, *City Close Up*, Penguin, 1971, p.158.
22) See Mike Brake, *Sociology of Youth Subcultures*, 1988.
23) Owen Jones, *Chavs: The Demonization of the Working Class*, 2011, p.8. Allegedly, the initials CHAV stood for 'council house and violent'.
24) Quoted in Owen Jones, ibid. p.95.
25) It was Margaret Thatcher who secured the funds to raise the school leaving age to sixteen when she was Ted Heath's Secretary of State for Education in 1971.
26) Terry Powley, *Detached Youth Work in the Community; Youth in Society*, November 1974. Powley was also involved in the grassroots story of a community youth work approach on an estate in Spitalfields, East London, later published as *Avenues Unlimited* by John Edginton in 1979.

Chapter 4: Becoming a Youth Officer
27) Alan Rogers, *Starting Out in Detached Work*, National Association of Youth Clubs, 1981.

28) *Providing for Young People: Local Authority Youth Services in the 1990s*, National Federation for Educational Research, 1996.

29) Howard Williamson, *The Needs of Young People and the Youth Work Response*, Wales Youth Agency, 1996; Sue Robertson, *Youth Clubs*, 2005.

30) D. Ritchie and J. Ord, *The Experience of Open-Access Youth Work: The Voice of Young People*, *Journal of Youth Work Studies*, July 2016.

31) Mark Smith, *Developing Youth Work*, 1988.

Chapter 5: Numero Uno: Head of Hampshire

32) Her Majesty's Inspectors, *A Survey of School Based Youth and Community Work*, 1991.

33) Dr Elizabeth Hoggarth, Assistant Director of Leisure Services, Wolverhampton Council, 1990.

34) 'By befriending and supporting young people, by offering them challenging opportunities to develop their social and life skills, by helping them to build up the personal confidence they need to take their place in society… youth workers are the unsung heroes of our time.' Nigel Foreman, Parliamentary Undersecretary of State, 1992.

35) The terms 'disputatious' and 'passion and panic' are Tom Wylie's in *Young People Now*, August 1999.

36) Tony Jeffs and Mark Smith, *Youth and Policy*, 1993.

37) Coopers & Lybrand, *Preventative Strategy for Young People in Trouble*, 1994.

38) Bernard Davies, quoted in a review of *History of the Youth Service*, *Young People Now*, November 1999.

Chapter 6: Ofsted: An Inspector Calls

39) Neil Ritchie, *An Inspector Calls: A Critical Review of HMI Reports on Youth Provision*, National Youth Bureau, 1986.

40) Examples from Ofsted inspection reports, 1997–1999.

41) Adrian Morgan, *My First Visit to a Youth Club*, *Youth Service Scene*, November 1982.

42) Ofsted report, *Effective Youth Work*, 2005. Of the thirty-one services inspected, six were good or very good, seventeen adequate and

eight inadequate. Value for money was good in four, satisfactory in nineteen and unsatisfactory in eight.

43) Marilyn Lawrence, Portsmouth City Council youth service manager, interviewed by the author, August 2017.

Chapter 7: 'New Labour', Connexions and West Sussex

44) Tom Wylie, *The Origins and Development of the National Youth Agency*, 2007, p.6.

45) David Blunkett, Secretary of State for Education, 2001.

46) This variability was confirmed by the Youth Service Audit undertaken by Mary Marken and published by the National Youth Agency in 1998.

47) Bernard Davies, *History of the Youth Service*, Vol. 3, Ch. 10.

48) Bernard Davies and Bryan Merton, *Squaring the Circle? The State of Youth Work in Some Children's and Young Peoples' Services*; *Youth and Policy*, 2009, p.26.

49) Howard Williamson, *Youth and Society*, 2003.

50) Jeremy Brent, *Communicating What Youth Work Achieves*; *Youth and Policy*, Summer 2004.

51) *A High Performing Service*; *Young People Now*, April 2001.

52) Tom Wylie, ibid., p.8.

53) Quoted in *Young People Now*, December 2006.

Chapter 8: The Private Sector: The Final Curtain

54) The themes were Be Healthy, Stay Safe, Enjoy and Achieve, Make a Positive Contribution and Achieve Economic Wellbeing.

Chapter 9: Bringing the Story Up to Date

55) For a valuable analysis of the perennial and damaging impact on government policy of 'turf wars' and 'silo mentalities' between Whitehall departments, see Anthony King and Ivor Crewe, *The Blunders of Our Governments*, 2013.

56) Tania de St Croix, *Grassroots Youth Work: Policy, Passion and Resistance in Practice*, 2016, Ch. 2.

57) Tim Loughton, quoted in *Children and Young People Now*, July 2016.

58) Network of Regional Youth Work Units, *Youth Services in England*, November 2014.

59) Sian Berry, Green Party Member of the London Assembly, *London's Lost Youth Services*, January 2017.

60) Tom Wylie and Tony Jeffs, *Articles in Youth and Policy*, May 2015.

61) These were the recommendations of the National Youth Agency's *Vision for Youth Work in England to 2020*, NYA, 2014.

62) Paul Oginsky, quoted in *Children and Young People Now*, December 2016.

63) This analysis is indebted to Bethia McNeil (*Youth Impact: Whose Game Are We Playing?*) and Tania de St Croix (*Questioning the Youth Impact Agenda*), Centre for Youth Impact, 2016; and to *Shared 3 Measurement: Rethinking Impact*, Osca Associates, 2017.

64) Reported in *Children and Young People Now*, 14th August 2017.

65) Tom Wylie and Tony Jeffs, *Articles in Youth and Policy*, May 2015.

66) Reported in the *Guardian*, August 2016.

Chapter 10: Conclusion: Whither a Fragile Occupation?

67) Howard Williamson, quoted in *Young People Now*, July 1999.

68) Jayne Senior, *Broken and Betrayed*, 2016, p.88.

69) Jayne Senior, ibid., p.338.

70) Bernard Davies, *Beyond the Local Authority Youth Service: Could the State Fund Open-Access Youth Work?*; *Youth and Policy* No. 116, May 2017.

71) Ian McGimpsey, *Understanding Youth Services Reform: Beyond the Language of Austerity*; *Youth and Policy*, May 2017.

72) Tom Wylie, quoted in *Young People Now*, March 2005.

A Note on History and Sources

73) Richard Hoggart, *A Sort of Clowning*, 1990, pp.211 and 220.

LIST OF PHOTOGRAPHS AND ILLUSTRATIONS

Cover photos: young people in Gosport, Hampshire. Photos: Matt Stevens, 2017, reproduced with kind permission of *Motiv8South*.

p.XV: Youth work/youth services chart, Tom Wylie, National Youth Agency, 2006, reproduced with kind permission of the National Youth Agency.

Chapter 1

p.4: Kelvin Flats, late 1970s. Photo: Peter Jones.

p.13: Greenhill-Bradway Youth Centre. Photos: Sheffield City Council, 1971.

p.15: Withywood design youth centres, Ministry of Education pamphlet, 1963.

Chapter 2

p.20: Kelvin Youth Centre members. Photos: Tim Caley, 1972/73.

p.21: *Youthwise* cartoon by TB, *Youth in Society*, 1982. (All material taken from *Youth Service Scene, Youth in Society* and *Young People Now* is reproduced with kind permission of the Editor, *Children and Young People Now* and *Mark Allen Group Publishing*).

p.23: *Youth Club Leader*, sketch by Phil Brown, 1972.

p.25: *Youth Work Trolley* cartoon, CartoonChurch.com, copyright Dave Walker, 1999-2018 and reproduced with permission.

p.27: *Youth Club Programme* cartoon by RGJ, *Youth in Society*, 1983.

p.29: *Working with Youth* booklet, BBC TV, 1972.

p.33: Press report, *Sheffield Star*, October 1974 reproduced with kind permission of the South Yorkshire Press.

p.34: Press report, *Sheffield Star*, October 1974, reproduced with kind permission of the South Yorkshire Press.

Chapter 3

p.46: *Identikit Guide for Detached Workers; Youth in Society*, 1980.

p.47: *'The Unattached.'* Mary Morse, Book Cover, Penguin 1965, reproduced with kind permission of Penguin Books Limited.

p.48: Ray Gosling as a young man. Photo: the *Independent*.

p.58: Press report, *Sheffield Star*, May 1976, reproduced with kind permission of the South Yorkshire Press.

p.60: *Children and Play on Kelvin*. Cover design by Phil Brown, 1975.

p.63: *'When I Was Your Age'* cartoon, Wilf Roberts, *Young People Today*, 1980 and *'Rumour has it...'* cartoon, Sebastian Buccheri, *Youth in Society*, 1996.

p.67: Buchanan Road Information Centre. Photo: Tim Caley, 1976.

Chapter 4

p.80: *A Sense of Community* article by Tim Caley, *Youth in Society*, November 1982.

p.84: *Down at the Club: Diaries of a Youth Worker* article by Anne Clode, *Youth Service Scene*, 1981.

p.86: Emmer Green youth exchange. Photo: *Reading Chronicle*, 1981.

p.100: Portsea detached work report, Marilyn Lawrence, 1984.

p.105: *Youth Provision and Factors of Social Deprivation by Portsmouth Wards*, Tim Caley, 1983.

p.105: Press report, *Portsmouth Evening News*, September 1983, reproduced with kind permission of *Southdaily Press*.

Chapter 5

p.111: Hampshire County Youth Service logo design, 1991.

p.114: Hampshire County Youth Service policy documents and reports, 1990/1995.

p.126: Hampshire County Youth Service: 1st Birthday Party; *Young People Now*, August 1991.

p.128: Letter in *Scouting News*, Tim Caley, 1995, reproduced with kind permission of *The Scouts Organisation*.

p.131: Lasham Gliding Club visit, *Southampton Echo*, 1995, reproduced with kind permission of the *Southern Daily Echo*.

p.132: *The Youth Disservice*; *Times Educational Supplement*, 1993.

p.134: *Beyond Graffiti* foreword, Tim Caley, 1992.

p.141: West End Youth Club: laying the foundations. *Hampshire Chronicle*, 1996, reproduced courtesy of the *Hampshire Chronicle*.

p.143: Hampshire Youth Conference. Photo: Tim Caley, 1997.

Chapter 6

p.150: Ofsted identity badge, Tim Caley, 2000.

p.164: *'Sorry I can't help you, too busy'* cartoon, Colin Reeder, *Youth Service Scene*, 1982 and *'Can I say something that needs sorting out...?'* cartoon, Sebastian Buccheri, *Youth in Society*, 1999.

Chapter 7

p.174: *Young People Now* cover, June 1997.

p.184: Southmead Youth Centre, *Young People Now*, 2005.

p.187: Connexions logo, 2000; and Connexions montage, Chris Nash, 2006, reproduced with permission.

p.196: Articles from *Young People Now* and *The Buzz* (West Sussex staff magazine), April 2001.

Chapter 8

p.210: Coldingley Crime Diversion Scheme and Youth Moves project evaluation reports, Tim Caley, 2006.

p.213: *Tim's Ten Commandments*, Tim Caley, 2007.

p.216: Enfield Youth Support Service curriculum documents, Tim Caley, 2007.

p.230: Motiv8: Rowner Youth Centre, Gosport. Photo: Kirsty Robertson, 2012, reproduced with kind permission of *Motiv8South*.

Chapter 9

p.236: *London's Lost Youth Services*, London Assembly, 2017, reproduced by kind permission of the London Assembly Green Party Group.

p.244: *The Milltown Boys Revisited*, Howard Williamson, 2004, reproduced with kind permission of the author/publishers.

p.251: Kirsty Robertson and young people in Leesland skate park, Gosport. Photo: Matt Stevens, 2017, reproduced with kind permission of *Motiv8South*.

AUTHOR'S NOTE

The author gratefully acknowledges the permission(s) granted to reproduce the copyright material in this book. Every reasonable effort has been made to trace copyright holders and to obtain their permission for the use of copyright material. The author apologises for any errors or omissions in the list above and would be grateful if notified of any corrections that should be incorporated in future reprints or editions of this text.

INDEX